Gratuitous Adventures of
Phillip H. Screwdriver,
Last of the real men private investigators

Tonight's Episode:
Slaughter of the Sacred Herd

by
Deus X. Machina

©2014 Deus X. Machina (Tim Leahy and Matt K. Baker)
All Rights Reserved.

www.lastoftherealmen.com

ISBN: 978-1-304-76461-4

DEDICATION

Dedicated? More like committed, as in: to an asylum. But since we're not calling out names here, we'll just say we're dedicating this to the ones we've chosen to be committed to.

COURTESY WARNING

This is your last chance to put the book down and walk away. If you are easily offended, pregnant or nursing, abnormally litigious, operating heavy machinery, or jump to conclusions before finishing the last page, we cannot be held responsible (especially if you're pregnant — don't look at us).

Table of Contents*

PROLOGUE	1
THE BOTTLE YEARS	7
INTERLUDE ONE	24
THE FETTUCCINE FILE	28
INTERLUDE TWO	48
THRYMMSKVITHA (or The Viking Saga)	54
INTERLUDE THREE	86
HIGH SCHOOL	91
INTERLUDE FOUR	104
THE COLLEGE YEARS	114
CHAPTER ONE	161
CHAPTER TWO	174
CHAPTER THREE	189
CHAPTER FOUR	200
CHAPTER FIVE	209
CHAPTER SIX	224
EPILOGUE ALPHA	237
EPILOGUE OMEGA	243

*Please note that theses are not the actual page numbers, but they're close. Horseshoes, hand grenades, and now tables of contents! Just one of many innovative literary techniques in this book!

PROLOGUE

A blade carved through the darkness, a flickering sliver of death that would have signaled the end for me – except that, in the back of my mind, I knew this was only the first sentence of the Prologue.

Instead of death, or an early stage of stigmata, the blinding lights that danced off the surgical steel did no more damage than to cut away the fog in my brain. In the nick of time, I heaved my body to the right and twisted on to my side.

With a gratifying twang, the knife snapped in two as it struck the ground.

This is a hell of a thing to wake up to, I thought. *Whose husband or pagan god have I pissed off this time?* I wanted to roar a defiant laugh but what gurgled out of my mouth sounded like a beer fart. I tried again, this time for a feral cry of fury; and this time, I think I burped. So much for the intimidate-the-bad-guy-by-shouting routine – time to take action!

My hand shot up like a cannonball and grabbed the gloved wrist of a man in a light green overcoat. The fashion plate jerked back, pulling me up. I got my legs under me and used a judo throw to take him down. Hard. I wrapped one paw around his throat and drew back my other, ready to drive a fist through his masked face. Fear and shock danced in his eyes as I started swinging like DiMaggio after too much coffee. But before I could knock his pearly whites into the cheap seats, my knees buckled, and I dropped me to the floor. Hard. Convulsions wracked my body, forcing me to release the bad guy. Blood, breakfast, and my last supper sprayed out of my mouth and spread out on the floor beneath me like a halo.

It's just the Prologue, I reminded myself as I saw my assailant's blade slash again. I felt a sharp prick, and then warm exhaustion gave me a Swedish massage. It could have been worse. I could have been left for dead in a cave somewhere. *It's just the Prologue*, I thought. *Gotta take it easy on the similes.*

A booming female voice screamed, "Doctor, doctor!"

A second voice answered, "More anesthetic, dammit! Christ! Nurse, do your damn job!"

A pair of smooth hands flipped me on my back in time for me to see the butcher—the thug called "Doctor"—coming for me again. This time, I knew I couldn't stop him. The little strength I had was spread out in a lumpy puddle on the floor. Even from behind his mask, I could see the "Doctor" smile.

It'sh . . . jusshht the pro . . .

I thought about trying another defiant laugh or feral cry. Then I thought about crying like a little girl. But *last of the real men private investigators* didn't cry- at least not since I was seven and a half, and certainly not while anyone was watching. I thought about what Bogey would do and tried to scream as the "Doctor" plunged the knife toward my chest for the third time in as many minutes. But before the steel slid into my flesh, I heard the familiar staccato of gunshots. The assassin's blade dropped from his fingers, and a field of blood-red flowers blossomed on his light green chest. They were very pretty flowers. I thought about picking them and bringing them to Judy just to show her I wasn't such a bad guy to work for. But as I reached toward them, the hypnotic red spots grew larger and darker, enveloping me.

The woman I knew only as "Nurse" grabbed me with her beefy paws, looked into my eyes, and asked "Now?" I don't know why, but she reminded my of an overweight Valkyrie who was choosing me from the battlefield to drink and wench in Valhalla until the final war between the gods.

With my last ounce of strength, I shook my head. "Not yet. It's ... just ... thuhhh ... Prolog ... "

* * *

Darkness embraced me with tender warmth until I became aware that I was still living. I cautiously opened one eye, not sure I was going to like what I saw.

But there was nothing to see, except darkness. The walls hugged me like a cheap leopard-print miniskirt, pulsing around my curled up body as if alive. I pushed, and the walls gave a little. Curious, I fumbled inside my London Fog trenchcoat for a Zippo and used it to illuminate my prison.

I wished I hadn't.

The walls were slick with blood, and slime seeped from everywhere. Someone had scrawled, "Glory was here" in the ooze.

Great. I was trapped in some damn Glory hole just waiting for the gates of Hell to open up. Hell might be right; I wouldn't be surprised if I was next in line for the altar. (That's "altar" as in sacrifice, not as in marriage. Though, I've heard some guys wish they'd chosen the former over the latter.) Dammit! The light bulb in my brain flashed on like a Zippo lighter in a womb. I was still in the Prologue! But what happened to the Doctor who'd been trying to slice me up? And who'd saved me? I didn't have answers yet but I was going to find them.

I pulled out a Lucky Strike (unfiltered) and touched it to the lighter. After a few thoughtful drags, I crushed my cigarette out against the wall—which contracted and spasmed in response. *Time to blow this joint.* I twisted around and finally caught a break: there was a literal light at the end of this tunnel. I made for it.

Halfway down the slimy hole, the shrill sound of a woman's screams echoed above me. The blood-curdling screams were ragged and raw like David Hasselhoff on a bender, and the woman sounded like she'd been at it awhile. The hair on my neck stood at attention. I knew those blood-curdling screams! I couldn't place her name or her face, but, dammit, those screams were as familiar as apple pie, baseball, and Jerusalem's Wailing Wall!

I doubled my efforts as the tunnel got smaller, making me feel like a Vietnamese Tunnel Rat. I stripped off the London Fog first, then the suit jacket. By the time I breeched the opening, I was down to my birthday suit and fedora.

As I struggled through, someone grabbed my head and yanked me clear, knocking my hat off in the process. Behind me, the screaming woman sighed with relief. I sighed too.

It was quiet for a moment. Crosby and Bowie's *Little Drummer Boy* played from somewhere. The world seemed to pause, as if something monumental had just transpired. If I hadn't left my clothes in the hole, I would have fired up a Lucky and bought everyone a Coke.

Just as I remembered the Lucky Strike tucked behind my right ear, rubber-gloved hands snared my ankles, hoisting me in the air like Hercules would a prize fish.

"Thanks, Herc. I owe you one. Now could you put me down? I'm hanging on a string. I'll do anything." At least, that's what I wanted to say, but the words got stuck. I clutched at my throat and flopped around like that prize fish until Hercules got the message. He slapped my firm buttocks, and I screamed, clearing whatever was caught in my throat and lungs. It did the job, but it hurt like hell. I like that in a man.

Just my luck! Judging from the cheap light-green overcoat Herc was wearing, he was a member of the same gang as the rat-bastard who had tried to dice me up earlier. I didn't know who these guys were, or why they wanted me dead, but it looked like they were going to succeed in painting me out of the picture with a bloodstained brush.

Still holding me up by my ankles, the thug reached over to a small table and selected one of a collection of knives. I struggled, vainly. Another knife. Didn't anyone use a gun anymore?

As he inspected the weapon, lights danced seductively off the blade, calming me. I realize that my reaction might seem odd given the obvious murderous bloodlust of my assailant, but small, shiny objects have always fascinated me.

Satisfied with his choice, Herc turned to me, knife raised. His arm started toward my exposed gut. I tried to twist away, but was too weak for acrobatics.

I guess this is it!

For once in my career as a PI, I guessed wrong. He missed.

Hercules smiled warmly and handed me to the familiar-looking, if enormous broad, whose previously bloodcurdling screams had become gentle grunting, like a pig rooting for truffles. She was soaked with sweat and looked as if she'd been through a ringer, but there was a satisfied smile on her puss.

I heard a voice say, "Congratulations, Miss—I'm sorry, Ms. Steinman! You are now the proud mother of a beautiful baby girl!"

I looked to see what they were talking about and noticed that, for some reason, they were gawking at me, stupid grins splattered across their mugs.

Baby girl? What the hell are you talking about? I'm a man! And with the possible exception of the time I was seven and a half, and considered the operation, I've always been a man. And I've always enjoyed it. And who are you calling "baby"?

A hunch hit me on the head, trying to get my attention. I looked at Hercules again, and then at the dame. The hunch had been right. It smiled smugly and, having made its point, went away.

"Herc" was really Dr. E. Wisemann, III, the doc who dragged me out of the womb and into the hard, cold world of Bethlehem, Pennsylvania's General Hospital. The chick was my mother. Dr. Wisemann was telling my mother I was in stable condition.

In reality, I was having a near-death experience. I was probably lying face down in a puddle of my own blood in an alleyway somewhere, my body just oozing life with someone sneaking 'round the corner again. That meant my assessment at the beginning of this Prologue could have been wrong. The knife might be the end. Here I was, just like in those supermarket tabloids, my life flashing in front of me, replaying scenes that I wished had stayed on the cutting-room floor; all the events that made me the man I am today:

Phillip H. Screwdriver, *last of the real men private investigators*!

Or I'd been reincarnated. Of course, the odds of me being delivered by the same doctor and to the same mother were about as good as the Giants beating the Patriots in the 2007 Super Bowl or Elvis Presley winning a limbo contest. That's 1970's Vegas scarf-throwing Elvis and not 1950's Elvis the Pelvis, by the way.

My mother wrapped her arms around me in a tender embrace. I was in good hands; she would protect me and bring me worms until I was strong enough to fend for myself. I relaxed, and a smile crept across my face.

"You are my special angel, sent from up above," my mother whispered to me. "The Lord smiled down on me . . ."

As I closed my eyes, reality began a spin cycle. A cup of vertigo and nausea washed through me, rinsing out memories of my life. The lid opened, and I was hung out to dry. After a while, a dark hand grabbed me from the clothesline. I was fluffed, neatly folded, and then stuffed into the clothesbasket of unconsciousness.

THE BOTTLE YEARS

A face rushed out at me from between a skirt of darkness and a jockstrap of emptiness. The face of Mrs. Geshtappo, my first grade teacher, focused surrealistically before me, floating in the void.

Her horrible features clicked everything into place: I wasn't reincarnated; my life *was* flashing in front of me. Here, in this flashback sequence, I was seven and a half again. But I knew that, in reality, I was standing on the threshold of the Final Abyss with the Angel of Death poised behind me, ready to give me the Big Heave-Ho. But, before she did, she was going to sit next to me with an extra-large Diet Coke and eat popcorn and Twizzlers and enjoy the chaos and misery and insanity that I had proudly called my life. And just so you know: she talks on her cell phone constantly, screams at the movie screen when someone's about to get killed, and doesn't share snacks. Bitch.

* * *

The place was Mickey Spillane Elementary School. Specifically, room thirteen. I sat in the last seat of the third row, the collar of my London Fog turned up and a black fedora pulled low over my eyes. Mrs. Geshtappo stood by the blackboard, babbling about the rules of English grammar in her thick Italian accent. It was a typical day, and I was typically bored; her incessant droning was lulling me into a deep sleep. To keep myself awake, I pulled a Lucky

Strike from my pack and lit it, inhaling deeply. Nicotine worked its way into my blood stream, reviving me a little.

As I did every fifteen minutes, I patted "Richard," making sure she was still tucked snugly in my trousers. The cool, damp feeling of my forty-five caliber, semi-automatic, rotating bolt, double safety, government-issue water pistol was reassuring in the face of today's grammar quiz. My mind wandered to the day when life would bless me with my Private Investigator's ticket, and I would get the opportunity to blow away some scumbag, avenging my best friend's senseless-yet-poignant death and putting my career on par with the other great hard-boiled detectives of our time: Sam Spade; Philip Marlowe; Mike Hammer; Rigby Reardon; Disney's "The Great Mouse Detective"; Ace Ventura, Pet Detective—

My reverie was rudely interrupted when Mrs. Geshtappo slapped her riding crop on my desk.

"For dein last time, Jimmy," she bellowed, "dere is no smokink in class! And take off dat shtupid hat und empty your vater pistol; the *verdamt* t'ing ist leakink everyvhere!"

I pushed my hat back far enough to give her the eye, exhaling a spear of smoke.

"Screwdriver, toots," I said smugly. "Phillip Screwdriver, last-of-the-real-men private investigators. Got it, sweetheart?" I pronounced "sweetheart" like Bogey would; it came out more like "shweethot."

From somewhere, trumpets sounded a dramatic, heraldic call to arms. Probably the loudspeaker. The principal always did have an inflated sense of self-importance.

"*Nein!* But *you* are goink to get it!" she exclaimed as she yanked me out of my seat. In a flash, she had pulled down my trousers, bent me over her knee, and started paddling my firm, young buttocks. I whipped Richard around and shot her in the eye.

She screamed and released me, clawing at her face with her hands. I rolled off her knee, stood, and pulled up my pants, denying her satisfaction. Richard dangled casually in my right fist.

"Look, kitten," I consoled her, "I know you want me, and I know that you like the rough stuff. But it would never work. You're three, maybe ten times my age. These January-December romances don't last. Trust me, kid, it's better this way."

I lit a Lucky and took a nice, deep drag. She just sat there, bawling her peepers out. She wanted to pretend that the water in her eyes came from the gun, but I was wise to her. I knew I'd hurt her, but I could never let anyone get close to me. As Marlowe once said, "Guns don't kill detectives, love kills detectives." In my line of work, people were bound to cross or double-cross me. I could be dead tomorrow. Even the people who loved me would always be in danger. I didn't want anyone to have forsaken me three times before the cock crowed at dawn. And I didn't want anyone to cry at my funeral. Well, not her, anyway.

I had just crushed my cigarette on the dirty, warped linoleum when Mrs. Geshtappo grabbed me by the collar of my London Fog and hauled me out of the room, heading for the principal's office. I was going to see the Big Man himself. Again.

Sheesh, dames.

As she was dragging me down the hall, I said, "Oh, and one more thing: these public displays of affection have got to stop. The children are at a very impressionable age, and this may not be good for their social development."

With the strength of an Austrian bodybuilder, she opened the door to the principal's office and heaved me inside, muttering Italian obscenities under her breath. Without looking up, Judy, the secretary, said that the Big Man would see me in a few minutes.

Judy S. (I never got her last name) was a long-legged beauty with an alleged, never legally proven, passion for underage *last of the real men private investigators*. She was the kind of dame who didn't need to wear make-up. Tight leather and a body that wouldn't quit—even if I begged it to—said more about her than any female war paint could.

Making myself comfortable in the semi-rigid plastic chair, I fired up my last cigarette and tossed the crumpled pack down the front of Judy's revealing blouse. She tittered and, looking up, gave her long, blonde hair a carefree, slow-motion toss. Her angel-blue eyes sparkled as her luscious red lips gave me an inviting, come-hither smile. I smiled back.

"Hi, Phil. Busy tonight?" she breathily whispered. I shook my head. "Call me later, then?"

"Sure, kitten," I replied, knowing that no matter what I did, my kiss would always be on her list.

We sat there making goo-goo eyes as I smoked my Lucky and she pretended that three of her blouse buttons had come undone by themselves. I took a last puff of my cigarette and ground it out in the pot of decaffeinated coffee. No one would notice anyway. With a tip of my hat to Judy, I kicked in the principal's door and strode confidently inside. I plopped myself down in a Barco lounger and propped my Florsheims on his desk, spilling a bottle of prune Schnapps. I watched as the alcohol soaked the stacks of paper before the dregs ran across the principal's desk, off the edge, and began pouring into the trashcan.

As it passed through the venetian blinds, sunlight and shadow striped the office like prison bars. A single lamp rested on his desk. Reflexively, I opened a fresh pack, stuck a Lucky in my mouth, lit it, and blew a wreath of second-hand smoke around the Big Man's face. His Charlie Chaplin moustache twitched.

After I had poured a healthy shot of his best scotch and used it to rinse out my mouth, I said, "What can I do for you, chief?"

The principal stared at me from behind his cast iron curtain desk. The nameplate said *Adolph Geshtappo*, and he was my English teacher's husband. Renowned as a strict disciplinarian, he genuinely hated himself and got his kicks taking his anger out on others. He despised the hand that life had dealt him, and the resentment gnawed at his guts like a rabid tapeworm. Back in the Old Country, he'd been a big bratwurst, but here, he was just another wiener.

"I vould like to talk to you about your paper," Adolph said

with a resigned tone in his voice. He searched briefly through a couple of stacks until he found what he wanted. He held a few stapled pages out to me, still dripping with the spilled schnapps.

"Vould you read it for me?" he asked.

"Sure," I replied, taking the paper from his hand and glancing at it. It was the composition that I'd turned in last September.

I cleared my throat and started reading, "'What I Did During My Summer Vacation, a five-hundred-word essay by Phillip H. Screwdriver. I smoked, I drank, and I killed a few people.' Do I have to read all of it? It gets kind of monotonous."

Adolph half-smiled, adjusting the shade of his desk lamp so I could see the numbers "666" written on it. "My point exactly. You wrote dat same sentence *funf und funfsig* ...uh, fifty-five times."

"Yeah, but," I shrugged my shoulders, "that's what I did. Between gigs, so I kept myself busy. You know how that goes."

"Unfortunately, ve vanted a little more detail. Vas did you drink? Whom did you kill? Vere any of dem Jews? Dat kind of t'ing."

I eyed him suspiciously. "And why would you want to know all that? I may not have done it. Nobody saw me do it. Can't prove a thing." My hand snaked inside my waistband, toward Richard. "Has someone been asking?"

Before he could reply, the phone rang. He snatched up the receiver with an annoyed look on his pale features. I noticed apple strudel crumbs around his mouth.

"Hallo, dere," he said, kicking spit-shined jackboots onto his desk. "Geshtappo speakink . . . Vas? . . . Mein Gott! Ven? . . . Ja, ja . . . nein . . . I'll be dere in zwei shakens of eine schnauzer's tail!"

He dropped the phone in its cradle and stood up, unsteady in his boots. The rest of the blood appeared to have drained from his face, and beads of sweat popped out around his moustache.

"I'll be back!" he said in his thick Italian accent.

I helped myself to more of Geshtappo's scotch. After a

couple sips, I sat back in the chair and lit a coffin nail, throwing the match in the Schnapps- and paper-filled trashcan.

I was relieved when Geshtappo finally came back. Watching fire climb out of the circular file and up the curtains was amusing, but it could only hold my attention for so long.

The principal seated himself behind the fire-scorched desk and took a long pull from the remains of his bottle of prune Schnapps. "He's dead, Jim."

Adolph didn't have to say who it was; I knew. It was Johnny. My best friend in this cruel, vicious world: Johnny. The name brought back a flood of memories. Johnny: the man who took a spitball with my name on it during recess. I had been standing by the jungle gym, making a highball from the wet-bar in my "La Cage Aux Folles" lunchbox. Johnny screamed a warning. Thinking nothing of himself, he dove in front of a hurtling wad of saliva-laced paper that was meant for me.

The image was still vivid: shreds of white paper peppered his face, spit mixed with blood ran down his injured cheek. Tears, mine and his, fell like bombs as I cradled his head in my arms. The school nurse took forever getting there.

Blood rage shook me. Johnny was never the same after that fateful day on the playground. Sure, the doctors managed to patch up his face, restoring it to its previous looks; but the emotional scars never healed.

Dammit, Johnny! Why'd you have to go and get yourself killed? Why, dammit, why?

Johnny's face faded and was replaced by Geshtappo's.

I looked at Adolph, fire blazing behind my eyes, and in front of them. "How'd it happen? Who did it?" I demanded.

He had a sad look on his drawn features. He shook his head slowly and said, "Johnny caught an *apfel* meant for mein vife, Frau Geshtappo! It exploded in his face! He didn't feel a t'ing."

"An *apfel*! An exploding *apfel*!? What the blazes is an *apfel*?" I screamed as the cold fog of hate rolled into my brain.

He scratched his head thoughtfully and said, "Let's see . . . An apfel is red und falls from trees und hits physicists on der noggins."

I fired up a Lucky and let the tobacco smoke mix with the hate-fog. The miasma formed a thick soup of rage that tasted foul and bitter in my mouth. I savored the flavor. It needed salt. Maybe a pinch of oregano. But no bay leaves. God, I hate bay leaves. I mean, who puts leaves into a soup? Maybe a platypus, but not a real man. The thought of a platypus, a twisted freak of nature, made me even angrier. It could only have been another twisted freak of nature that would try and kill with an exploding apple. For Christ's sake, the last person who tried to take someone out with an apple was Cinderella's wicked stepmother, and even she wasn't twisted enough to do more than use a sleeping poison.

"Who did it, Geshtappo?" I spit. "Who murdered my best friend Johnny?"

"I know nothink," he whined, his eyes white with the fear of what he knew was coming. "Nothink."

My hand darted across what was left of his desk and snatched the lapels of his uniform. I yanked him toward me until our faces were 3.14 inches apart (as required by *The Private Investigator's Handbook*).

"Ve haff vays of makink you tock," I said, before realizing that the goose-stepping bastard had me speaking Italian.

Adolph's bony frame shook like that trailer you don't knock on when it's rocking. "I swear it! Frau Geshtappo vas showink ein film; dere vas no one avake, you fool, except for Johnny. He vas correctink papers, the brown-noser. Ven he saw de apfel land on de desk, he threw himself on it. It exploded und he died. Dere vere no vitnesses."

"No witnesses? Wrong, pal. There was a witness! Someone threw that *apfel*—that person is a witness! I'm going to find him. I'm going to find him and make him pay! Pay in spades, mister! You had better believe that I'm going to stand over him and make him suffer.

Suffer and die a slow, painful, lingering death. I'm going to enjoy watching the lights go out behind his eyes as I squeeze Richard's trigger. Bet the whole schnitzel on it!" I said through clenched teeth.

I shoved him back into his chair, stuffed my hat on my head, and stormed out, leaving Geshtappo a blubbering mass of jelly. My trenchcoat flared behind me as I exited, like the cloak of the Grim Reaper. Or my idol, Batman!

AUTHORS' INTRODUCTORY NOTE:** The Batman section following has no real bearing on the story, but we liked it and this was the only place we could force it in. Besides, we figured you could use a break from the above tripe, which is clearly sub-par, manufactured melodrama in the guise of a loving homage.*

Everyone has a hero. Even a last-of-the-real-men private investigators like me. My hero was the caped crusader: Batman. Not Christian Bale's Dark Knight or the Michael Keaton-Val Kilmer-George Clooney Batmans, but the Adam West 1960's TV Batman.

His sidekick Robin was okay, but I often wondered about a teenager who ran around in tight shorts that would make a porn queen blush, Peter Pan slippers, and called himself the "Boy Wonder." Besides, his real name was Dick.

Batman was the epitome of the tough guy, but he really shouldn't have been hanging out with Robin. Child Protective Services must not have had the address for the Bat Cave.

The TV show didn't have rubber-nippled bat suits or unnecessary brooding of the movie versions. They were fine, but didn't really capture the bat essence. In one TV episode, the Boy Wonder was tied up (a Batman standard) and dropped from a seven-story building. Batman threw his bat-a-rang, which Robin caught in his mouth *while falling*! Batman then hauled him up five stories to safety. Once untied, Robin thanked him and said, "Holy dentures, Batman! It's a good thing that I brush and floss daily!" To which Batman replied, "Yes, Robin, you owe your life to good dental hygiene."

The horror. The horror.

I have no respect for anyone who didn't immediately start spitting out bicuspids and screaming, "Holy shit, Batman! That hurt like a bitch!" while pummeling Batman about the head and shoulders.

Robin aside, Batman was the greatest. Why? Because he's a scofflaw. Maybe not on big crimes like murder, kidnapping, and jaywalking, but on lesser things. Not one show went by that Batman wasn't trespassing, breaking and entering, and wracking up several hundred accounts of aggravated assault and battery. He also violated every traffic law in the book at least once an episode. You always saw the Batmobile flying by, as Chief O'Hara scratched his head and said, "There be goin' Batman. And right as rain he'll be chasin' some villain."

In all actuality, the caped crusader was probably trying to get his spare costume back from the drycleaner's before it closed.

And the Batmobile: A 1962 Lincoln concept car with an atomic engine and . . . and fins! That car was an accident waiting to happen. Fire came out of the back every time he stepped on the gas. Obviously, he was in with someone at the emission control board. If he'd read Al Gore's *Earth in the Balance* or seen "An Inconvenient Truth," he didn't care because, hey, flames shooting out the back of your car are way cool.

Yeah, the Caped Crusader was great and did much to influence my tough-guy image. At one point, I was going to put bat-ears on my fedora, but I couldn't make mine stand up like his.

****APPRECIATIVE AUTHORS' NOTE*: Thank you. Now that we have that off our chest, we can get on with the main story.***

After I left the principal's office, I headed straight for Spillane Elementary's cafeteria, the local dive, to get a drink.

Velma was behind the counter, polishing glasses as usual. When she saw me heading her way, she pulled out a single malt scotch. She looked at me again, made it a double, and handed it over without a word.

"Thanks, kitten," I said, as I shook the little cardboard container and peeled back the twin tabs on my Glen Fiddich.

"You looked like you could use the drink, Phil."

I looked up at her and took a swig of scotch. Booze, and her comforting personality, soaked into my system like bats in a belfry on a summer night, hanging upside down and letting the warm breeze waft over their little, furry bodies. *Hey, if you're gonna do a simile, do it all the way.*

Velma was one of those broads who was so gorgeous it hurt just laying eyes on her. Looking at her was like looking at the sun for an hour and a half. When she smiled with those ripe, red lips of hers, birds sang, flowers bloomed, and I got an urge to grab Richard and start shooting. I often dreamed of being the explorer who first conquered the hills and valleys of her landscape. But I was a private dick, not Lewis and Clark.

I put my hat on my lap and played it cool.

"The bastards got Johnny!" I snarled.

Her hands flew to her mouth as she recoiled in horror. Tears welled up in the corners of her eyes, glittering like diamonds caressed by the first rays of the sun. But the tears couldn't quench the fires of sadness that burned in the depths of her irises. I stood up and put a comforting arm around her. She needed someone strong. Johnny meant almost as much to her as he did me. Once, there had been a food fight in the cafeteria. A meatball had been lobbed by some sinister coward. Johnny had dived in front of it and took the meatball meant for Velma right in his chest. Yeah, he survived, but he had never been the same after that.

"*(Sniff)* Uh, Phil?" she asked after a few moments of torrential sobbing. "Why *(sniff)* why does your hat stay attached to your pants like that?"

I looked down and mumbled something about Richard's barrel. Just then, her husband, Tyrone, came in swinging a dung-covered plunger. He looked like he meant to snake my drain permanently.

"Git yo' hands off my cotton-pickin' wife fo's I kick yo' lilly-white ass!"

Obviously, our Oriental custodial engineer was insecure in his manhood. But, being a real man, I released Velma and picked up my hat.

"What's your problem, Ty?" I asked, lighting a coffin nail.

"B'sides dis fool accent you make me use? Why does the janitor has to be having a minstrel negro accent? My sanitation engineering degree is from Harvard. Dat aside, it's de third time dis week I'se caught you foolin' wit' my Velma," Tyrone shouted, pointing the plunger accusingly at me. "What's de excuse dis time? Yo' bes' frien' git hisself kilt again?"

Velma came to my defense. It was a good thing she did, too; I'd have hated to have to kill her husband.

"Lay off, Tyrone. It's fo' real dis time. Johnny done bought a one-way ticket to the Promised Land."

"Swing low sweet chariot!" Tyrone's brow knitted — not just a little, but a whole damn sweater's worth. Slowly, the words sank past his six-foot Afro and into his brain. He apparently reached a decision because the next thing I knew I was on my back. Tyrone stood over me and plunged my face like a newlywed husband does his bride on the first night of their honeymoon, in some plush hotel by a waterfall. You know the kind of place: red velvet on the walls, mirrors on the ceiling, pink champagne on ice, slippery satin sheets, and a revolving, heart-shaped bed that vibrates for thirty seconds if you give it two-bits. Outside, the bellhops are holding out their hands while the new bride is clawing her man's back in the throes of passion and lust. The roar of the waterfall is just loud enough to mask the screams of ecstasy that the bellhop makes when tipped a C-Note to leave the bottles by the door and go away. Inside, the newlyweds writhe and undulate, pumping up and down like Tyrone plunging the face of the last-of-the-real-men private investigators. (See what I mean about me and similes? Read that again — it's awesome, if I do say so myself even if I'm doing it because the authors want extraneous material in this book because they might get paid by the word for this manuscript.)

Velma jumped on Tyrone's back and started pummeling him. Her distraction gave me an opportunity to pull Richard out. I squeezed the trigger and unleashed a torrent of water into Tyrone's left nostril. He screamed and staggered backwards, his plunger flying into the cauldron, where it was later used to stir pizza.

I stood up and wiped the crap from the plunger off my face. Strangely, it tasted like the meatloaf the cafeteria served for lunch. I looked around and saw Tyrone being chased around the cafeteria by Velma. She was swinging a rolling pin and shouting words that would make a longshoreman blush.

I lit up a Lucky and then threw up into the pizza cauldron, dropping my butt. I learned later that my school had won the coveted "Best Pizza Award" that day.

I remember thinking that I needed a drink and a smoke to wash the taste out of my mouth and so I could look manly while debating my next move. That wasn't unusual because I always needed a drink and a smoke. I satisfied both cravings while looking manly and debating my next move.

The cafeteria angle was dead, so I decided to see if Adolph was holding out on me. I pushed several yellow-jacketed men with long firehoses out of my way and made it into the office. Judy rushed up and threw her arms around me, sobbing her pretty, little angel eyes out on my London Fog. This was normal for her, which was why I had had my trenchcoat Scotchguarded.

"Oh, Phil, it's been terrible! (*sob*) First Johnny, then the principal's office gets burned down, and now . . . and now (*sob*) Velma and Tyrone are dead!"

"Velma and Tyrone? But I was just there! Where's Adolph? I need to talk to that bastard; he's holding out on me."

"Oh, he left to run some errands," she replied with a casual wave of her hand. "He'll be back later." Then, she looked up at me with liquid eyes and said, "Hold me, Phil, I'm scared. I . . . I may be next. Will you stay and protect me?"

"I can't," I replied.

This newest twist told me that things were getting way out of hand; I was going to need more firepower than my trusty water pistol could provide. I pulled Ol' Richard from my holster and pointed it at Judy.

Her eyes got wide, and she stammered, "How . . . how did you know it was me?"

I flipped it over so that I was holding it by the barrel and handed the gun to her. "Know what was you?" I asked.

She took the gun from me with a relieved look on her face and said, "Oh. Never mind."

"Do you know how to use one of these?"

"Yeah," she replied. "I learned how during the war."

"Good, 'cause there's a madman running around here, and he's got a bone to pick with someone. Take this and use it to protect yourself, doll."

She nodded and then hosed me down. Thank God for Scotchguard. Judy apologized profusely, saying her gun skills were a little rusty, and then went to a water fountain to reload.

Having made sure that Judy was safe, I decided to see if the school store was surviving the fire that was slowly burning the school to the ground. After several minutes of dodging burning timbers and screaming students, I arrived at the store to find Becky Fettuccine standing behind the counter and staring at me blankly with wide eyes. Somehow, today, she looked different; there was a radiant quality about her that I'd never noticed before. I had seen her a thousand times before: arriving at school in her father's limo, or with her faithful bodyguards, Donny "Soldier of Love" Osmondo and the cast of "Growing up Gotti."

Sometimes, I would intercept the notes Becky passed in class. Without fail, she always wrote wonderful things about me to her friends. Of course, she called me Ares, Yahweh, Ah-Puch,

Buddha, Crom Cruach, Hanuman, Thor, or Bob in those notes--Becky was a bit of a gold-digging whore. However she tried to disguise her lust for me, I knew who she was writing about. Still, I couldn't place my finger on what was different about her today. It could have been her dress, or the way the light from the flames in her hair flitted merrily across her eyes. I really didn't know; she just looked different.

I pulled a Lucky out of my deck and tapped it on the counter.

"Hey, kitten, I need a heater. Something big like a .45, but small enough to hide from those anal-retentive Nazi hall monitors. You got anything like that?"

She turned in an almost robotic manner and stiffly swayed in her suede skirt over to the back of the room where they kept those kinds of things since Columbine. *Can't be too careful today with a bunch of psychos in trenchcoats roaming the schools.* She grabbed a large, cardboard box and returned to the counter with it.

Just as I was opening the box, a support beam burned through, fell from the roof, and pinned Becky to the floor. A shaft of sunlight streamed in through the newly-formed hole in the ceiling and fell upon the .45 M-1911A-1 Colt semiautomatic pistol that rested inside the box. A heavenly chorus that must have come from what was left of the school intercom sang from above my head. Geshtappo must be back. Just in time.

I picked up the pistol, caressing it gently in my hand. A thin sheen of oil and Cosmoline covered the pistol. I traced a finger lightly over her, feeling her slick, firm form.

The choral music grew louder and louder. I chambered a round, aimed, and fired in the general direction of the intercom squawk box and the heavenly chorus choked on some lead. Sparks returned my fire until they eventually fizzled and died.

I really hate heavenly choral music, I thought.

Leaning over the counter, I looked at Becky. The flames on the fallen support beam were slowly climbing toward her.

"Hey, kitten, can I have a light?"

She screamed and then passed out. Even at a young age, I had that effect on women.

"Someday, Becky. Someday, but not today; not yet. Today I have a job to do. Because I know now who the killer is. I have to stop him, and it's not going to be a pretty picture. It never is."

Becky didn't respond; she just lay there, resigned to her fate. I couldn't blame her, really. I wouldn't want to be me either. I wouldn't want to walk around with the weight of the world on my broad shoulders. But someone had to do it.

I threw her a fire extinguisher and left. I hadn't taken a dozen steps before I saw THEM. Their jackboots struck the ground in rhythm to their gut-churning rendition of "Deutschland Uber Alles."

Italian patriotic music made me even more nauseous than heavenly choral music. I unholstered the new Richard and smiled a feral smile.

The leer left my face in a hurry when it realized that, with the exception of boots, aviator goggles, and spiked helmets, the Geshtappos were both buck-naked. I told you that it wasn't going to be a pretty picture.

I drew a bead, decided that it wasn't a very good drawing, crumpled up the paper, and threw it on the ground. Then I sighted in with Richard.

The pair came to a halt and looked cross-eyed at me. Crazy looks did a polka in their eyes. It may have been the fire raging through the hallway that gave their eyes an insane glint; but I didn't think so. Somewhere along the line, the Geshtappos' train had jumped the track.

Just what I needed: my principal and my English teacher were both mad as rabid weasels!

"You killed Johnny, Adolph!" I screamed, Richard shaking accusingly in my steady hand. "You killed my best friend because he was on to you. Yeah, he knew your little secret; and now I know it too. You went through a lot of trouble to cover it up, but you made a few minor mistakes."

Geshtappo had a surprised look on his face. "Vas? What are you talkink about?"

The smile returned. I had him now. "Come on, Adolph, admit it. All the clues are there: the little Charlie Chaplin moustache, converting the cafeteria into a beerhall, the Oktoberfest last autumn, just to name a few. No one but me noticed that the Jewish students had to use separate showers after gym class, or your plan to replace the school uniform with lederhosen, or making *Mein Kampf* required reading for everybody. The straw that broke the camel's back was making the school store sell Lugers instead of good ol' American forty-fives." I nodded at Richard. "This is the last one. Fitting, eh?"

"I know nothink. Nothink!" Adolph groveled.

"Spare me the innocent routine, pal. Who would change the football team's name from Spillane Sloths to Spillane Stormtroopers? Who would replace the American flag with a swastika? It all points in one direction: you, Adolph Geshtappo, are really Benito Mussolini, the fascist scourge of Italy!"

The principal's rigid posture slumped. "It was only a matter of time. Ach. But it vas not I who did de killink of Johnny."

"What the Hell are you talking about, you bastard?"

"I mean dat I am der innocent man!" he sniveled as tears welled in his beady eyes.

I couldn't stand to hear anymore of his damn lies.

"I, the judge, I The Jury, I, the executioner, pass judgment and pronounce sentence."

I pulled the trigger and Richard brought the gavel down and closed the case of Adolph "Il Dulce" Geshtappo.

Mrs. Geshtappo/Mussolini looked at me with glazed, teary eyes.

"You fool! He vas mit you vhen de apfel kilt Johnny! He couldn't have done it!"

"Oh," I replied, scratching my head with Richard's smoking

barrel. "Then it must have been you."

Bang!

I gutshot her so that she would suffer for her crimes. Turning my back on the nauseating scene, I lit up a Lucky.

The distinctive cocking sound of a Browning water-cooled, .30-caliber machinegun extinguished the smoking lamp. I took a final drag of my coffin nail and flicked the butt at a platypus swimming in a vat of gasoline. I whipped around and shot the machinegun out of Eva's hand, just as she squeezed the trigger.

Her machine gun went spinning out of control. Bullets sprayed into a crowd of students who had mindlessly gathered like a herd of cattle. By some Act of God none of them were killed although four score and seven students were grazed by bullets, their scars an eternal reminder of the fate of all those who rubberneck.

A stray round struck Judy's desk, sending applesauce everywhere in a large explosion.

I looked at the destruction and smiled. Mrs. Geshtappo lay on the floor, crying; her eyes dripped like a leaky faucet.

"Kill me, Jimmy," she pleaded. "I cannot go on like dis. It doesn't matter if Eva Geshtappo ist innocent of dis crime; dere are others. Ach, pull de trigger und end dis madness." She wheezed, coughing up blood before continuing. "I vanted to lead a gut life, but, ach, it vas never to be. Don't hate me, Jimmy. Don't hate me for what I haff become. Just remember me as I was: innocent."

I was tired of her mindless babbling. Innocent, she said. Hah.

"Nobody's innocent," I said, finishing her off like a tall glass of lemonade on a hot summer day. The impact of my bullets made the same sound as a sea gull exploding after being fed Alka-Seltzer by kids vacationing at the beach with their parents.

Exhausted by all the death, I sat down in the burning ruins of Spillane Elementary. The acrid stench of burning applesauce filled the hallway, mixing itself with the stench of death. I finished off a bottle of Jim Beam and half a carton of Lucky's before an overweight, blond Valkyrie popped her horned-helmeted head out from around a burning corner and asked "Now?"

I threw the Jim Beam bottle and shook my head. "Not yet."

The blond shook me out of my bourbon and nicotine induced stupor and I finally reached the blind alley at the end of Memory Lane and got up to leave.

I thought of Johnny as I walked out the door and across the playground. I thought of how he used to lick my face when he was happy, and how he'd scratch at the door when he wanted to go for a walk, and how he left me a Christmas present at the front door every year. Johnny was the best friend a man could ask for. I was going to miss him.

As I left the playground, an earthquake struck. The ground opened up and swallowed the burning ruins of my elementary school.

Then the ground, and my first case, closed.

INTERLUDE ONE

As the flashback from my childhood released me, I saw Jay's face wavering above me. I swam through the murky pools of my mind, toward him. I breast-stroked and butterflied as I swam, occasionally changing strokes to see which worked more effectively.

I finally broke the surface and gulped the sweet air of consciousness. Shooting pains wracked my entire body, telling me that reality wasn't all I had it cracked up to be. I was too weak to argue and went under again.

I knew what I was up against as I regained consciousness the next time, so I screamed like a girl.

Jay was leaning against the far wall, staring at me with tired, bloodshot eyes and puffing on a Kool Mild.

My lips were cracked and dry like Ronald Reagan in *Death Valley Days*, but they grudgingly managed a smile and said, "Give me a cigarette, will you, Jay?"

Jay grinned at some private joke and pushed off the stark white void of the wall. He savored a last drag from his smoke before grinding it out in a pot of colorless flowers.

"Forget it, Phil. These things'll kill you."

"Alright then, get me a nurse. I'm in pain."

In response, Jay pressed the creme-white buzzer on the bone-white Formica table next to my eggshell-white bed. It occurred to me that Jay's tan trenchcoat and wrinkled blue suit violated the white on white color scheme of the room like a Catholic priest violated an orphanage. Acting like he didn't notice, he then pulled another slim, white cigarette from his pack and proceeded to make a big production of lighting it. Bastard. He knew the tobacco smell was driving me crazy.

"That's cruel, Jay, I'm having the worst nicotine fit of my life."

"Consider yourself fortunate to even have a life."

"True. Thanks for saving me again, buddy. That's two I owe you."

Jay looked at me quizzically and said, "Two?"

"This one and the one in the war. Don't think that I'll ever forget that one, Jay." I thought he'd smile, but emotions played Monopoly across his face. Jay frowned, obviously landing on Marvin Gardens. He became serious.

"Phil, what are you talking about?"

"Nam! The war! Remember? Never mind, I need to tell you about my latest brush with death. How long was I out this time?"

Jay shrugged. "The usual: three days."

Just then, a heavy-set, Caucasian woman, perhaps Nowegian, in a pale white dress, with hideously mismatched ghost-white stockings, entered the room. Her over-starched nurse's uniform snapped, crackled, and popped as she waddled across the marble-white floor. Fat crinkled around her eyes as she cast a disapproving look at Jay, probably because he wasn't wearing white.

She had a booming voice that was tiny even compared to its vessel. She asked Jay in a squeaky tone, "When did he regain consciousness?"

"Half an hour ago for a few seconds and then just now."

She nodded and most of her kept nodding long after she intended to stop. This woman was large. (How large was she?) She was so large that the Law of Irony demanded that she drive a Mini Cooper.

Hers was a kind voice, though; her words soothing and safe. They reminded me of a time when I was but a wee lad, and my father would sing to me, just before bedtime.

She looked at me with a questioning smile: "Now?"

I looked around and shook my head.

"OK then. We're happy to see that we're awake, Mr. Steinman. How are we feeling today?"

"Steinman? Who are you talking to, sister?".

She looked at Jay, who nodded his head slightly.

"Phil," Jay said, looking from me to the nurse and then back to me, "we've been over this before. Just let it go."

I wasn't sure what I was supposed to let go, so I changed the subject. "To answer your question, lady, how would we feel if three million people were starving in Africa?"

"Hungry? But then, I'm always hungry. Suppose, for a minute, that the whole world is as well fed as I am--then how do we feel?"

I smiled and let the leash on my tension play out a little. This kid was all right. "Great," I said, "except my chest wants to talk to you about its current job description."

"Well, that's good," she said. "We're lucky we can feel pain, it lets us know that our nervous system still works."

Before I could tell her where she could stick my nervous system, she added, "Of course, the doctor has prescribed some medication for the pain—"

"Give it to me!" I snapped.

She gave me a look and pulled out an opaque white bottle from her milky white apron. She handed me two sperm-white pills, and I gulped them down faster than a lawyer chasing an ambulance leaving an accident scene caused by drunken CEOs.

"Don't get used to them," she warned.

"Sister," I snorted, "these aren't anything compared to a couple of highballs."

She poured me some water from the spill-proof pitcher and handed it to me.

"Try this straight, tough guy." She watched me take the rest of my medicine and gave me the spiel on how to ring if I needed her. Her parting words, as she waddled back toward the antique-white door, told Jay not to push me too far. She was humming as she closed the door. Jay decided to ignore her advice and resumed his position by the bed.

"All right, Phil, spill it: whodunit?"

I wasn't up to a brow beating so I told him I was suddenly very tired. Relaxing and pretending to doze, my body took this as a convenient excuse to lapse back into a nonsensical coma.

I saw a fleeting glimpse of the Authors as I was going under. They were dark shadows that cackled gleefully; the ruggedly handsome one was vigorously wringing his hands together. I had never actually seen anyone wring their hands before, so I took it to mean that I was in big trouble with a capital "B."

It was obviously time for another strange flashback sequence that would allegedly be relevant in retrospect to someone with enough time on their hands to read this literary travesty a second time. So for the sake of readers who weren't doing Life Without Parole, I just hoped that the flashback wasn't as bizarre and difficult to understand as the last one.

THE FETTUCCINE FILE

As I slipped back into my coma, I got that nauseating feeling again, like I was on some kind of twisted joyride to Oz. I rode out the vertigo and bumped into a strung-out looking chick and her Scotty dog. The dog was singing "Somewhere Over The Rainbow" off-key. Before I could get her phone number, the ride was over.

I looked around to see where the Angel of Death had dumped me this time. By the streamers hanging from the ceiling, I knew that it was the day of the big freshman dance.

Becky Fettuccine was lucky enough to be my date. Her pretty little face lit up when I informed her that she would be accompanying me.

"So, kitten, now that all of your other potential suitors are in the hospital, how about I pick you up at eight?"

"Not if you were the last prospective date on earth, you maniac!" she said, playing coy and hard-to-get. Her sweet, Southern lilt was like music to my loins.

"The name's Screwdriver, doll-face. Phillip Screwdriver, *last of the real men private investigators*. And about that 'last prospective date on earth' thing, I can arrange it." Richard's cold steel was more reassuring than another taunting Western Union telegram from EHarmony or Match.Com.

After the heraldic trumpets had quieted down, her eyes

became wide and wet like the River Styx. My sweet-talk finally convinced her adolescent hormones that it was the right thing to do. She whispered the three letters that I wanted to hear, her grand-parents were returned to her, unharmed. We were young and we were in love.

* * *

That evening, I dressed to the nines in my best suit and hat. After picking up my trenchcoat from the dry cleaners, I stopped by Eddie's for a quick buff job on my Florsheims. Eddie could have been a rich and famous Hollywood minstrel star but when racist stereotypes went out of fashion had to fall back on the fact that he was the best shoeshine boy in town, and, more importantly, my ear to the underworld. I stopped by his stand at least once a week to keep tabs on who wanted me dead in an alley, a zucchini shoved up my left nostril, and a Spam wig on my head to feed the fishes.

"Golly, Phil!" Eddie exclaimed. "You sho'nuff be lookin' sharps! You gots a hot date tonight, Boss?"

I nodded and fired up a Lucky. People who graduate summa cum laude from Harvard don't talk like Eddie was talking. He sounded like a character from a DW Griffith parody. He was trying to tell me something, but what? Was he saying that the white authors of this book were too chicken in today's politically correct world to portray a black man as poor and uneducated and felt the need to write Eddie as a Harvard valedictorian to prove they weren't racists or to assuage some sort of racial guilt?

"What's wrong Eddie?"

"I'll tell you what's wrong. You really done ticked off Becky's folks, Boss, they's got a contract out on you fo' da gran' parents thing."

"How much am I worth this week, Eddie?" I asked, blowing a nonchalant plume of smoke.

"Two hunnert, Boss." Eddie started doing a soft-shoe for no other reason than he was a stereotypical 1930s Negro and his character was designed to guarantee that this book didn't make it on the list of required reading for Orcah's Book Club.

A lousy two C's, that was it? Well, hell! I was still young. I took another drag off my cigarette and held it in my lungs. The smoke nestled there comfortably, like a bear hibernating for the winter, until I got light-headed and my face turned blue.

Eddie looked at me with concern and started reapplying shoe-polish on his face. "You okay, Boss? You looks kinda shaky." He reached beneath the shoeshine stand and pulled out a jug with three X's on it. "Here," he said, offering me the container, "try some o' dis. It'll steel yo' nerves."

I took the bottle from Eddie and poured half of its contents down the hatch. Liquid fire warmed my insides and shook up the world outside. It must have been some powerful stuff because everything kept shaking until I volunteered my dinner to the ground.

"Let them come, Eddie," I said, wiping my mouth with the back of my hand. "Let them try and stop me. They've tried before and they'll try again. Take last week, for instance. Three that wanted to stone me, two that wanted to own me, and one said she's a friend of mine. They won't get me, Eddie. They won't. Do you know why?"

Eddie nodded his head and didn't do anything stereotypical. "Sho'nuff, boss. I'se could tell from the smoky-fuzzy thing roun' the edge o' the page that we was in a flashback."

"Because we're in a flashback, Eddie, that's why. That means I'll live past tonight. Pretty good detective work, huh, Eddie?"

"Yowsah. Uh, boss?"

"Yeah, Eddie, what is it? And hurry up, because I've got that feeling again."

"Does I gots to talk an' act like somes 1930's Negro stereotype shoeshine boy every time that we'uns meets?"

"What a dumb question, Eddie. Frankly, I expected more from you. Everybody knows that the stereotype Negro shoeshine boy was the underworld connection of choice for real-men private investigators. It helps meet those Equal Opportunity laws while not really interfering with the story. Besides, what else were you going to do? Go to law school?"

"I'se could be a rogue lawyer in state's attorney office and pass youse information I ain'ts supposed to buts I does it anyways 'cuz I knows you'sah helps us solves 'da case!"

I let out a deep-throated laugh and continued, "What's the big deal, anyway? This is the 1930's; you have to speak like a stereotype."

"But, boss, it ain't da Thirties. It's da—"

"Early thirties, late thirties, whatever. Same time tomorrow?"

"Sorry, boss. Can't make it. I'se gots this big test in criminal law class, 'n' I'se gots to be a-studyin'."

That Eddie, what a kidder. He even had an attaché case right next to the footrest. Some poor sap must of left it there by accident.

"Say, Phil? Dids ya see dat 'Commandant Lugarson's Neighborhood' show on de tube last night? It sho'nuff sets a colored man back a piece."

I laughed. "Silly Negro, television hasn't been invented yet. See you around, Ed."

"Sees ya', boss," Eddie replied. "May yo' chariots always be swingin' low."

I flipped him two-bits and then hailed a cab. The Hack saw me, and, trying to stop his for-hire Edsel, plowed into a light green sedan next to me. The owner of the sedan, a dapper and limp-wristed but manicured man, opened his door, stood up, and burst into flames. The flaming man rushed toward me, screaming and flailing maniacally, but with a certain element of panache'. I pulled out the last cigarette from my pack of Lucky Strikes, crumpled the empty pack, and proceeded to litter.

"Got a light, mac?" I asked the flaming man as he ran up to me.

He screamed something unintelligible, and his car and my cab caught on fire. The flaming man continued screaming as he ran past me and toward the gas station. I had the thought that a flaming man running toward a gas station was probably a bad idea and wondered briefly about how what was likely to happen would affect the global price of a gallon of gasoline.

I walked over to the cab driver's flaming Edsel, reached in the window, and pressed the cigarette lighter. I waited for it to pop out into my hand. Then I stuck a cigarette in my mouth and touched the glowing end of the lighter to the fag. The fag screamed. I don't know where he came from or how he got between the lighter and my cigarette but assumed the authors just liked homophobic puns. The fag, now flaming himself, went running after the green sedan's flaming owner and toward the gas station. This time I was sure that a flaming man, let alone two flaming men, running toward a gas station was a bad idea. It's a good thing I'd sold my oil stocks and invested in a firefighting supplies manufacturer. Funny how things just seem to work out sometimes.

I chuckled, lit my cigarette, and put the lighter back into its little slot on the quickly melting dashboard.

My cabdriver had just gotten his engine fire under control, so I got in the back seat and gave him Becky's address. The nerves in my body were still a little rough, so I took another long pull from Eddie's tonic. And then another. Polishing it off, I threw the empty bottle out the window. It sailed gracefully through the air, reminding me of the flight of the *Enola Gay*. And then everything got blurry and I started seeing double. Eddie's tonic became two bottles and both impacted on the windshield of two police cruisers, smashing both. Fortunately, the two flatfeet were in the two Doughnut shops side-by-side across the streets. They shrugged at the carnage their vehicles had become and went back to their Bavarian Creams and coffees.

My two hack drivers turned around and asked, in unison, "Hey, kid. Aren't you a little young to be drinking?"

I don't know where the other guy came from, but I replied, "What's it to you, pals? I'm older than I look."

Actually, I looked ten, but I was really twelve or thirteen. But I looked like a really tough ten-year-old, and that's what mattered.

The cabbies rolled their eyes and simultaneously turned around to watch the road.

I felt a sudden wave of nausea and stuck my head out the window for some air. The wind yanked my fedora off my head.

I told the hack and his twin, "Stop, so I can get my damn hat."

They hit the breaks, and a couple of limousines rear-ended us. I got out and started looking for my hat; the cabbies could handle the limo drivers.

I was on all fours, looking under the cars, when I bumped into two burly, German toughs wearing black dress shoes, dark suits, and darker glasses, standing beside the limos. One of them was holding my hat, and the other was holding a hat that looked just like mine.

What the hell is with all these twins, I thought.

<u>ANOTHER EXPLANATORY AUTHORS' NOTE</u>: In case you haven't figured it out by now, Phil is drunk and seeing double. There are no twins. It's a gag, albeit not a very good one. He's twelve, people, and he's loaded on Eddie's moonshine. If you've already deduced this fact, skip the rest of the Authors' note. Go on. Nothing else to be learned here. Are they gone? OK, the rest of you, kindly read on. You are dumb. The directions on toothpaste are for you. But, in the interest of fairness, we will write more slowly, as we know you cannot read very fast.

The hoods asked, "Hey, kid, youse wouldn't by any wild chance be da Fruitcake that kidnapped the Fettuccine grand-parents, would youse?"

"The name's Screwdriver, pals; Phillip Screwdriver, last-of-the-real-men private investigators." Heraldic trumpets trumpeted again, just like in the last flashback. I wondered if they meant something. I shrugged. Maybe it just meant the hoods were playing heraldic trumpet music on their limo stereo systems.

They looked at me and asked, "What's with da trumpets?"

"I don't know," I replied thinking so much for my theory that the hoods have heavenly chorus and trumpet music on their Ipods. "Every time I say my name like that, they blow the horns in a triumphant and heraldic manner."

The goons grabbed me and threw me into a couple of hotdog stands. Pickle relish broke my fall. The torpedoes loomed over me, their simian silhouettes eclipsing the streetlights. They cracked their knuckles and said, "Stay away from Becky, Fruitcake-boy. Or else."

"Or else what, you paperless dagos?" I snapped after blowing some sauerkraut out of my left nostril.

"Gee," they stammered, scratching their heads, "I don't know. Nobody's ever not obeyed. Don't worry, though; I'll think something up. And it will be plenty nasty, too. Really vicious. I mean it. See? Somethin's already comin' to me. So, stay away from Becky."

They turned and walked back toward the cabbies.

"Hairy, WOP bastards!" I screamed. "Your mothers have mustaches that Tom Selleck is jealous of! Shave her back for me, you linguini-breathed goons!"

They snorted and, shoving my hack drivers aside, got into their limousines and left. The cabby and his twin brother started jumping up and down in a macabre, synchronized swimming act on dry land, screaming about insurance.

I grabbed a couple cups of coffee from one of the two hotdog vendors, and asked, "Hey, pal, are they shooting a Doublemint commercial around here?"

The vendor, and his doppelganger, merely shook their heads in disbelief.

I downed the first cup of coffee and reached in my pocket for some change. I went to hand the vendors my two-bits when I noticed that one had disappeared.

"Thanks for the java, pal. Where'd your brother go? He a magician, or just light in his loafers?"

The vendor shook his head again, "I am an only child, señor," he whined in a thick Canadian accent. "Here, amigo, have another cup on me."

"Make it two cups, pal, and while you're at it, throw in a hotdog. I'm not stupid, you know! I know what's going on here. I didn't just get off the boat," I paused, and then raised my voice, "like you're illegal alien brother! Where's your Carte Verde? I'm Emigré, pal, Buenos Tacos, border patrol, *comprende*?"

The vendor dumped two cups of steaming hot coffee over my head and tried to shove a wiener up my left olfactory canal. The Scotchguard on my hat and coat made them coffee-proof, and nobody shoves anything up this twelve -year-old's left olfactory canal! I took the hot dog, brought it down like a pimp cane, and left it in a place that would remind the vendor, and anyone else who peddled meat on the streets, that private investigators were the original Mac-Daddys who wore a fedora. Maybe next time the hot dog vendor would remember to pick on someone much larger than himself. Or at least not this last-of-the-real-men private investigators!

As I got into the cab, a gas station exploded in the distance.

"The Fettuccine place, pal. And step on it! I've got a hot date."

I slipped the hack an extra fin for his troubles as I got out in front of the Fettuccine mansion. The impressive structure stood quietly under the stars, like an impassive guardian of the night; its lit windows staring at me like all-seeing eyes. From the Victorian design, it must have been originally constructed in the early 1300's, but had been remodeled and was obviously well-kept.

The waning half moon smiled down on the landscape like a slavering platypus, shining a cold light on the newly blossomed trees. Pink flamingos scattered about the lawn cast twisted shadows onto the ground, making them look like pink flamingos casting twisted shadows. My simile skills were still a little weak but Richard made sure no one would point that out. I took another sip of coffee and tried to shake it off.

As I strolled up the inlaid-brick walkway toward the front door, I noticed a black limousine parked in the portico. My head pounded like a jungle drum, and my tongue felt like it was wearing a toupee. I made a mental note not to get coffee from those vendors again.

I slipped around the far side of the limo while the flamingos danced to Hannah Montana's' cover of *Achy Breaky Heart* on the lawn. God, how I hated that song! Hannah Montana was nowhere near as talented as her sister, Miley Cyrus. I ignored the bumping and grinding of the frolicking flamingos and turned my attention to the limousine. I examined the grille; flecks of yellow paint confirmed my hunch. Like a good detective, I gave the paint a fair shake. I took some hair from the toupee on my tongue and wiped the yellow. It was fresh and came off easily.

This clinches it, I thought. This is one of the limo's that rear-ended my cab.

Suddenly, the door to the house started to open. I ducked behind the limo. A familiar simian silhouette stood in the door opening, talking to someone inside.

"I'll takes care of him, boss. Youse ain't got nuthin' to worry about," the shadow said. It was one of the goons who had tossed me like a salad into the hotdog stands.

The voice inside the house replied in a language I'd once heard Alfredo the pizza man use. *So*, I thought, *the boss is German.*

Grunting, the goon shut the kitchen door and got into the limo. I opened the passenger door and slid in next to him, rod clenched in my fist. (That's rod as in gun, not as in penis, so don't get any wise ideas. Although I have had a penis since at least before I was seven and a half, and I'm damn proud of it, I don't go around waving it at strange men.)

I pulled a Lucky out of a fresh pack and stuck it in my yap. "Got a light, pal?" I asked the startled gunsel.

He reached under his jacket, and I grabbed his arm. "You had better be going for your lighter, pal, because I've got a real itchy pointer finger."

"Trigger finger, youse moron."

"What?"

"Youse gots a real itchy trigger finger."

"Who told you?" I asked through clenched teeth. This guy is tricky. I'd better keep an eye on him.

"Never mind, get on wit' it. What do youse wants?"

He gave me a strange look, and I gave him back a mean one. I snarled, "Leave Becky alone. This is your last warning."

"That's my job, pal, to keep youse away from her. Youse really pissed off da boss when youse went and snatched his parents. He don't like youse no more. Youse or that two-bit hood father of yours. What's his name? Oh, yeah, Frank 'the Pansy' Antipasto."

"That's 'Screwdriver' Linguini."

"My name ain't 'Linguini.'"

"No," I said, becoming annoyed, "Frank's is."

"Is what?"

"Never mind."

"You never mind," the goon replied, oh-so-cleverly.

"So what are you saying?" I asked.

"I'm sayin' this, kid," he replied and started drawing his arm out of his jacket. I shot him in the left nostril and watched the smirk melt off his face.

I reached my arm inside his Armani jacket and pulled out his little surprise. It was one of those shiny, nickel plated deals; the kind that doesn't even waver in the wind. It was a Zippo. The bastard was going to set me on fire. I used it to light the only irreplaceable part of my anatomy: my Lucky Strike unfiltered cigarette.

After pocketing the lighter, I switched places with Guido and turned over the engine. The motor roared to life, and I kicked the transmission into "Drive." Smashing through the kitchen door, I found myself staring at a hippopotamus in a black dress. The poor beast was apparently made up as a woman.

"Where's Becky?" I screamed, getting out of the car. The Ultimate Secret of Life flashed through my brain as I finished computing pi to the last place. I shook off my momentary dabble into intellectualism and fired three rounds into the air.

"WHERE IS BECKY?" I screamed again in a high-pitched, feminine voice.

The fat lady in the black dress put down her copy of "Songs for Swinging Scandinavian Lovers," stared at me with saucer eyes and pointed with one her ring laden meat hooks. I checked Richard's ammo supply.

As I charged the door the hippo had pointed at, a scarecrow in a three-piece suit opened it, saw me, and stepped aside. Momentum carried me through the hall and into the bathroom.

Becky was sitting on the porcelain throne in all her heavenly splendor, applying lipstick to those ripe, luscious lips that I so yearned to kiss. As I came barreling in, she turned her head toward me and left a red trail of Revlon across the left side of her face. My appearance must have startled her because she screamed and made another trail into her left nostril.

I stopped hurtling forward when my shins impacted on the onyx bathtub. My hands grabbed the curtain rod to break my fall. It was too weak, and I fell into the tub, pulling the curtains on top of me. I lay there, staring at the little blue platypi and red duckies pattern on the curtains.

Gee, Becky sure had class.

After going fifteen rounds with the web-footed warriors, I finally got them off of me.

"Hi, kitten. Miss me?" I asked, climbing out of the tub.

"No," she replied, not missing a beat, "you missed me. But not by much. What the hell are you doing here. . . er, What was your name again?"

"Screwdriver, toots," I replied, smiling. "Phillip Screwdriver, last-of-the-real-men private investigators."

The heraldic trumpets sounded from Becky's shower radio. Then, without warning, the music of the damned started playing in my head. Heavy jungle drums made sounds that would drive a man to the precipice of insanity, leaving him to stare at the dark void of his soul, where the reptile rested in its comfortable slime.

". . . Uh, Phil? Could you turn off the radio?" Becky asked, her voice like a light from above.

I reached over and yanked the cord from the wall.

Just a word of advice from your friendly, neighborhood last-of-the-real-men private investigators: If you've just rushed into a room, slammed your shins on an onyx bathtub, grabbed a curtain rod to break your fall, only to have it break and set you down as gently as a Buick going off of a cliff, fought fifteen rounds with blue plastic platypi and duckies, heard the music of the damned in your head, and been asked to by a gorgeous, half-naked blonde with lipstick lines bisecting her face, never, never, ever take your dripping wet hands and yank the frayed power cord of a radio from the wall. Like I did.

I flopped around in Becky's tub like the mime I hit with my Fiat last week and buried in Elton John's backyard. Lights flashed everywhere, and I swear I could see my skeleton, like in those old Warner Brothers' cartoons.

The next thing I realized, Becky was standing over me and asked, "Are you all right?"

As required by the Private Investigator's Handbook, chapter 3.14, I did not look up her slip. I sat bolt upright and grabbed her arm.

"Becky," I hissed, "we have to get out of here. I don't have time to explain, but there's a couple of toughs after you. We've got to make tracks twenty-three skiddoo."

I had Richard in my hand again; his hardness felt reassuring in my mitt. I knew that soon, if Becky and I were lucky, Ol' Dick would be spitting like a cat with a hairball in its throat. Richard seemed to be smiling at the thought. Oh yes. Yes! YES! I smiled with him.

"Uh, Phillip, right?" she asked. I nodded and put a finger to my lips, signaling her to keep her voice down.

She continued in a whisper, "What the hell are you babbling about? I live here; this is my house."

They really had her scared. Shrinks called it Stockholm Syndrome, but then shrinks name everything after cities: New Jersey Schizophrenia, New York Finger, Hong Kong Phooey — you get the idea. They still hadn't come up with a name for the Massachusetts mania that manifested itself in an entire State by continuing to elect Kennedys who'd made their fortune as illegal liquor bootleggers and fired their secretaries by driving off of the Chappaquiddick bridge. So Becky was either scared with Stockholm Syndrome or the tremendous stress she had been under had finally made her brain hop the first train out.

"Look, kitten," I said, smiling reassuringly, "just stick with me and Richard and everything will be jake."

I cracked the door open and stuck my fedora out. No takers. I stuck my mug into the hall and took a quick glance. The place was empty.

With Richard in my right hand and Becky's hand in my left, we crept out of the bathroom and into the hall. Wait, I think it was Becky's hand in my right and Richard in my left. No, no, that wouldn't have worked since my right hand was my shooting hand. So, it was definitely Richard in my right and Becky's delicate hand in my left as we crept out of the bathroom and into the hall.

STRAIGHT FORWARD AUTHORS' NOTE: *The above paragraph is not, we repeat, not an attempt to artificially lengthen the manuscript by inserting frivolous text, such as we are doing here, to increase book length and, thus, our paychecks, since we are not, repeat, not being paid by the word. Really. Have we ever lied to you? Ad infinitum.****

After we had taken half a dozen steps, a voice sounded from above. The masculine, bass timbre of the voice sent shivers up my spine as it echoed in the empty hall.

"Rebecca? Rebecca, mi canoli, is-a that youse?"

I slapped my palm over Becky's mouth before she could respond, and she bit down. Hard.

I wanted to scream like a girl, but I knew that our survival was depending on my silence.

"Becky," I whispered, "act like everything's jake, and we'll be able to bluff our way out of here."

The voice continued, "Rebecca, what was alla that racketeering going on down-a there?"

Becky whispered in my ear, "Who the hell is Jake?"

"Never mind," I whispered through clenched teeth, "just say everything's all right."

"Papa?" Becky asked the voice upstairs.

"Si, what is it?"

"It's the head of the family, usually masculine, and used in a familiar form. But that's not important right now."

"And what is important, mi little garlic bread?"

"Well, Papa, there's a maniac down here trying to kidnap me—"

I put my hand over her mouth and made for the door. I would have made it, too, if a fat man with snowy hair wearing a pinstriped bathrobe hadn't burst into the hall carrying a violin case.

"Dammit! It's that Fruitcake punk again! Whatsa matta wit' you? Youse want a war between the Linguini's and the Fettuccine's, you stupid freak?!" Joseph Fettuccine screamed as I dashed through the hall with his daughter.

He started to open his violin case. Violin case! Damn! That was the oldest trick in the book! Sure as the sun will come up tomorrow, he had a Tommy gun in there.

I didn't wait for a second invitation; I fired Richard and hit him where it hurts men the most: the wallet. I fired a second time and Joey Fettuccine dropped to the floor.

I had to give him credit for cleverly disguising his weapon in the shape of a violin. It even sounded like one getting crushed beneath a dead body when he landed on it.

I smiled. Becky screamed. I slapped her face—hard—and then threw her unconscious body over my shoulder and made for the exit.

About ten feet from the door, the scarecrow in the monkey suit reappeared. This time, he was holding a genuine M-1921 .45 Thompson, or "Stradavarius" for those of us in the know.

"What's going on here?" he demanded, waving the gun at me. His voice sounded as if it were filtered through a cheese grater, reminding me that I was hungry. I shifted Becky's dead weight to my other shoulder.

"Nothing out of the ordinary," I replied. "You wouldn't happen to have any pizza around here, would you? Pineapple with extra anchovies would hit the spot."

"I thought I heard gunfire."

"No, just bad Fettuccine backfiring. About that pizza?"

"Hold on, I'll see what I can do about it." He turned and yelled into the kitchen, "Mabel!"

Good German name, I thought.

"Mabel, could you fix our guest a large pineapple pizza with extra anchovies?"

Mabel grunted something from inside the kitchen, and the Scarecrow turned and said to me, "About twelve minutes. Do you want some wine with that?"

"Yeah, that would be nice. What goes well with pineapple and anchovies?"

"Nothing," replied the Scarecrow.

"That's what I thought. Now confess: what did you do with Dorothy, the cowardly Lion, the tin guy, and that lovable, scene-stealer: Toto, the wonder dog?"

His brow knotted in anger, his pasty face flushed, and his

hands began to shake.

Scarecrow was clearly upset and shocked by my accusations. I watched him spill his guts, making sure he didn't try to spill mine with his Stradivarius.

"That wasn't me in the Wizard of Oz. I'm Jay Bolger, Ray's little brother. But all the other stars got their goddamn contracts renewed by the studio. With Ray's new brain, he was too smart to sign for what they were asking. I was going to be a star, dammit! I was working' security for the studio and signed to be a Keystone Cop! When Ray tried to renegotiate, the heartless bastards blacklisted him and sent me packin' for being' his brother!

"I was walkin' the streets one day, when Mr. Fettuccine found me. He was a big fan of mine, and seein' me down on my luck, he offered me a job. I tried to get the Don to give me one of those Sinatra deals but he said I'd make a great straw man some day for sham transactions"

The Scarecrow lit a cigarette, something not all-together intelligent for someone made of straw, and continued, "It's a great employee advancement plan that the mob has. Start out as a butler, get used as a straw man, hear a few secrets, blackmail the Don, and move up, you know?"

"Really? How long have you been a butler?"

He grumbled something unintelligible.

"What did you say?"

"Thirty-seven years, okay? There, I said it. Are you happy?" he shook his head slowly. After a moment of silence, he continued, "Too many bad breaks, you know how it is. And then after all his promises the Don told me that because I was a scarecrow I was over-qualified to be a straw man."

"Yeah," I replied, "I know how it is."

I stuffed Becky in the recliner and then realized that she would probably be more comfortable if her firm, round, nubile buttocks were placed on the cushion, instead of being displayed in the air. I turned her upright. It was a shame, though; she had a great butt, and it would have made a great conversation piece over dinner.

I fired up a Lucky and flicked a match into the exotic fish tank. The goldfish didn't complain.

An idea popped into my brain. I looked at Scarecrow and said, "So you want to move up, eh?"

"Well, yeah. Thirty-seven years as a butler really blows."

"What would it be worth to you if I could get you that promotion?"

The Scarecrow looked at me incredulously. "It'd be worth anything you want. But you're a ten-year-old kid; how're you going to get me that?"

"I'm twelve or thirteen," I replied, indignant. "Anyway, straw for brains, if I get you that promotion, you owe me a favor; got it?"

"Yeah, yeah, sure. Whatever, kid."

"I've got your word on that?"

"I said 'yeah' didn't I?"

I sat back in my chair, smiling like the cat that just ate the canary. "Go look in on Mister Fettuccine."

He gave me a strange look and left with his violin. Twenty seconds later, he was whooping and hollering with joy. Abruptly, the yelling stopped, and he came running back in where we were sitting. There was a look of terror drawn on his potato sack face.

"Wh-what about Meatball, the boss's right hand man?"

"Go look in the limo. It's in the kitchen."

I took a drag on my smoke as he left for the kitchen. I passed up the bottle of twelve-year-old scotch for the fifteen-year-old stuff from behind the fully stocked wet bar and enjoyed a quick belt. I made it a rule to only drink scotch that was older than I was. The Don's hooch tasted like a watered down version of Eddie's nerve tonic. I had just poured myself another drink when the Scarecrow came rushing back in. Between pumping my hand, hugging me, and making me his partner in an Irish jig, I never did have that second shot.

After a few minutes, he had sufficiently regained his composure enough to ask, "What's your name, kid?"

"Screwdriver, pal. Phillip Screwdriver, last-of-the-real-men private investigators, and don't you forget it." Trumpets sounded again.

The Scarecrow and I looked around for a second to see if we could discover the source of the heraldic trumpets. Then he said, "Don't worry, Phil, I'll remember your name. I owe you big. Any time you need a favor, you just ask your old pal Scarecrow. Sorry I can't stay, but I've got to go practice my gravelly accent. Mafia union standard, y'know."

He started to leave and then turned back toward me.

"You want to come with me, Phil?"

"No, I want to be alone," I replied, nodding my head at Becky.

"Oh, I get it," he said. "You want me to take her with me."

"No," I repeated, "I-want-to-be-ALONE, you putz." I nodded toward Becky again, adding a knowing wink to it. "I've got an immaculate conception of my plan for the rest of the evening and you're not in it."

"Oh, right. The Polaroid's in the desk. See ya! And thanks again!"

He went through the kitchen door and yelled gleefully at Mabel to get into the limo. As they were walking through the door, Mabel, who was fat lady in the black dress I'd encountered in the kitchen and who was as large as someone named Mabel ought to be, paused, looked meaningfully at me and asked, "Now?"

I shook my head, and the Scarecrow grabbed her hand and yanked her across the threshold.

I didn't remember Becky fainting. I guess the relief at finally being rescued was too much for her delicate constitution. I went into the kitchen and got a glass of ice-cold water. Returning, I threw it in her face, hoping that it would revive her. The cold water made her white teddy quite transparent. It was obvious she was happy to see me.

Her sea-green eyes shimmered as they opened. Her little, pink tongue snaked across her lips, leaving a glistening trail behind it.

"I-is it finally over?" she asked in a quavering voice.

"Yeah, kitten," I assured her, "it's over."

She still looked a little uptight. She buried her face in her hands and started sobbing. "He was so mean; he tried to electrocute me, he didn't give me any privacy, he kidnapped me at gun point. I was so scared."

"I know, kitten. But you're in good hands now."

"Thanks, Daddy. I knew you weren't really dead."

"Daddy?" I asked, taken aback. "Joey's dead, kiddo. It's me: Phil." Not wanting to alarm her further, I didn't complete the name, and spared her the heraldic trumpets.

"Wh-what?" She looked up at me, and her eyes went wide, and I swear to this day that I saw smoke come out of her ears. Her face went slack, and she started babbling and drooling.

"You see, kitten, the way I figure it, we're like Romeo and Juliet; you're Romeo, of course, and I'm your Juliet. We're a couple of crazy, mixed-up kids in a crazier, more mixed-up world. Like the Jets and the Sharks; Tony, Maria, and the rest of the West Side Story gang, we're a couple of crazy, mixed-up kids in a . . . well, never mind, you get the picture. Huh? . . . What's that about poison? . . . Ours' is a truly romantic tale, transcending the bounds of reality as Cupid blasted his way into our hearts, only to splatter our souls together against the memory of my mother. Cupid's a punk. Trust me, I know. It's like Oedipus and Jocasta, Batman and Robin, Abbott and Costello, Godzilla and Mothra, the Three Stooges. Unrequited love, baby, that's you and me, that's what it's all about; this is crummy writing, but that's life. Yeah, that's what all the people say. You're riding high on Monday, shot down in May, and I wouldn't want to change my tune, cuz I'm back on top, of you, in the month of . . . Say, is it hot in here?"

Becky was drooling and rolling her eyes. She went limp as her head lolled to the side. Becky had packed her bags and left sanity far, far behind. She was crazy, crazy in love with me. I knew then that I had to end it. Anybody who got to close to me would only end up hurt or dead. But I knew that this would be a moment we would always treasure. Not wanting to ruin it, I kissed her forehead and left.

I walked out of her house that morning, and shot every damn dancing flamingo I saw because now I had an Achy-Breaky Heart but I certainly wasn't going to do the Hustle to prove it. Those pink bastards looked like they had been dancing all night. Not content with simple disco dancing, they had moved to a more difficult step: line dancing. The flamingos were gyrating lustfully when I gunned them down. I guess they didn't realize just how much I hate Serbo-Croatian religious dances.

Looking back, I wonder if I should have let them live long enough to teach me the flamenco.

* * *

Incidentally, Scarecrow brought the Mafia to its knees within a year through sheer incompetence. Uh, of course, I planned it that way. The brain that the Wizard had given him was a Wal-mart yellow dot special, and, therefore, crap. I should know; I had to return mine three times before I got this one.

The doctor said that Becky would probably never recover. I had that effect on women. Her inheritance gave her the best room at St. E's that money could buy; she even had a special nurse to come in hourly and change her drool buckets. Occasionally, I'm told, she would see my face on the tube or hear heraldic trumpets and go into spasms of uncontrollable passion.

Yeah, like St. Pauli Girl Beer, you never forget your first girl.

INTERLUDE TWO

The Angel of Death got up to get more popcorn and drink refill. Knowing she would be in line for hours trying to get the minimum-wage drones to actually do their jobs, I took a chance and floated back into consciousness. It had been nice seeing Becky again, but it was even nicer to see my hospital room.

When I opened my eyes, I found my room deserted. Muted sunlight peeked through the panes, giving my cheery, antiseptic white room a gray tint. Motes of dust floated lazily about in the shafts of sunlight, unconcerned with the dangers of exposure to ultraviolet radiation.

I slipped out of the starched sheets and almost collapsed to the floor. Steadying my atrophied legs, I crept over to the closet and found my fedora, shoulder rig, and trenchcoat. A bouquet of roses was tucked in my holster beside Richard. The card told me what I already knew: Judy had sent them and wished me well.

What a doll, I thought, and a fleeting smile sweetened my usually sour lips. I smiled again when I realized that the Authors were engaging in a pitiful attempt at character development. Why did they even bother? Phillip H. Screwdriver is an archetype—not some three-dimensional character to be given ethos, pathos, and nachos. My stomach grumbled. If the Angel of Death came back from the concession stand with chips with extra pathos that would hit the spot.

I wandered over to the mirror to get a good look at myself. The upper half of my body was covered in fresh bandages. If I put on my trenchcoat, buttoned it up and belted it, the gauze might pass for a shirt. Hopefully, the casual observer wouldn't notice that I was sans trousers.

A quick search of my trenchcoat failed to produce a deck of Lucky Strikes. Really needing cigarettes and pathos and tracking down the hit man gave me three swell excuses to leave this two-bit hospital. I buttoned up as best I could and walked out.

Upon reaching the street, I saw that it was only half a block to a bar and decided to hoof it instead of calling a cab. The cool morning breeze wafted through my toes and across my bare calves before gaily flitting up my trenchcoat. The wind gave me a cool, refreshing sensation, like that of a York Peppermint Patty.

I was trying to act casual and not draw attention to myself when I stepped on a wad of chewing gum that squished through my toes. Just one more reminder that Phillip H. Screwdriver was no ordinary gumshoe. I didn't even need shoes. I picked the stuff off my toes and kept walking. By the taste, it was either regular or well chewed watermelon.

I checked my wallet and decided that I needed to grab some cash before I grabbed a drink. I knew that the church next to the hospital cashed checks, so I slipped in and scribbled out an IOU for the pastor who put the "rev" in revenue and reverend. After I handed him my marker, he told me in his sanctimonious way that the institution charged a convenience fee of $6.66, in addition to any fees my own bank charged. Christ, that was more than any ATM fee. Disgusted, I told him to forget it, drew Richard, and emptied 666 rounds into his lockbox. It sparked, fizzled, and started spewing twenties at me, like it was tithing me. Ah, the riches of Heaven. I picked up a handful of bills and left the church.

I walked down the street and when I finally walked into the 21st Amendment Bar & Grill, it hurt like a bitch. I decided to try the door.

The bar was a cozy, family owned tavern. The mother, Hillary, was slumped against the cigarette machine; drowning herself in liquid pity after another failed Presidential run. The father, Bubba, was at the bar, face down in a bowl of beer nuts, an oddly smelling cigar smoldering in the ashtray next to him. Junior, who looked like Bubba but not Hillary, was playing mumble de peg with a swabbie wearing a black eyepatch. Sis was hooking, hawking her wares in her normal spot: the men's room. Besides them, the joint was deserted. Good, because I needed some quiet to sort things out.

My favorite bartender, Norm, was behind the oak bar and whistling a familiar tune. I pulled out a cheap wooden stool, dropped myself onto it, and asked him for a double.

Norm looked at me and said through half sneered lips, "Don't do what your big sister done!"

Norm had worked behind that bar for as long as I could remember. His slicked-back hair and outrageous sideburns were reminders of better days. As were the diamond-studded sunglasses and the shiny jumpsuit that strained to contain his massive gut.

"Look, Norm," I said, "I've had a rough day, so start singing a new song and leave the bottle."

A hurt expression creased his plump features. "Take my advice, treat me nice."

He sounded like Ann Landers, but I knew he was right. We were friends from way back, but right now, I didn't want friends. My edges were frayed and rougher than a Velcro codpiece. That little simile reminded me that I wasn't wearing any underwear.

I crossed my legs and pulled my trenchcoat down a little. "Sorry about snapping at you like that, pal, but I'm looking for the guy who tried to give me lead poisoning."

Norm smiled, letting me know that everything was jake. He set a glass of amber liquid down in front of me and went back to polishing beer mugs. I sat there, sipping the scotch and contemplating my situation.

There wasn't much to go on. Flashes of people, a few voices. I remembered some guy wearing a light green overcoat trying to stab me, but I didn't think he was the Big Cheese. It didn't seem right: he must have been working for someone; but who? The Fettuccine family?

A beautiful face darted across my mind's eye. Long, honey blonde hair framed her features like a halo, high lighting emerald green eyes. I had visited her last month in St. Elizabeth's. She hadn't changed much since the night of the prom. When she saw me, she had gone into convulsions, screaming my name and pointing a dainty finger at me. Poor Becky. I guess my appearance was too much for her. Maybe it had brought back feelings about me that she wasn't prepared to feel. With one final scream, she had broken free of the restraints on her bed and come rushing toward me for one last embrace. Unfortunately, she also had been tethered at the neck, and Becky's tortured life ended with a snap. Her lifeless body dropped at my feet like a marionette with no strings, drool mixed with blood puddling on the floor.

Nah, it couldn't be the Fettuccine family. The Scarecrow was still the head of the family and he still owed me. Even if he hadn't brought the mob to its knees he would have had me shot, not knifed.

But I was shot, so who was the guy with the blade? Maybe just a no-name bum trying to roll me after finding me unconscious in an alley? I just couldn't remember any details. I had left who? Was headed where? I couldn't remember.

Norm brought me a frosty mug of dark beer and back to reality. Having finished my Scotch paragraphs ago, I accepted it gratefully.

"What is it?" I queried. He pointed to a bottle marked "Viking Lager," and smiled. I took a sip and let the bitter, manly ale go berserk on my taste buds. I had a hunch that this beer was another pitiful attempt by the Authors at proving that they actually knew what literary devices were.

"Smooth," I rasped, referring to the ale and not the

foreshadowing. Norm smiled and then went to tend another customer. I returned to my thoughts.

Adolph and Eva Geshtappo crossed my mind, but I moved them along, certain they were dead. The only one left was . . .

The Platypus! Of course!

"Hey, Norm," I asked hopefully, "has a man in a navy cap with webbed hands been hanging around?"

Norm came over, leaned his beefy mass across the rail, and whispered, "A very old friend . . . came by today. He was tellin' everyone in town of the—"

The report of a gunshot cut him off.

As I hit the floor, I saw the round shear off one of Norm's sideburns, sending it sailing across the room. The fur was really flying, so I rolled under a nearby table and had Richard out before I took a breath. The saloon doors flapped open and closed but I caught a brief glimpse of a peacoat; the gunman had left in a hurry!

I charged the door and dove out headfirst. I did a quick roll and ended up crouched behind a parking meter, playing my gun all around me. The maniacal laughter of The Platypus drifted down from above. His evil mirth seemed to eat into my soul; it seemed to taunt me like those big kids in kindergarten did. But, like them, he would only do it once.

I looked around and discovered that the laughing came from a fat, Norwegian meter maid who was staring at my private dick (excuse the pun). Damn, my trenchcoat had come open.

Mortified at having revealed myself to a woman before she had wantonly thrown herself at me, I rushed back into the bar. If the guys ever heard about this, I'd be kicked out of the union and have to get a Real Job. *The Private Investigator's Handbook* specifically says, chapter 11, section 8: "In detective novels, any woman shall be immediately overcome with lust and remove all clothing, including undergarments, in front of the detective. That detective will immediately show the emotional reactions of a long-deceased monk."

All right, The Platypus was still somewhere in this two bit berg; and he knew that I was still alive and kicking. This was it: one of us was not going to live to see tomorrow. Or at least next Easter.

I released the magazine from Richard and checked the ammunition for dramatic effect. It was full. Good, because I hadn't fired a round. I slammed the clip into the magazine well and jacked back the bolt. The satisfying metallic clang of a round slamming home calmed my nerves.

I was going to find me a killer, just as soon as I got some pants on. I shoved Richard back into the shoulder rig and noticed sticky, red liquid on my hand. Dammit! I was bleeding again! All the action must have ripped open my sutures.

I became dizzy, and my world was spinning like a draedel, letting me and anyone who bought my book know that I was about to go into another flashback sequence. The edges of my vision darkened, and my legs buckled. Waves of pain crashed brutally upon the sands of my body, as the undertow of unconsciousness dragged me beneath the pounding surf. Rainbow trout swam before my eyes, snickering at me and frolicking in the tide. Their iridescent scales shimmered and flashed.

From out of the miasma I heard a woman's voice ask "Now?" My last conscious thought as I shook my head was: Dammit! I'm not wearing dirty underwear.

THRYMMSKVITHA (or The Viking Saga)

The collage of colors gradually blended themselves into a uniform white. For a moment, I thought I had lucked out and was coming to again in my white hospital room. But it wasn't hospital white—it was snow white but there weren't any dwarves in sight. Snow covered everything and was falling from the sky with a vengeance. Full, dark clouds smothered the heavens like a shroud. The feeble glow of the sun did little to warm the frosted landscape.

I looked around and noticed that everyone was decked out in fur trenchcoats and antlered hats.

A voice like rolling thunder boomed from behind me, shaking the ground and my feet in their fur-covered(?!) Florsheims.

"Be that mine belov'd, yet tortured, son gazing 'bout the frozen land like a lost sheep? Hast thou newly come from the drycleaners?"

I turned around to see who the voice belonged to and noticed that I was holding a bear-skin trenchcoat, wrapped in plastic. I filed that in my keen detective mind for future use. Turning my head left, I saw the owner of the voice: a large, over-muscled man wearing a horned, sky-blue fedora pulled down over his left eye. He was clad from head to toe in deerskin, and his long, gray beard was laced with frozen spittle and blood, reminding me of a wild cherry Slurpee. Crumbs from the ham hock he carried decorated his outfit.

"Didst thou rememberest to retrieve thine mystical hammer,

Mjolnir, or didst that thought vacate thy tempestuous skull, son Thor?" he asked, his words shaking the nearby mountains.

I looked around. It was just he and I standing out here in the frozen tundra of what I was certain was not Lambeau field. Though we were clearly two warriors. He had called me, what again--Thor? That explained a lot. Then the god who called me son must be Odin, my father. I must have flashed back into a previous life (which really rattled my cage because I don't believe in reincarnation). Worse was that, up until now, my life had been going by in sequential order. The Angel of Death must have hit the wrong button on the remote-- either that, or the Authors were on crack.

AUTHORS' JUSTIFYING NOTE*: We are not currently on crack, nor any other illegal narcotic. By the way, the word "narcotic" comes from the Greek Narcos, the god of sleep or something, and means: to sleep. The Federal Drug Administration (FDA) labels any legal or illegal substance as a narcotic, even if, as in the case of crack cocaine, it accelerates one's adrenal output and excites one's metabolism. Perhaps the FDA should refer to Webster's Unabridged Dictionary before making such an onerous boner and kicking down the front door to our Colombian chalet. Who are the idiots now? But we digress, again.****

So, I was no longer, or wasn't yet, Phillip H. Screwdriver, last-of-the-real-men private-investigators; I was Thor, last-of-the-real-gods-of-thunder! This holy insight made me remember that I was mad. Damn mad! It all came rushing back like a bolt of lightning.

I had just returned from Thrymm's Drycleaning and Hammer Repair. There I'd picked up my freshly-blocked fedora helmet and my Valhalla Fog trenchcoat (which had been altered to conceal the bulge made by Richard, my trusty hammer). But after taking off the plastic overwrap, I discovered that Odin's hunch was right: Richard was missing!

Just then, a man galloped up on a horse and spoke in

reverent tones to Dad.

"'Tis time for thine nap, m'lord Odin," he whispered.

Odin studied his Rolex sundial for a moment. "Verily, 'tis so. The All-Father doth need his rest if he is to run the Heavens and Earth." He turned toward me. "And Thor, go seeketh thine hammer. Thou wert born to have it."

Yeah, I was born to have a hammer in my hand, Lord, Lord. Born to have a hammer in my hand.

When they had gone inside the house, I went to the stables and borrowed Sleipnir, Dad's V-8-legged Mustang, and set out for Thrymm's at a full gallop. If all went as planned, I'd have her back in the stables before Dad got up from his nap.

I set the cruise control, fired up a Valkyrie Slim, and relaxed, spinning the dial to Radio Free Asgaard and taking a pull of mead from the flagon I kept in my hip pocket. The disc jockey, Casey Kayson, said that ABBA, Roxette, and Bjork were still climbing the charts, and that Diana the Supreme had left the Valkyries to pursue a solo career.

What a moron, I thought. She's nothing without back-up. I bet she goes on to do some really lousy disco tunes, maybe even a tribute album before fading into obscurity. Why, she—

A loud, wailing noise sounded from behind me and interrupted my train of thought. I noticed Jay Heimdahlson on his police stallion approaching in my rear-view mirror. I reined in my steed and pulled off to the righthand side of the snow-covered path. Shortly, Jay pulled up beside me, coughing and wheezing.

I took a pull from my flagon and asked, "Want a hit, Jay?"

"Thou shouldst refrain from imbibing the fruit of the vine whilst thou art behind the reins, friend Phil. Tho', verily, mine throat be parched as the siren hath yet to be invented. But, alas, I am on duty."

I looked at him like he was crazy, and I said, "What? Why are you talking like some guy out of a Shakespearean tragedy?"

"Every tongue in the vale doth so wag, Phillip. Art thou

feeling ill?"

"Yeah, I'm fine. But the name's Thor, pal. Thor, last of the real gods of thunder. Got it?" Jay shook his head wearily as trumpets thundered in the distance. "Good. Anyway, Jay, I'm glad that you came along. I'm on my way over to Thrymm's place. That dirty frost-giant bastard stole my Richard."

"I hath finally remember'd to hail thee as Phil not Glory, and now those damned Authors, borne of the bovine and kin to the still-born calf, wish thee to be anointed as Thor?"

"Yeah," I replied. "That about sums it up. Anyway, could you—"

"Hast they lost their freaking minds?!" Jay screamed. "Hath they naught anything better to do than to maketh mine life a living Hell? Jesus H. Christson, where be mine agent?"

I fired up a Valkyrie Slim and pushed my horns back far enough to give him The Eye.

"And what be 'Richard?'" Jay continued. "Dost thou mean the mighty Mjolnir, the mystical hammer bestow'd upon thee by thine most high and half-blind All Father, Odin?"

"Yeah, Dad gave it to me for the Feast of Yule last year, but I changed the name because I like Richard better. There's just too many damn consonants in 'Mjo . . . Mjol . . . What you said. Is the 'j' silent?"

That Jay was silent, fuming at something. He took off his horned homburg and ran his fingers through his long and braided hair.

"Hey, Jay?" I asked. "When did you grow the beard? And those locks? A little longer than police reg's, aren't they?"

Jay sighed and looked past me, toward the frozen North Sea. I followed his steely gaze to a large Red Star liner running full force into an even larger iceberg. I could even hear the distant strains of the orchestra playing.

He looked back at me and said, "Be ye certain Mjol—uh, Richard 'twas purloined?"

I nodded an affirmative, took a deep drag on my cigarette, and spit. I watched my downward-hurtling phlegm turn to ice in the frigid Scandinavian air. I mentally kicked myself for not making some kind of Flemish joke. The frozen glob struck Jay's steed in the hoof with tremendous force, causing the stallion to rear and bolt. We watched in horror as the horse ran right off the fjord's edge and begin plummeting toward the icy waters far, far below.

I tried to look casual.

Jay snatched the flagon out of my hands and took a long, long pull. And then he took another. "Dammit, Phil . . ."

I gave him a hard look, and he corrected himself. He knew who he was dealing with.

"Uh, damn thee to Rightgaard, Thor! That be thrice in a single fortnight that thou hast driven mine steed to the abyss. Thou wilt fill out the runes upon the damned report and parlay with the police chieftain, beseeching him to spare mine mortal coil!"

"Yeah, I'll take the heat for you. There's no love lost between me and Chieftain Beowulf that a box of Norwegian Creams can't find. We can pick some up at the Danish Donuts on the way to Thrymm's Drycleaning and Hammer Repair shoppe."

"Donuts! Donuts? Thou wouldst placate my chieftain's ire over three lost stallions with . . . donuts? Thou wilt sucketh upon mine porcine saber ere this calamity doth approach the curtain!" Jay swore.

"Yeah, whatever, Jay. Saddle up, cause we're out of here."

As Jay swung up behind me on Dad's mustang, we heard a distant whinny and a splash. I could feel Jay's eyes burning a hole in the back of my head.

I tried to look casual.

With a flash of light and a cloud of snow, I heartily yelled, "Hi-ho, Sleipnir! Away!" and then turned and whispered to Jay, "Y'know, I've always wanted to do that."

We galloped down the snowy path toward the village of Fjkrl, by the Fjord of the Vowelless. The frozen tundra and craggy landscape reminded me of earlier times: building Vikings out of snow and playing with my childhood companion, Johnny the platypus. We used to frolic through the icy fields, laughing at life, singing operas, drinking from mead-horns, and chain-smoking Valkyrie Slims. We had the best times—that is until Johnny fell in with the wrong crowd.

Johnny had started hanging out at Loki Lemming's Poolhall more and more frequently. I later discovered that he had fallen in love with a beautiful, but emotionally disturbed, lemming dame. We had started to drift apart as Johnny began palling around with her and her friends, doing lemming things, like cliff-diving.

One day, I had awakened to a note pinned to my pillow. Johnny had written that he was going on a roadtrip and that he would miss dinner for a few days.

I never saw Johnny again.

* * *

Jay and I stopped at Eddie's boot-fluff stand on the outskirts of the village. We dismounted, and I dropped myself onto Eddie's stool.

Placing my reindeer-skin boots on his footstool, I said, "Just a quick fluff job, Eddie. And the drift on Thrymm's latest icecapade."

I pulled out a Valkyrie Slim, and Eddie was there with flints before I could think to ask. I took a nice, deep drag, and let Eddie fill me in.

"Sho'nuff, boss. Verily, it doth seem that Thrymm hath become of addled mind. The drycleaning mogul hath not seen the light of maidenhead since she who borne him. His ears hath been filled with tales of thine much-cherished Richard, thinking 'twas thine daughter and not thine mystical hammer, Mjolnir. Therefore, he hath kidnapped thine mallet to hold as ransom against thine daughter's hand in matrimony, boss."

I mulled over what Eddie had said, and it just didn't sound jake (was the "j" silent in jake?). First of all, Richard was a boy's name. But that wasn't what was bugging me. An idea was kicking around inside my brain. Suddenly, it kicked hard enough to put it through the uprights for three points.

"Say, Eddie, aren't you supposed to talk like a 1930's (A.D.) Negro stereotype throughout the entire novel?"

"Well, boss, this tome doth be pregnant with paradox. To wit, thine Norse brethren speaketh in the iambic pentameter tongue of Shakespeare to suggest the ancientness of these proceedings. Verily, the true speech of the ancient Dane was of the trochaic rhythm."

SHORT AUTHORS' NOTE: *We enjoy educating our readers as we entertain them, as we are more intelligent than all of them put together and feel the need to parade our superior intellects in front of them.* ***

I flipped Eddie and the two Authors two bits and thanked them for the info. Jay and I remounted and began galloping down the expressway.

Eddie called to me as we rode out of sight, "Perchance, wilt thee picketh up and returneth to me, on the morrow or the next week's genesis, mine judicial robes? Thy father hath elevated me to the bench and I hath left them at Thrymm's to be clean'd."

That Eddie, what a kidder. He was the best boot fluffer in the land but liked to think that he was a law school professor and now a judge. I let him live out his little fantasy. "Sure, kid."

Silly Negro.

Jay called over my shoulder, "Learnst thou what thee seeketh?"

"Yeah," I replied, "As near as I can translate, Thrymm, that dirty yellow snowball, couldn't get a date, so he decided to steal Richard and trade it for my daughter's hand in marriage."

Jay stroked his beard thoughtfully and mused, "Verily, Thor, it doth ring true."

"There's only one problem, Jay: I don't think I have a daughter."

He again stroked his beard thoughtfully and then pointed ahead, through the blowing snow. "Ye Olde Danish Donut Shoppe draws nigh. We must rememberest the chieftain's Norwegian Creams."

Through the front window of the store, I saw King Norm of the Graced Land shoveling jelly donuts into his mouth, hand over fist. He was the barkeep at the Great Hall, Flagsheim's, and could schlep mead with the best of them.

Jay went inside and emerged a few minutes later with a bag under his arm and two Styrofoam chalices in his hands. He handed me a cup and took a sip of his. "Mrs. Olsen's coffee grown of the mountain be good to the last drop."

"It's all right. I like the lattes from Starbjuck's better, though." I gulped some down and said, "You know, Jay, we really ought to stop using Styrofoam products; they're bad for the environment. Didn't the campaign of the Bifrost Berserkers teach you anything?"

***<u>AUTHORS' EARTH NOTE</u>: *Not only are we intelligent, artistic, witty, and handsome, but we are ecologically responsible, too. This book was printed on 100% recycled trees made from recycled pages of old Al Gore speeches and Earth in the Balance. We should know, as we nurtured and hugged these trees from mere saplings in anticipation of this novel's printing to enhance your tactile enjoyment. We care, really.* ***

We finished the coffee and tossed the cups over our broad Viking shoulders. The fierce Norse wind blew them over the edge of the fjord, where they came to rest among the carcasses of Jay's steeds. We rode quickly across the snow to the station hall, where I paused to let Jay off.

Apparently, Jay's mother never taught him any manners. With a mouthful of donuts, he said, "I hath great deeds to perform and lofty mountains of recycled trees to push. Fare thee well, friend Thor, in thy quest for thine magick hammer. But fail not to returneth to yon station and bespeak with Beowulf."

"Yeah, yeah. Is the chieftain still coming over for a game of bones on Thursday?" I asked.

"'Tis already planned. But do not bring thy landlord, Grendel, as he and Beowulf do not get along well."

"I'll think about it. See ya," I said, firing up a Valkyrie Slim. I opened up my flagon and took a long pull.

This God of Thunder crap was getting on my nerves. When you're the BGOC (Big God on Campus), every Thrymm, Dickson, and Harry has a big, nasty-looking axe with your name on it.

I lit up a smoke before realizing that I had one going in my other hand. I shrugged and stuck them both in my vice-like jaw, inhaling deeply. I let the smoke gently waft through the caverns of my lungs--and passed out from oxygen deprivation.

When I came out of the smoke-filled haze of unconsciousness, a beautiful, long-legged brunette was smothering me with sloppy, wet kisses. Her deep, soulful brown eyes gazed longingly into mine. Her perfume was a heady and intoxicating mix of oats and barley. She languidly tilted her head back and whinnied.

It was at that point that I realized that I was lying in a yellow snowbank, staring up at Sleipnir's underside.

I lit a Valkyrie Slim by summoning a lightning bolt and then stood up. I reached into the saddlebags and pulled out a towel to dry myself off with. The eight-legged horse had a satisfied smirk on its face. I don't know what Sleipnir was smiling about: he was a gelding. If I were without mine, I'd never smile.

I thought of Richard and frowned. I decided to head back to my office and check in with my secretary before making my next move. I mounted and fired up a Valkyrie Slim before realizing that I already had one smoldering in my other hand. I put them both between my teeth, started to inhale deeply, and then thought better of it. I took one of the butts out of my mouth and flicked it toward the donut shoppe.

By a strange twist of fate, the lit fag sailed into the open mead horn of King Norm, who was just leaving the store. The horn burst into flames, causing him to exclaim, "Lord Amighty, I doth feel mine temperature rise! Higher and higher, it doth burn through to mine very soul!"

With that, he tossed the flaming horn into the air. By another strange twist of fate, the lit flagon landed in the chimney pipe, slid down into the stove, and blew up. The explosion sent donuts, cream filling, and jelly (not to mention two-thirds of the Fjkrl police force) flying into the air and over the fjord's edge. Everything and everyone began plummeting toward the arctic waters far, far below.

I tried to look casual and kicked Sleipnir into a casual trot. A very fast casual trot.

I arrived at Bilskinir, my office, tied up Dad's nag, and was inside in record time. Judy S. Audhumla, my faithful secretary (who was secretly in love with me, but whose affections I could never return, because it says so in the *Thunder God's Handbook,* Chapter 11 of section 8), had a steaming chalice of hot cocoa waiting for me as I strode casually through the door.

I stripped off my trenchcoat and threw it and my horned fedora onto the chair by the window before accepting the cocoa. Judy S. Audhumla gave me her usual disgusted look as she hung my Stockholm Fog jacket on the coatrack. She discreetly inspected the collar for lipstick stains.

After taking a sip of the steaming liquid, and letting it defrost my insides a little, I asked, "Anything happen around here, Dollface?"

"Nay, milord; thy telephone hath been cloaked in a shroud of silence since the morn."

The bottle of good mead was kept in the bottom right-hand drawer of my desk. I used it to sweeten my cocoa.

After a few swallows, I said, "Judy, we don't have a phone; it hasn't been invented yet."

"That doth explain its strange silence, milord. Mayhaps, thou shouldst retrieve thy promissory to the phone company."

I chuckled and patted her on the shoulder. "Consider it a done deal, doll. I never sent one in the first place. And please, call me Thor, last-of-the-real-gods-of-thunder."

Thunder beat out a drum solo in the air tonight.

I looked around the office and admired my taste in decorating. I'd been doing some interior work on the side to make ends meet, and, dammit, I wasn't afraid to admit that I had a flair for color schemes. I was particular to dark palettes.

The Venetian blinds cast dark, horizontal, and ominous shadows on everything, giving the office that "homey" feel. Judy had stoked the fire to a roaring blaze, and the heat melted my bitter disposition.

I parked myself behind a desktop covered with recycled trees (bills more likely than not). I absent-mindedly scooped them off my desk and into the fire. Flames roared and spit angrily, devouring the paper. Sheesh, nobody likes bills.

I was just starting to get a little better outlook on life when Conan-Edison, the local power company, had the out-and-out gall to cut off my electricity.

Usually, a god of thunder such as myself would merely strike his mystical hammer on the ground, causing lightning to strike the flying chariot of the sun god and send it careening into the power company's administrative offices. This would usually result in that god of thunder's electricity being turned back on. Unfortunately, I did not have my mystical hammer, which made me think that maybe the power company is in cahoots with Thrymm. In fact, Conan-Edison was probably behind the abduction of Richard, using Thrymm's frustration to eliminate the only other power generator in the city: myself, Thor, last of the real gods of thunder! I'd have to remind myself to have Hela, last of the real mistresses of the underworld, open the ground beneath the house of ill repute that the Conan-Ed executives' frequented.

This wasn't the first time that Conan-Edison had screwed me. If the patent had been invented any earlier, I would have owned electricity and Conan-Edison would have had to pay me royalties. But their lawyers were better than mine, which is why Eddie shines boots. And I don't want to hear about Zeus having a claim because of his thunderbolts. That horny old goat was always too busy turning into showers of gold and impregnating young girls, kind of like Donald Trump, to give a damn about patents. Yeah there was going to be some ground opening up under some buildings. Nobody, but nobody, ever crossed this god of thunder and got away with it. Of course to be fair, the guy who really got screwed was the guy who invented the patent.

*** AUTHOR'S HISTORICAL NOTE: We know it ruins a joke to explain it but we've ruined plenty of jokes so far and see no need to stop. The first successful patent was probably given in 1449 by King Henry VI of England to John of Utynam for glass-blowing. Unfortunately, the King forgot to patent the patent. ***

Judy stood up, showing me her long, sensuous legs as she informed me, "A missive of dire import didst sail through yon window earlier this day. Wouldst thou liketh to read it?"

My eyes glanced over at the far window and noticed that the bottom left pane had been smashed and then boarded up. Judy must have done me the favor of cleaning up the glass. One of these days, I'd have to remember to pay her. Judy S. was always asking me for pieces of silver and I was always handing her a line about Dad rewarding her in the next life and the dangers of materialism, etc . . . It couldn't last forever but she still hung around.

"Sure, Dollface. But it's probably just from Thrymm, the frost giant, though. It's about Richard, right?"

She handed me a slip of paper with chicken scratch on it that I couldn't read. Before I had a chance to ask her for a quick run down, she gave me one.

"It doth seem that Thrymm, king of the frost giants, hath kidnapped thine mighty Mjol . . . uh, Richard—"

"Yeah, yeah," I muttered, cutting her off. "I got the same

skinny from Eddie."

"Art thou referring to thine law professor, Edward Shysterson?"

"No, Eddie, the stereotyped, colored boot-fluff boy. He doesn't have a last name because minor characters, especially stereotypes, aren't important enough to bother making one up for." I cast my peepers in her direction and asked, "Say, have you been talking to him?"

"No," she replied, looking at me quizzically. "Why doth thou ask?"

"Never mind, Dollface," I muttered. "Do you have an old wedding dress sitting around somewhere?" A foolproof, real-man plan was beginning to gel in my remarkable gray matter.

I fired up a Valkyrie Slim, inhaled deeply, and felt dizzy. I decided right then and there, as I stubbed out the butt on my desk, that it was time for an Authors' Note on "the evils of smoking."

INDIGNANT AUTHORS' NOTE: Who us? Sorry, Phil, but we both smoke. We particularly enjoy lighting up in over-priced, snooty French restaurants. Savoring the taste of a fine, high-quality blend of tobacco in crowded elevators makes us feel like last-of-the-real-men-Authors/ despisers of quiche. So, Phil, why don't you tell the readers of the dangers of lung cancer, emphysema, and yellow teeth, instead of pawning it off on us. We'll take a break and fire up a couple of Luckys.

I lit a coffin nail and watched the end of it burn like the rage rising inside me. I thought that the Authors must be real pinheads if they couldn't even remember the name of their main character. Sheesh. Why couldn't I be written by Robert Parker or Stephen King, instead of these two hacks?

THREATENING AUTHORS' NOTE: Look, you ingrate, psychopathic bastard, we own you. We stop writing, and you're fish wrap, pal. We could kill you off in two sentences; one, if we really felt like it. So you'd better watch out, you'd better not cry, you'd better not pout, we're telling you why: we haven't decided how this particular piece of literary history is going to end yet. Get the picture, laughing boy?

I muttered something under my breath and decided to play patsy. For now. The corners of my mouth turned up as I realized that I had them by the short hairs: if they don't finish this book, they'll have to get **Real Jobs**.

My attention was drawn back to the "plotline" when Judy exclaimed in a breathy voice, "A wedding dress?! I hath yet to be betrothed."

She got a starry sparkle in her eyes, and her body quivered in anticipation. She looked as if she were about to burst wide open.

"Milord Thor," she stammered in one of those high, squeaky voices dames use when they're excited, "ha-hath thee something in thy mind?"

She was really acting strange; I'd never seen her so wound up over one of my plans before. It must have been her time of the month.

"Yeah, Kitten," I answered finally. "Here's my plan . . ."

She was holding her breath now and looking at me as if I was about to propose marriage to her or something. I hoped my plan would live up to her expectations.

"I'll put on your wedding dress, some make-up—just a little rouge, some eyeliner, and a dab of lipstick—not too much; I don't want to look cheap —and borrow a wig. Then I'll pass myself off as my non-existent daughter, marry Thrymm, and when he falls asleep, as all men do after having sex, I'll grab Richard and smash his skull into a million slimy pieces!"

I looked at Judy to see if my plan met with her approval. She had a resigned look on her face and was staring blankly at the ceiling.

"Milord, would it not be of greater ease if I were to disguiseth mineself as thine daughter in thy stead, leaving the door to the matrimonial chamber ajar so that thou couldst enter after

Thrymm hath retired?"

I shook my head. "Sorry, Dollface, but I never send a woman to do a man's job."

"Methinks that thou truly doth enjoy donning womanly garb. Thou hast done so in nine of thee last ten cases."

"I had to, Kitten," I protested. "I do what I'm paid to do. No matter what. Sometimes dames can get into places that guys can't. You know that. Besides, I look better in a dress than you do."

I could tell that she wasn't buying a word of it.

"Verily, Thor, I doth believeth that I wouldst be more appealing bedecked in bridal garb. And that thee, milord, wouldst be striking in matrimonial skins."

"Yeah, Kitten, I know," I replied, inspecting my fingernails. "I look good in anything. Some people can wear clothes, some can't. I can. It's not something I chose, it's just something I am. I look good in clothes."

Judy sighed dramatically, "Alas, dear Thor, I fear that the sun shalt ne'er dawn uponst The Day. I hath not a gown for thee as I hath ne'er been betrothed."

"Damn!" I swore. I was going to have to get my paws on a white dress soon, or I'd never caress Richard's beautiful form again.

Turning to Judy, I said, "Hand me the phonebook, Ver. I've got to find me a twenty-four hour dress shop. Maybe I'll be lucky and find a gown on such short notice."

Judy looked at me with a strained expression on her pretty face. "Thor, didst thou not recently remindeth me that the telephone hath yet to be invented? Forsooth, thy blindness to my desire might yet be a blessing in disguise."

"Oh yeah." The old thunder god luck was running true to form. "Is there a place where I could rent one nearby?"

"A phone?"

"No, Kitten, a dress. What the hell were you thinking about?"

"Thine hammer in a sling, milord."

"Yeah, I miss Richard, too, kid. I can't wait to feel him strapped to my leg again. But first, I need a dress shop, and I need it fast. You know where one is?"

"Strangely enough, milord, this maiden doth possess knowledge of one such shoppe. 'Tis on Lief Erikson Lane, next to Loki Lemming's Palace of Instant Divorce and Pool Hall. Verily, it be the shoppe of least expense. I hath often gazed longingly upon its frosted panes."

What a dame. I certainly got my money's worth with this secretary. She didn't have to look up the address or anything. I bet she even knew the phone number.

I grabbed my hat and stuffed it on my head as I made for the door. "Thanks, Dollface. While I'm gone, go down to the super's office and see if Grendel's in. Tell him to fix the glass and remind him of our bones game."

I walked down the creaky wooden stairs and out into the cold, Norse air. Sleipnir whinnied, acknowledging my presence. He stomped his hooves in complaint about being left outside in this weather. I told him to shove it. The wind whipped past me, following the weenie-wielding mob on their way to the burning Danish Donuts Shoppe.

A light snow began falling as I swung into the saddle. Spurring Sleipnir on, I decided to take the long way to the dress shop, avoiding the arson squad and their accusatory tones. Besides, it was a nice night. A quiet ride through town might give me some new ideas about how to handle Thrymm. The waxing moon lit the sky and the landscape, showing me the way.

I shivered a little and noticed that my bearskin trenchcoat wasn't cutting the mustard against the plummeting temperatures. It was too cold to continue riding, and I knew that Flagsheim's was just ahead. I decided to stop for reinforcements in my battle with Jack Frostson. A bite to eat would go down well, too.

I double-parked Sleipnir by the frozen water trough and slapped a month-old parking ticket between his ears. The trick was an oldie but a goodie, and it worked every time.

A wave of heat greeted me as I opened the door. As usual, King Norm was behind the rail. He was gyrating his hips, which, for some strange reason, at that moment I thought of my mother.

Let a shrink get a load of that one, I thought.

King Norm saw me and drew a chalice of my favorite poison. He set it down on the bar with three shot glasses next to it.

"What are these," I asked, "more King Norm originals?"

He nodded, and I pointed at the first one. "What do you call this one?"

"Devil in Disguise," he replied with a half-sneer, half-smile.

I threw my head back, and my hat flew off as I downed the drink, the horns thumping on the wooden floorboards.

I bent over to pick up my fedora and discovered just why he called it Devil in Disguise. Its smooth taste was deceiving: it went down easy and came back hard.

"The Devil and I don't get along," I wheezed. "How about the next one?"

He swiveled his pudgy hips and crooned, "Ye Ole Kentucky Rain."

I knew about Kentucky, some thousand years and three thousand miles away because I'm a god. But how did King Norm? Suspicious, I sniffed the shot glass and took in the heady aroma of the drink. Noticing that the liquid was dissolving the pewtered bottom, I chugged it quickly, before the drink could eat its way out and escape.

I made funny faces for a couple of minutes as the concoction assaulted my liver, kidneys, stomach lining, and guts.

"That's good stuff," I hacked. "What is that: whiskey and battery acid with just the slightest hint of vermouth?"

King Norm chuckled and pointed a ring- and fudge-encrusted finger at the final glass.

"What the hell's in that one?" I warily asked.

He looked sad and moaned, "We canst go on together, with

suspicious minds!"

"Alright, alright, you haven't steered me wrong yet," I admitted. "What do you call it?"

"Latest Flame," he said, whipping a torch off the wall.

I watched in horror as he dipped the torch into the flagon and set it ablaze. I liked Norm but how stupid did you have to be to put open flame in the same room with me. It's like he wasn't reading this book or had purchased more insurance on this dump of a meadhall than it was worth.

My knuckles whitened on the rail of the bar. "You're kidding, right? That isn't fit for man or beast, let alone thunder gods!"

"Doth not be cruel," Norm said, feigning hurt.

"Alright, you over-sequined polar bear, here goes nothing."

I took the shot, and my life, in my right hand. The flames from the glass highlighted King Norm's face, making him look almost evil. I drank it down quick, pulled out a Valkyrie Slim, and lit it with my breath. I took a deep drag. "You're still the King. Could you throw me another beer, a couple of your famous greasy cheeseburgers, and a paramedic?"

For several hours, I sat at the bar, sipping my drinks and mulling over the finer points of my plan of attack. Occasionally, a friendly free-for-all would break out, distracting me from my thoughts, and forcing me to snap a couple of spines to get some peace and quiet.

My cheeseburgers came, and Norm had taken his usual ten percent off the top. Not hungry anymore, I shoved both burgers down the throat of some gabby punk trying to sell fire insurance.

Before the salesman could swallow my sandwiches, and I could finish my thoughts, King Norm ambled over and started reading to me from the latest issue of *Rolling Runes*. The article compared an up-and-coming bard with the legendary King of Bards, who had apparently died in an outhouse some years back.

While Norm worked his way through the article, saying the

new bard was "nuthin' save a mongrel cur," I worked my way through a twelve pack of mead.

As I finished the last flagon, I stood, deciding it was time to drive over to the dress shop. I thought, *It's getting late. I'd better hit the road.* Then I remembered how cold it was out there, and thought, *I think I'll have one more.* I sat back down and polished off another half-case of mead. Between flagons, King Norm would use me as a guinea pig for his latest unpatented alcoholic invention.

I had a terrible case of the spins by the time I got up to leave. Using the rail for support, I asked Norm for directions to the front door.

"Your *(hic)* highness, how the he-*(hic)*-hell do you get out of here?"

Norm and his twin (oh no, not again) shrugged.

"That's okay, Normie. You *(hic)* you are the greatest publican in the entire land. I didn't know you had a twin."

They looked at each other, confused.

I fell to the floor and crawled toward the wall. My face let me know when I'd made it. Using my hands, I started crawling, hoping I'd find the door.

When I finally found it, I congratulated myself on my ingenuity. The difference between common mortals and this last-of-the-real-gods-of-thunder, I thought smugly, is that a common mortal can only think on his feet, whereas a god like myself can think on his hands and knees wading through two inches of beer.

Pulling myself up on the doorframe, I crashed through the door and staggered out to my horse. Some patrolman had had the unmitigated gall to slap another parking ticket on Sleipnir. I shoved both into the glovebox, vomited, and eventually saddled up. I spurred Sleipnir in the direction of the dress shop and immediately wrapped him around the closest telephone pole.

By One-Eye, I swore, Dad's going to be pissed! That's the third time this week I've wrecked his Mustang.

Fortunately, Sleipnir only had a ding in his fender; Dad

probably wouldn't even notice. I told the horse to head to the dress shop and then passed out.

When I opened my eyes, I saw a sign that said: "Ye Olde Dress Shoppe & Liquor Store. Est. 1492 B.C. Open 24 Hrs To Serviceth Thy Matrimonial Needs."

I fell off Sleipnir, opened the door, and staggered up to the counter. An elderly Zulu man, in a platypus tuxedo, looked at me and smiled.

"Milord Thor," he said, "I hadst expected thine presence earlier."

"Sorry, I stopped off for a beer."

Then it dawned on the foggy peaks of my brain. I grabbed him by the lapels and yanked him across the counter, 3.14 inches from my face.

"Alright, wiseguy, how did you know that I'd be coming here at all?" I demanded.

"You've been thrown out of every other dress shop in town. This establishment is the only left who'll still take your Asgaard Express Platinum card." I released him and shoved him back against the counter. "Besides," he continued, "your secretary called us earlier. She said you'd be here after stopping off for a drink. By the way, your office is by the Danish Donuts, do you know what happened? It burned to the ground."

"Why, no. I don't. Why do you ask?" I queried, trying to look casual. Then a realization hit me, "Wait a minute, brightboy," I growled, "what happened to your damn accent?"

His chest heaved up a sigh, and he said, "Our Authors art of weak mind, sloth-like prose and . . . erk!"

The dress-shoppe man had a sudden heart attack and dropped over dead. I knew I'd never get a dress fitted in time without the shoppe-keeper's help, so I appealed to THE AUTHORS.

AUTHORS' IRED NOTE*: *We are not to be trifled with. Snooty, punk, dress shop men, who probably have homosexual* *tendencies, are not going to question us! Unless, of course, they're literary critics with no talent of their own, and, more likely than not, stick their fingers into their own orifices just to smell themselves. We just don't take that kind of crap from bit players. But, fear not, Phil, the stiff has a twin in the back room. Just ring bell for service.*

I looked down and noticed a bell on the counter where there wasn't one before. I rang the bell and an elderly Zulu man in a platypus tuxedo came out of the back room, and nervously said, "Ah, Milord Thor, I hadst expected thine presence earlier."

Eager to get on with "the plot," such as it was, I decided not to rehash the last page, despite pleas from the Authors about being paid by the word.

"Do you have anything in a size twenty-three wedding gown? It has to be conservative; not too much in the lace and frills department, yet pleasing to the eye. You know, maybe a provocative slit up one of the legs, not too high though. I don't want to look like a slut. How about a low-cut back? Do you have that? And a long train. A real long train."

I thought a little bit more and decided that that was about it. The shoppe keeper made a few notes on his pad of paper and excused himself to the back room.

While he was gone, I looked around the store and picked out a veil. It was gorgeous and covered most of my face, allowing only a little of my beard to show. Then I picked out a magnificent bouquet of flowers and a fabulous garter. With an eye toward thriftiness, I decided to reuse a pair of white stockings left over from my last case, and save a few bones.

As I finished looking around, the shoppe keeper returned, carrying a large bundle of white. With a grunt, he heaved it onto the counter for my approval. Hoisting the dress, I held it in front of me and looked in the mirror.

The shoppe keeper came up behind me and said, "Verily, thou art smashing!" He lisped. "Any frost giant in the land wouldst be proud to burst thine maidenhead!"

"What?"

"Uh, you look great."

"Hey, pal" I barked, "what happened to your accent?"

He looked nervous. "Uh, thine Authors art of deep character and twisting plot. They hath done it for reasons we canst not begin to comprehendeth."

AUTHORS' MERCILESS NOTE: Uh-uh. Ain't gonna work, pal!***

"Erk!" he said, and slumped over dead, the victim of a sudden, inexplicable heart attack.

I thanked him for the wedding gifts and stepped out of the store.

Outside, I looked up and saw babes in flannel breastplates swooping down from the snow-washed sky on winged horses. Those women were always picking up losers and going mead-hall hopping with them. I tried to steer clear of their kind. All they wanted to do was pick up dead-beats, get drunk, and go to the fights.

One of the Valkyries, Rosie O'Donnellson, a chick I'd run into at a dive called Loki Lemming's Poolhall, hovered above me. When I'd first met her, she'd been playing eight ball and playing it hot. She'd bought me a drink and said she liked to know what I could do with a stick and balls.

"Hiya, Thor-ey, remembereth me?" she grunted through a mouthful of chewing tobacco.

"No, Rosie, I don't."

She smiled broadly, and I noticed her nasty brown teeth. She flexed a massive left biceps and pointed, "How ya liketh mah bran' new tattoo? 'Tis a skull with a knife through it. Say's 'Dad' on it. That's 'casin I findeth the yella-bellied bastard who knocked up Mama!"

I looked around for an escape; not finding one I asked "You, uh . . . have a mother?"

Insulted, she reared her mount, hit me in the face with a glob of Redman, and then flew off at redneck speeds.

"Wench!" I screamed, attempting to draw Richard.

Unfortunately, I didn't have my trusty hammer or a winged horse to catch her with. Powerless, I watched her fly out of sight.

I lit a cigarette and smoked it down to the butt. Finished, I tossed it into a snow bank, before realizing that it was still lit. After a few moments of waiting, I congratulated myself on a traditional "tossing of the butt" without causing a major disaster.

Smiling, I got back on my horse and galloped back toward my office. After I left, unbeknownst to me, the wind blew the cigarette into a pile of gas-soaked snow. The butt rolled downhill, gaining size and fuel as it became an ever larger, flaming snowball. The unsuspecting town of Hjindenberg slept peacefully below . . .

As I walked in my office, Judy handed me Thrymm's latest note, which had been delivered via rock express. She told me that the note said for Richard to be at Thrymm's palace by eight o'clock the next day and ready to tie the knot.

I guessed the old frost giant was getting a little anxious for female companionship. It's a damn good thing that I wasn't sending out any invitations.

* * *

Judy stayed late, coaching me on the finer points of Viking damehood and Show tunes. I learned about breastplates, hairstyling, and how to end an opera on a high note. Surprisingly, damehood wasn't much different than manhood, except for the toiletry habits, of course. She complimented me on the ease at which I mastered her lessons, and even went so far as to say that I was a natural.

After Judy left, I grabbed twenty winks.

Twenty-two winks later (I'd hit the snooze alarm twice), the sun reared its ugly head. As the light hit my face, I cursed fate and made a mental note to have Dad fire the god in charge of mornings.

The crowing roosters and the gaily chirping birds accompanying the sun wouldn't get off with just a pink slip.

Still vowing revenge, I dragged myself out of bed and through my normal routine: I chugged coffee, smoked heavily, and read the morning paper: *The Midgaard Messenger*. There wasn't anything of interest in the news: no wars, no hammer throwing maniacs on watertowers, no gangland warfare, nothing; just some squib about a nationwide manhunt for the arsonist who burned down the town of Hjindenberg and a local donut shop. There was also an article about a catfight in the preteen maternity department at the Val-Mart.

I put down the paper and let out a long sigh. It looked like just another boring day in the life of the last-of-the-real-gods-of-thunder. I was still sighing when a rock came crashing through my kitchen window. Glass showered the floor for the third time in two days. If this vandalism kept up, Staked (Through the Heart) Firm Insurance Company was going to raise my rates, and I would be forced to kill those greedy, blood-sucking bastards.

The note attached to the rock reminded me that today was my wedding day.

I decided to celebrate by smashing in the rest of the windows with a T-ball bat. Thrymm's boys had shattered most of my glass, so I decided to keep things uniform. I smashed outward, so the glass shards showered the pedestrians on the street below.

I hung the bat where I usually kept my hammer. As I stared at the empty spot where Richard usually hung, a tear of sorrow would have come from my eyes, if I wasn't so damn masculine.

I forgot my tears, and remembered that, even though he was Catholic, I had to get married to Thrymm to get my Richard back. Since I'm one of the leading figures in the Norse pantheon, there was going to be a major uproar among my following. To tell the truth, I wasn't so fired up about it either.

We gods of the Aesir could do anything we damn well

pleased, but Catholics weren't allowed to have any fun. And why don't guys wear panties? Does anybody use that stupid flap in our briefs? I can't even begin to count the times my balls have gotten caught in that damn—

*** *KOWTOWING AUTHORS' NOTE: We apologize profusely and seek to render ourselves obsequiously deferential. We do not wish offend the Catholic Church and be damned to hell by The Pope. But as Salmon Rushdie found out: screw with Islam, go into hiding; poke fun at Catholicism, some guy in a dress will sentence you to purgatory. If you don't know what purgatory is, it's like being stranded in an airport terminal with only this book to entertain you, only not as bad. So once again, we wax apologetic for our protagonist's unmitigated tirade. Don't think he's going to get off scot-free for his impure thoughts. Just between you and us, we're going to blow up Phil's limo, which he doesn't know he's getting yet, later on in the novel. Believe us when we tell you this, he won't get a chance to enjoy it. We certainly hope this incident won't affect book sales and thus decrease our royalties.* ***

I pulled my balls out of the little flap in my underwear and finished reading the paper. I had some time to kill so I decided to smoke some Valkyrie Slims and wane philosophic. I was the son of the All-Father, King of the Norse gods, and I was about to dress up as a woman, again, to get my magic hammer back. Why? Couldn't I just storm Thrymm's fortress with the help of a few of my drinking buddies? After all, we were gods, Viking gods, were we not? Wouldn't that be much easier--not to mention more manly?

The answer was blatantly obvious: never send a man to do a woman's job. Real men, such as myself, did things once, did it as violently as possible, and removed anyone or anything that got in our way. However, this job required a feminine touch.

Having once again justified my cross-dressing tendencies, I got up and mulled over what Judy had shown me. After blowing another hour reviewing the finer points of all things feminine and Norse, I started getting dressed for the big event.

It was 5:30 in the afternoon when I finally got the whole outfit on correctly. Judy had told me that she'd be at the hairdresser's all day if I needed help. I didn't, of course, but it was swell of her to offer. At 5:45, Viking Standard Time, about 11:36 in Los Angeles, I left my office on Dad's steed and galloped toward Thrymm's place.

My fiancé lived at Jotunheim, in the northern hills, about a hundred and eleven miles from town. I put the spurs to Sleipnir, turned on Dad's radar detector, and cruised the ride in about half an hour, not worried about speed. Even if I did get pulled over, Dad was All-Father, had appointed all the judges, and could fix the ticket for me.

The terrain was mostly frozen and deserted tundra. This came as no surprise to me, as most of Scandinavia is frozen and deserted tundra. I filled the vacant miles with satisfying images of Thrymm's skull split wide, stomped into guacamole pudding.

*** <u>HELPFUL AUTHORS' NOTE</u>: *We now leave Phil's perspective and delve briefly into the realm of the third person. When the point of view is again shifted, we will have returned to the first person. This knowledge of grammar techniques is certainly not to prove that we are artisans who utilize the various tools at our disposal and not just hacks.* ***

Sparkling spheres of light constructed columns that defied the icy wasteland. Five figures coalesced from the luminescence, and each struck a bold and heraldic pose. The apparent leader, garbed in a golden tunic, said, "Spock," dramatic pause, "Bones," dramatic pause and then quickly added, "you're regulars on the show," dramatic pause, "stay here with me." Dramatic pause, "Yeomen Johnson and Hershel," and then added quickly, "whom no one has ever seen on the show before," dramatic pause, followed by yet another dramatic pause, "Nor, will they ever see again," dramatic pause, "go behind that boulder and," dramatic pause, "get killed or something."

Yeomen Johnson and Herschel fell to their knees, supplicating themselves before their commander. The wails of the yeomen's mothers, beseeching Captain Kirk to spare their progenies' lives, and make them show regulars, filled the airwaves.

But Kirk stood his ground and thrust his right arm outward with his palm upwards and fingers half curled, and said, "Go," dramatic pause, "and get off my set," dramatic pause, "it's in the script," dramatic pause, "and a *Star Trek* formula," dramatic pause, "I," dramatic pause, "can do nothing for you."

Yeoman Hershel leapt to his feet and said, "Yo, Captain! As the Chairmen of the *Star Trek* Non-Regulars' Union, Local 3.14, I have to protest. I can add so much to this worn-out show. I can put us on the cuttin' edge of the music scene. Check out this rap, Home-Kirk."

Kirk sighed and looked at Spock.

Hershel crossed his arms sloppily across his chest and said, "Kick it one time, Yo-Jay!"

Yeoman Johnson began making rhythmic noises with his mouth.

Hershel began rapping:

"We-e-ll, I'm the new crewman, My name is Hershel

"And I'll be dead before the next commercial!

"Break it down, Spockee Spock!"

Spock pulled out his Vulcan harp and began strumming to the beat. Kirk stared with disgust.

"Et tu, Spockee Spock?" Dramatic pause, "I hate rap!" Dramatic pause. "Now, if you want to hear," dramatic pause, "real spoken word poetry," dramatic pause, "allow me to do Rocket Man."

The two crewmen's faces paled and their eyes widened in terror.

"I see." Dramatic pause. "Hershel, Johnson, go!" Dramatic pause, "And Trek no more!"

The two hapless crewmen joined hands and shuffled

dejectedly, their heads hung low, around the nearest snow-covered boulder.

*** ANOTHER HELPFUL AUTHORS' NOTE: We now return you to Phil's point of view. Aren't you giddy with excitement? You do know, dramatic pause, what's coming, don't you? ***

I was just about to light up a Valkyrie Slim when two fairies, holding hands and wearing sparkling red outfits, came waltzing around from behind a large boulder. I tried to steer clear, but they were directly in my path. All eight of Sleipnir's legs tapdanced across their frail torsos. I looked around quickly and saw that there were no witnesses. I wiped the blood and flesh off of my horse's bumper and windshield, tossed the bodies in the fjord below, and left the scene casually.

The temperature dropped steadily as the sun climbed in the sky and my destination drew ever closer. The cold gnawed through my bearskin trenchcoat and my baby-sealskin wedding gown. I'd have to remind Dad to get the heater on this filly fixed.

Pulling my trenchcoat tight, I reached into the saddlebags for some of my anti-freeze. I took a couple of swigs and then stashed it in my garter. I fired up a cigarette and thought about having another drink. I decided against it, as I didn't want to be two skins to the wind on my wedding day.

I approached the gates to Thrymm's palace right on schedule. The guards gave me little trouble when I showed them my invitation. The cute one pinched me on the butt. Being an upright Viking dame, I backhanded him, snapping his spine and leaving him a heap on the snow bank.

"I'm not that kinda frail. Besides, you cheek, it's my wedding day!" I left him and his lolling head with his more prudent partner and entered the foyer.

I was quickly escorted to the altar and shown to a goathead-wearing priest. He was just finishing lacing his platypus leggings when I arrived.

The priest's tiny, black Charlie Chaplin mustache accented the fire blazing behind his beady eyes. An evil gaze lasciviously devoured my feminine curves, undressing me in its mind's eye. The mental strip search must not have gotten far or he would have discovered my ruse.

I fished under my dress for the pack of smokes tucked in my garter, next to the mead. I shook out a couple of butts and offered one to him. Greedy fingers snapped the cigarette up.

We lit our cigarettes in the ceremonial candles.

"So," I said in my best Lauren Bacall impression, "let's get this wedding deal over with."

"Ja, *mein liebchen*, der ceremony shalt commence uponst de striking of der eighth bell."

"What's with the Italian accent in the middle of a Swedish flashback, bub?"

He inhaled nervously on his fag; the end flared as bright as the sun's reflection off the morning's snow.

"*Ach, fraulein*, ich hast received meinen spiritual enlightenment in yon fatherland."

"So, you studied religion in Italy, huh? Probably the Vatican, too, right, big boy?"

"*Nein, nein*, ich received einen doctorate in endocrinology in der land from which der strudel cometh. I doth only dabble in der ways of der churchen."

I puffed on my cigarette and said, "So, this is only a part-time gig for you, huh?"

"Ja, but der time for die ceremony draws nigh. I must preparen thee for thy journey into thine new lifen. Thou shalt cease to be Richard Thordottir, und becommen der object of Thrymm's desires."

"Yeah, yeah, whatever. Let's get on with it."

I threw my smoke down on the marble church floor and ground it out with my high heels. I lit up another as the priest donned his light-green ceremonial garb. His assistants, oddly familiar Canadian migrant farmworkers, led me to an altar room and made me lie down.

The head priest came in, dipped his hands in a steaming bowl of unknown liquid, and began chanting while vigorously rubbing his hands together.

One of the assistants placed a ceremonial mask over my face and joined the chanting. I started to doze off.

What the hell, I thought, I'll catch a few winks while these bozos do whatever they're paid to do. Besides, I might come out of this flashback and get back to the main storyline.

No such luck.

When I awoke, I heard the priest ask if everything was satisfactory. Someone asked if he could get his money back if not. The priest said "Nein." The other voice replied, "Verily, thou hast outdone thineself in mine service. Thy toil hath rendered a masterpiece."

So, Thrymm was in the room. I reminded myself that it was bad luck for the bride to see the groom before the wedding and kept my eyes shut.

The rest of the day seemed to fly by, and my wedding was the stuff that dreams were made of.

The dream ended when I realized I was in Thrymm's bedchambers, wrapped in foreskin sheets and about to consummate the marriage.

He stood before me, wearing a commodore's cap and a black peacoat. So he was a longboat man. His weathered face smiled at me with paternal pride as he stroked my hairy legs.

"Thou hast the legs of the ash Yggdrasil, mine bride," Thrymm said as his hands worked their way up to my inner thighs.

"You sure are a smooth talker, sugardrawers," I said and discretely looked about the room. I didn't see Richard anywhere. "But where's the hammer?"

"Verily, thou art an eager bride!"

"No, pinhead, the hammer you stole from Thor, last-of-the-real gods-of-thunder?"

Trumpets blared, as usual. I was used to them, but Thrymm flinched and looked around for a moment. He shrugged and turned back to me, fire burning in his beady eyes.

"Do not fret thine sweet brow, my little love moose. 'Tis in a safe place."

"Hey punk, no hammer, no Screwdriver, if you catch my drift."

Thrymm looked resigned and hurried over to a trunk at the foot of his four-poster bed. After punching in a code on the keypad, the lock released.

As Thrymm raised the lid, a preternatural glow shone from the box like the dawn's early light. What so proudly we hailed by the twilight's last gleaming was . . . Richard, in all his glory! He seemed to be singing a song that was meant only for me. "Give it to me!" I screamed in ecstasy.

"Ye gods!" he exclaimed, dropping Richard and tearing off his clothes.

"Calm down, Commodore; I meant the hammer."

He picked the hammer up and gingerly presented it to me. I gingerly presented it to his skull. Then I reverently offered it up to his groin.

Thrymm doubled over, gurgling words of passion, like, "Oh god, beateth uponst me, maketh me crawl, do unto me as no other hath done. Treat me like the swine that I truly be!"

Great. A weirdo. A man can't even beat down a pervert those days without the damn sicko enjoying it.

Thrymm had recovered with a smile and found a Louisville Slugger, complete with rusty nails.

"Verily, 'tis better to giveth than to receiveth. Bendeth over, mine little reindeer of love. Here cometh Santa Claus!"

I was starting to get a little worried. I'd hit him with everything I had, and the moron was still up for party games. I lit up a Lucky and hoped that pin-the-tail-on-the-donkey wasn't next.

Suddenly, the window shutters burst open, light streamed into the chamber. Johnny, my long-lost childhood companion and platypus pal, came swinging into the room on a jungle vine, singing the Mighty Mouse theme song.

"Here I cometh to savest thine day!" he lilted in my favorite operatic voice.

Thrymm turned around, placed his feet approximately shoulder width apart, slightly twisted his upper body, and choked up on the bat.

I held my breath, and time slowed as events unfolded. Johnny swung ever closer, a sword appeared in one webbed paw. Thrymm spat tobacco and scratched his jock. He leaned in and swung mightily, but missed.

"Striketh one," Johnny taunted, but his sword also found only air.

Johnny's vine reached the top of its swing, and he pushed off the wall with a backflip. The mighty Thrymm raised his hand to silence the crowd. He smiled confidently. Johnny laughed in the face of danger and raised his sword high. Thrymm tapped the bat on the inside of his left cleat. He resumed a perfect batting stance and smiled knowingly.

Both swung in unison as Johnny rocketed past Thrymm's head. Thrymm missed, but Johnny's blade grazed Thrymm's left nostril.

"Foul tip and striketh two!" Johnny chuckled.

I grabbed a beer, some peanuts, popcorn, and crackerjacks from the vendor.

Johnny stood defiantly on the windowsill, preparing for his next attack. His Johnny began crooning, "Taketh me out to the ballgame!" His singing raised my spirits, and my soul flew to the window and landed beside him. Together, our hopes and fears leapt from the ledge, hurtling downward one final time toward destiny.

Thrymm spat more Redman tobacco, scratched himself

again, and raised a finger to test the wind. Satisfied, he brought his Louisville Slugger into position and then to bear.

Crack! Thrymm used Johnny like a piñata.

I cried out in horror and struck Richard on the floor in anguish. A lightning bolt shot forward and struck Thrymm in his left buttock.

He grabbed his keister and howled like Pat Boone singing "Tutti-Frutti." I got real worried, thinking I'd have to consummate the nuptials. Johnny was lying on the floor, his battered and bloody body barely breathing. I was wondering where the cavalry was, when Jay burst in through the door with the Asgaardian police force.

He yelled, "Halt! Thou art under arrest!"

Thrymm dropped the bat and threw his hands into the air.

"What be thine charge, o thee of swine descent?"

A couple of officers, including a fat lady cop wearing an operatic breastplate and carrying a 9 mm spear, threw themselves on top of me, for my protection, I guessed. I shoved them off enough to see Jay talking with Thrymm. Thrymm's arms were down, and I knew something wasn't jake.

The cops slapped a pair of cuffs on me and dragged me outside. Jay joined us in a few minutes, with Thrymm in tow.

Jay walked up to me, carrying my hammer, and said, "Thor, thou art under arrest for the destruction of Ye Olde Danish Donut Shoppe, Hjindenberg, and for horsetheft!"

I looked up at him and cocked an eyebrow. "Horsetheft?"

"Verily, Thor, thine father wants thine ass for purloining his steed."

Ass? I only rode the finest of steeds, not pack animals. I was about to protest when I realized what was going on. Jay was making up charges to help me escape from the lair of the frost giant. What a pal!

I winked and softly whispered, "Thank's buddy, that's another one I owe you. One for now, and one for the sword you took for me in Ragnarok."

Jay looked at me incredulously and said, "Thor, thou wert never in Rag—"

Thrymm was frantically calling me as I was unceremoniously shoved onto the back of Jay's latest police stallion. "I shalt get thee back, mine love! If I have to search the four corners of the Midgaard plane, I shalt get thee!"

Sheesh, what a loser.

The fat lady cop who'd pushed me into the police stallion asked me "Now?"

I shook my head at her and looked at Jay. "By the way, pal, what's a porcine saber?"

INTERLUDE THREE

I couldn't see anything yet, but I knew Jay was hovering over my prone body like a vulture. My tip-off was that cheap aftershave he always wore. Bobby, Jay's kid, always gave him a vat of the stuff for gifts. Not wanting to offend the little tyke, but willing to offend everyone else, he wore it every day.

"Phil? Hey, buddy, are you in there?" he asked.

I opened my eyes and saw white. But this time it wasn't the fluffy, yellow-stained white of snow, but the cold white of a hospital room.

"Thanks for pulling me out of Jotunheim," I croaked. "I was beginning to think that I'd have to consummate the marriage!"

Jay cocked an eyebrow, "Marriage? To who?"

"Thrymm, the Frost Giant King!" I replied, annoyed.

"Thrymm?" Jay asked, cocking his other eyebrow.

"Yeah, the drycleaning mogul! You saved me, remember? The horsetheft charge, my magic hammer..."

"How're you feeling, pal?" Jay inquired, a concerned look on his long features. "Before you ask, it's been three days. You good enough to answer a few questions?"

"I... don't... remember... anything," I rasped, pretending that I was worse off then I was. "Caught me... with... my pants down. I... was on my way... to the office, and then... I was...

here."

I wasn't exactly telling the truth, of course, but I didn't want Jay's law-abiding mitts on the assassin before I tried the bastard in the court of .45 caliber. The guy would get a slap on the wrists in Jay's book; but my book was written in blood by a much more unsympathetic author.

SYMPATHETIC AUTHORS' NOTE: *We don't want that last line taken incorrectly. The book that Phil is speaking of is not the one whose pages you are currently staring blankly at. He is talking about the much-acclaimed Private Investigator's Handbook, which is occasionally referred to in this novel. The Handbook was written by an anonymous author who is currently modeling concrete overshoes to aquatic life forms.*

We, your authors, on the other hand, are very sympathetic and caring people. We do charity work, we help old ladies cross the street, and we support Third World families by shopping at 7-Eleven. Not only that, but we still make time to sit down and write books that provide hours of wholesome entertainment for the entire fucking family. Having cleared up that little misunderstanding, we return you to your regularly scheduled novel. ***

Jay threw his arms up in objection, "Knock it off, I ain't buying the dead and dying routine. I want answers, and I want 'em now!"

"Ooooooo," I oo'ed, "Standard Cop Line number one-thirty-two. How textbook of you. Answers: you want 'em, I got 'em. I got pi figured to the last digit, I know how to end world hunger, crime, and poverty. I know tomorrow's lottery number. I know that people aren't wearing enough hats. What I don't know, but you do, is: What is a porcine saber?"

"Tomorrow's lottery number? Really? Not that I believe you, but, what do you think it is?" Jay asked casually.

I was telling him that it was 12-19-28-31-39-44 when the fat lady nurse in her starched whites walked in. My mouth slammed shut faster than a nun's legs on her first date.

The hippo-cum-nurse glowered and wagged a finger at Jay. "We thought we told you not to push him until after the doctors gave their okay."

I tried hard to keep my face poker, but my smile had a royal flush that won the game. I chuckled quietly to myself, glad that I wasn't the target of her ire. But I wasn't quiet enough. She turned on me like a rabid pit bull, glaring with eyes that could freeze Hell solid.

"And us, Mr. Screwdriver! We shouldn't laugh. That was a stupid trick to pull, sneaking out of here like that. We don't know how we did it, but we're lucky that the meter-maid found us when she did. By all rights, we should be in the morgue!"

"You know you're a dead ringer for the meter maid. You got a twin?" I chuckled at the thought.

"Do we still think it's funny, laughing boy?" the nurse said with a wicked grin on her face. "All right, then; let's roll over!"

I saw the nurse's chins migrate as the demented cackle worked its way from her throat to her lips—it was obvious that she wasn't used to things going in that direction. In her right hand she held a syringe that shone with an unholy light; her other pudgy hand raised a bottle of murky liquid. She inserted the needle into the top and drew out some of the dark fluid. She shot a jet of liquid out of the needle until confident that most of the air was out. Then she looked expectantly at me.

"What the hell do you plan on doing with that?" I asked in a calm, deep voice. Somewhere outside, a dog howled.

"Why, we're going to stick this in our derriere," she replied in a sedate, soothing tone. Somewhere outside, a dog growled.

"And just why the hell are we going to do that?"

"Because we'll be in a lot of pain if we don't."

I gave her the eye and chuckled without mirth. Phillip H. Screwdriver, last-of-the-real-men private-investigators, was no stranger to pain. Pain liked to drop by every so often just to let me know that he was still thinking about me. Sometimes, we'd go get a drink or catch a movie. No chick-flicks, though; Pain has his limits and doesn't think any guy should have to endure the agony of a chick-flick. Die a painful death from a gut shot infection, yes. Have to watch a chick flick, no. Unlike the Angel of Death—she loved crappy movies.

"Pain and I get along just fine. Lose the needle, twist."

She looked sad and said, "We're sorry that's our attitude."

Before I could respond, she feinted to the right and ducked back to the left, faster than someone her size ought to be able to move. Obviously, she had done this before.

I tried to roll off the far side of the bed and ended up exposing my flanks; in other words, exactly what she wanted me to do. With a thrust of her flabby arm, the needle struck home.

She withdrew the needle from my butt and I rolled back over. *Bad move*, I thought, rubbing my aching gluteus. I rolled back onto my side.

I watched the nurse bend the needle and chuck it into the trashcan. She looked at me with the corners of her mouth bent up slightly, and shrugged. "Doctor's orders."

While the nurse and I were struggling, Jay had been standing quietly in the corner, thankful that he wasn't the patient. After she was through with me, she turned her attention, considerable mass, and immense gravity field, toward Jay. For some reason, the hippo reminded me of a poodle turning on its owner. I don't mean one of those Paris Hilton sized toy poodles, but one of those large, steroid-using kinds. I guessed it was my turn to be thankful again.

"Visiting hours are over, mister. We're going to have to find a new place to haunt until tomorrow," she growled, grabbing Jay's homburg from the chair and stuffing it on his head.

Jay started to complain, but decided to save his breath. On his way out, he gave me the thumb's up and said he'd be back tomorrow. After Jay left, the nurse paused from behind the slightly cracked door to ask, "Now?"

I shook my head, and she closed the door.

Finally, I was alone with my thoughts. The thoughts were heavy and weighted down my eyelids, and the next moment I seemed to be flying through the night sky.

Oh no, I groaned, realizing that I was on my way to another flashback.

I looked down and noticed a stadium where a football game was in progress. The Astroturf below me was like a magnet, drawing me down, and into it.

HIGH SCHOOL

The big mountain of man squatted in front of me as I placed my hands between his thighs. I could feel his body heat and smell what he had for breakfast when the wind was right. My hands clenched and his thighs tensed. I looked up, past his massive shoulders, into the eyes of the other men watching us. I was quarterbacking the Mike Hammer High School Hammerheads against our archrivals, the Philistine Point Pilots. This must have been *that* game, and the Angel of Death was watching my highlights reel.

Flicking my eyes, I could see the entire stadium through the facemask specially fitted to my fedora. The crowd roared like enraged lions as the cheerleaders, including Judy S. formed a human pyramid. I couldn't help but notice that none of the cheerleaders were wearing underwear and suspected that was the real reason the crowd was so excited.

Too many distractions, I thought and stepped back to signal a time-out.

I lit a Lucky and looked over at my head coach, who was doing shots of whiskey by the warm-up bench. He nodded at me through bleary eyes, as if to say: "Do what ever you want, Phil. You are an offensive genius and a football god. I trust your judgment implicitly."

I flicked the remains of my cigarette at the line judge and fired up another. *I really ought to cut down*, I thought. *This is my third pack this game.*

I crouched down behind the center again and said, "Give me the damn ball!" This was my signal for the rest of the team to "Go long and I'll take care of the rest."

The center hiked the ball to me and assumed a defensive stance, bringing his massive arms up under the helmet of the brutish Defender who was snorting and charging at me. I stepped back into the pocket and pumped my arm. My black trenchcoat flowed behind me; the number thirteen was emblazoned on the back in ebony, like a grandfather clock in an art deco kitchen.

Three or four linemen came at me; I ducked to the right. Then came the linebacker and the second-string sax player; both missed me. Next I was charged by Kiki Lust, the Playboy play-by-play bunny of the year (who was hopelessly, tragically in love with me). I dodged left, but she still managed to cop a quick feel on my firm, adolescent buttocks. Kiki was followed by some hairy-legged dame named Patty Eerie, who claimed to be the leader of the Unshorn Sorority of the Apocalypse. The Blitz was ended by the Jewish Defense League, followed by the PLO. They were riding the *Orient Express*, which was ten minutes late, as usual.

Having successfully avoided the Blitz, I threw the ball long. The opposing team's star quarterback hit me with a cheap shot just as I released the ball. I whipped out Richard and shot him twice in the helmet at point-blank range. I kicked the quarterback's flaccid corpse three times to make sure he was dead.

The roar of the crowd told me that my pass had been intercepted. I sighted downfield and shot the cornerback who did it. He fumbled, and my receiver recovered the blood-slick ball for the game-winning touchdown, just as time expired.

The line judge had the unmitigated gall to throw a flag for unnecessary roughness. So I shot him. The referee, who had also thrown a flag, picked it up, apologized for it having slipped, and signaled for the score.

The local police arrived moments later to congratulate me on my win. They offered me a police escort to jail, where they thought I could be protected from my adoring fans.

"No, thanks," I told Chief Kumquat. "I can take care of myself." He was very insistent, but I managed to shoot my way out of Hammer High's astrodome.

By the way, I took the Hammerheads all the way to the state championships that year and won it for them. God, how they must have loved me.

* * *

Monday morning, in homeroom, I learned that Johnny had been murdered. He had been given the game ball to give to me, but it had exploded while he was on the way to my house. Johnny had died instantly.

I had thrown a bomb to win the game and someone had thrown it back. But something had gone wrong with their plan and Johnny ended up buying the farm. Oh sure, it was a nice farm. Forty-acres and a mule with a house and a white picket fence. There was even a little black jockey statue by the driveway. The John Doe tractor was parked there when it wasn't being used to plow the back twenty (depending on government subsidies that year). Yeah, Johnny had bought the farm, but they forgot one thing: Johnny was no farm-boy. And for that, they would pay!

CONFUSED AUTHORS' NOTE**_:_ *If you are lost, don't despair, so are we. So relax, grab a beer (regardless if you're over twenty-one or not; though we strongly recommend that you at least have a realistic fake ID), fire up a Lucky, count the royalties from your latest novel, have Inga, your Swedish maid, massage your thighs, have your accountant check your balance one more time, take a deep breath, and continue reading. Just like we, your much-heralded, literary geniusi authors, are not doing. Really. But we digress. But you knew we would, didn't you?*

I felt a fiery ball of hate twist my guts into granny knots and then add a sheepshank for good measure; the same feeling I got when I ate a tuna on rye with Grey Poupon while drinking a fifth of Jim Beam (which I had done the night before, but that had no bearing on how I felt now).

The cold, stiff fact was: Johnny was dead. Someone was going to feel the muzzle of my wrath shoved up their sphincter, watch as I gleefully pulled the trigger, and see the life ooze out of their . . . Well, watch them die.

Somewhere beyond the fog of my rage, I heard the teacher call for Friday's homework assignment. Johnny had always done my homework for me and let me copy off him during exams. Now he'd taken the final exam for me.

I'm going to find that guy who failed you, Johnny, and mark his paper with a big, fat, greasy, blood-stained 'F!'

I looked at the teacher with utter disdain and disgust. "Homework? How can you think of homework at a time like this?"

She looked puzzled and asked, "At a time like what? Monday morning?"

I stared at her with my cold, steel blue eyes and whispered, "Johnny's dead."

"Who's Johnny?" she said, and smiled in her special way.

Obviously she'd repressed his death. It wasn't that uncommon a psychological phenomenon, exhibited in times of extreme mental duress by those minds weaker than a real-man-private-investigator, such as myself. I could only envy her; it must be nice to live in a world of illusion and fantasy.

I would never know.

In my profession I had to look cold, hard reality in its blood-shot eyes every day, or lose the edge that kept me alive.

I fired up a Lucky.

"Son, you know there's no smoking in school," she chastised. "Go see the principal."

I blew a stream of light blue smoke into her face.

"Shut your pie-hole, Sister! The name's not 'Son.' It's Phil; Phillip Screwdriver, last-of-the-real-men private-investigators." I pursed my lips like Bogey would before adding, "Got it, sweetheart?"

From somewhere, perhaps the classroom intercom system, heraldic trumpet music sounded.

She rolled her eyes. "Whatever. Go see Principal Sodom and tell her your problems." She paused for a second and then added, "And then see the nurse for a special test."

I pulled out my hip flask of whiskey and slowly unscrewed the top. Alcohol vapors leaped from the spout and sensuously caressed my nostrils. Then, after savoring it for a moment, I poured the contents on the pile of collected homework. I took the cigarette from my lips and dropped it on top of the volatile mess.

Flames blazed to life, consuming the desk like a drag queen eats a hotdog: slowly and with love. Fire leaped onto my trenchcoat, hungry for more. It was a good thing that I was wearing a fire-retardant spare trenchcoat underneath my London Fog.

"Grade this, you old bat!" I exclaimed, throwing her my old, burning trenchcoat.

I picked up her grade book and used it as a cigarette lighter. Some kids had marshmallows out and were toasting them on the bonfire that used to be the teacher's desk.

I tipped my hat to her and left to the applause of the students. The roar of the crowd followed me wherever I went. I couldn't help it: I was a people pleaser.

* * *

Outside the principal's office, I took a pull of vodka from my vest flask. I wiped my mouth on my sleeve and stowed the sauce. I fished the last butt out of my deck of smokes and threw the crumpled pack at the overweight, sexually repressed, anal-retentive, president-of-the-chess-club, Nazi hall monitor. It bounced off of her nametag that read "Otis." She demanded that I pick it up.

I snickered at her bravado and calmly smashed in the glass

case on the wall marked "BREAK GLASS IN CASE OF OVERWEIGHT SEXUALLY REPRESSED, ANAL RETENTIVE, PRESIDENT OF THE CHESS CLUB, NAZI HALL MONITOR," and grabbed the shotgun therein. I mentally patted myself on the back for having had the foresight to install one of these stations near every hall monitor post.

Then I shot her. With both barrels. Cut her in half.

I smiled down at her ventilated body. "Nobody will notice a crumpled cigarette package on the floor, what with your guts splattered discretely about the walls, bulletin board, and the trophy case. Ingenious, if I do say so myself, and damn more fun than having to stoop and pick it up, don't you think?" Disgusted, I shook my head and sighed, "Get yourself together, sister."

She gurgled something that sounded like she only wanted to sing for me but now would try and get herself together. I shook my head "no" at her as I entered the principal's office. Her upper and lower halves scampered off down the hall.

Principal Sodom looked up over her latest copy of *Leatherboy Magazine*, and said in a breathy, bass voice, "Hmmm. I see a little silhouette of a man! What was all the noise about, sweetcheeks?"

"Littering laws. Did you know that your hall monitor is a real mess?"

Sodom was dressed in a conservative black camisole that highlighted the three-day growth of beard on her feminine features. The Marine Corps tattoo on her bulging left biceps made her look a bit trampy, but I'd seen worse.

She stood, her tight leather mini-skirt riding high on her unshaven thighs, leaned across the desk, and held out a cigar in her slender, calloused hand.

"Cuban?"

"No," I replied. "Mostly Chinese."

She looked at me oddly. "No, I mean do you want a cigar?"

"Thanks," I said, taking the stogie, "but I only smoke Lucky's. Private Eye Union rules, ma'am." I pulled a fresh pack from the carton I kept in my trenchcoat.

Ms. Sodom sat back down in the chair, propping her size-seventeen pumps on the desk. She asked, "What's a young, virile stud, with such tight buttocks, like you doing in a place like this?"

We lit our respective tobacco products simultaneously.

"You know, honey, you'd look a lot better if you had those gams waxed, and maybe your face, too."

"Not till after the operation, you silly," she replied coyly. "Now, are you here looking for a good time, or were you a naughty little boy?"

I inhaled on my coffin nail and let out a long plume of smoke.

"Listen, toots, I'm flattered, really; but you're not my type. I never go out with chicks that have a silver medal for dead-lifting in the Olympics. Besides, I hear they maybe transferring you to judge the International Dyslexic Spelling Bee."

She nodded her head in confirmation.

"What I'm really here for," I continued, "is to find out who gave Johnny that football meant for me."

"Who's Johnny?" she said and smiled in her special way. The smoke from her stogie curled like a caduceus around the few remaining wisps of hair on her otherwise balding head.

"Johnny's my best friend. You know, the one who took an exploding football meant for me?" The smoke from my Lucky billowed around my hat in a dense fog, making visibility, and breathing, difficult.

Wait a minute, I thought, all this smoke isn't coming from a cigar and a cigarette. Oh, yeah. Homeroom.

Sodom waved away some of the smoke between us with a limp-wristed hand and asked, "What's Johnny's last name, Buttercheeks?"

"My name's not Buttercheeks, it's Phil. Phillip Screwdriver, *last of the real men private investigators.*"

There was that music again. I made a mental note to find out where it was coming from.

"As for Johnny, he doesn't have a last name. Just Johnny. It's kind of like Madonna, only without the freaky pretentiousness or appeal to the gay community. By the way," I asked, getting a strange hunch, "are you related to Mr. Gomorrah, last year's principal? You look a lot like him."

"Wh-why no," she replied nervously, glancing around as if for a means of escape.

Suddenly it hit me; hit me the way an eighteen-wheeler hits a wounded, orphan puppy at eighty-five miles an hour, in broad daylight. Incidentally, eighty-five miles-per-hour is well above the posted speed limit and is punishable by a fifteen-dollar fine or being shot at dawn. The higher penalty if you hit a puppy.

Anyway, it became painfully obvious that Sodom had given Johnny the ball to give to me, because I was on to her little secret. She wasn't who she wanted everyone to think she was.

I pulled out Richard and chambered a round.

"Everybody knows Johnny. You shouldn't have played stupid. I know your little secret now."

As I said those last six words, she blanched, pounding the last nail into her coffin

"I, the judge, I, THE JURY, and I, the executioner, find you," I paused for dramatic effect, "guilty of murder and behaving in a way unbecoming a principal. And I sentence you, Ms. Sodom, or should I say Mister Platypus, alias Mister Gomorrah, to a permanent stay in the Deep-Six Motel!"

Her eyes got big and liquid as I leveled my forty-five caliber cannon at her dainty skull. She shoved a pair of tortoise-shell glasses in the planned flight path of my bullets and whined, "You wouldn't shoot a guy — uh, I mean lady with glasses would you?"

Richard repeatedly barked a staccato "Yes!" at her until the hammer fell on an empty chamber.

Hollow, blood-filled eyes stared up at me from the floor, and with her last breath she asked, "How could you?"

I smiled a victorious, but empty smile at her and answered, "To quote the school's namesake: It was easy."

She let out a terrible death-rattle and a hairy-chested Valkyrie, who looked an awful lot like the overweight, anal retentive, president of the chess club, Nazi Hall Monitor, escorted Sodom to the blackest depths of Hell, pausing only to ask me, "Now?" I shook my head and smiled.

Case closed, I thought and strode out of the burning husk of Hammer High.

I was suddenly awash with *deja vu*. Years ago, under similar circumstances, I had done much the same thing: Hammer High had been built upon the ruins of Spillane Elementary, virtually overnight. The industrious Canadian migrant farm workers who'd done the work were already on their way as I left the grounds. Tomorrow there would be a brand new school, and life would go on.

But there probably wouldn't be a brand new Johnny.

I started the long walk home, thinking of Johnny and all the good times that we shared: Johnny and I on our first double dates; Johnny and I touring Death Row at the local prison; Johnny and I on that water tower in Texas; Johnny and I with Mr. Capone on Valentine's Day; Johnny and I piloting the *Enola Gay*; Johnny and I cow-tipping on Mrs. O'Leary's farm in Chicago; Johnny and I . . . There were just too many memories.

"Johnny pal," I said, raising one of my sock flasks heavenward, "I'm going to miss you." And then I emptied the scotch into my stomach, hoping that it would quench the rage that still burned there.

My train of thought was derailed by an angry, torch-bearing mob, screaming behind me. It was obvious to my trained eye that this wasn't any ordinary torch-bearing mob chanting my name. They were clearly Ms. Sodom's accomplices, and environmental extremists to boot.

Fortunately, I'd had the foresight to predict such an event, and broke the glass on the case mounted to the tree next to me marked: "BREAK GLASS IN CASE OF ANGRY, TORCH BEARING MOB." I pulled out the fifty-caliber Browning air-cooled machine gun stashed therein and fired a burst into the air. The mob paused momentarily.

At the top of my voice, I yelled, "Ms. Sodom killed Johnny! She had to die! But you don't! I don't want to kill all of you! Go home! Leave me alone!"

The mob took a few tentative steps forward. I drew a line of lead in front of their feet with the machine gun.

"Hasn't their been enough death?" I yelled. "Jesus, I can't even look at Eggplant Parmesan anymore! Shuffleboard is death! I am the Walrus, coo-coo ka choo. Don't you see? Don't you see? It's as plain as tea, you drink with jam and bread, which will bring us back to do-re-me-fa-so!"

They stared open-mouthed at me. I heard one of them say, "Hey, man, he's right! Let's go home and pick up the tattered ruins of our lives. Let's try and mend the fabric of our previous existences, now that they've been torn asunder, like a lingerie sale at the Vatican City Frederick's of Hollywood."

The mob looked at themselves and then, heads hung low, turned to leave. However, I saw through their clever ruse and opened fire. I could barely hear their beseeching screams for forgiveness over the din of the Browning, as I wept for their immortal souls.

The carnage was amazing.

As I stood surveying the robble, I felt twinges of guilt and sorrow. Wait a minute, I meant rubble, not robble. Robble is the sound the Hamburglar makes. You know, "Robble, robble." But I felt sorry for the crowd, and the Hamburglar, too, because they just couldn't see things the way they really were.

I fired up a Lucky and walked home, into the setting sun.

* * *

I graduated high school *magnum cum laude*, in the summer of my senior year. Even though I was valedictorian, I had to kill the fourth principal of my high school tour of duty before he would let me deliver the commencement speech. Repeated questioning at gunpoint would not make Principal Fodder concede; at the moment of death, though, he decided to let me give the speech. I must give credit where credit is due: Fodder lasted much longer than the other heads of Hammer High. I still don't know why he didn't pick me to speak in the first place; I was the obvious choice after all of the other candidates had died mysteriously.

    On graduation day, I stood behind the podium and surveyed the unfortunate saps who'd survived the whole four years. These poor kids would have to go into the hard, uncaring world and carve out miserable existences for themselves. At least they'd been tough enough to make it this far. Those losers who'd died, for one reason or another, had gotten off light.

    I had stayed up all night with Johnny, writing my valedictorian speech. I helped him where he got stuck and modified it to fit my particular prose. It went something like this:

    "As I stand before you today, I am reminded of the hundreds of us who didn't make it to graduation. That hopeless sea of faces that I first saw at freshman orientation has trickled down to a mere puddle.

    "I remember that tragic bus accident that occurred in our ninth-grade year. Some maniac had cut the brake cables, causing the bus to go over a cliff and slaying every single member of the football team. Fortunately, the married players had taken a separate bus, and arrived home from the game safely, to the open arms of their loving spouses, and not . . . to Becky Fettuccine. I, and I alone, was the only single member of the team to survive that fateful day, as I had been called out of town on unavoidable business.

    "Then there was that terrible, terrible incident with the band at the Homecoming game of our sophomore year. I was, unfortunately, out of town that day on unavoidable family business. I still feel guilty about it. If I'd been there, maybe I could have prevented them from breaking into my locker and using my landmines on the football field. That first quarter was a terrible time for us all.

"That tragic occurrence at the junior prom comes to mind next. It was rumored that some nameless maniac massacred every student there after being told, 'Not if you were the last Real-man-Pri . . . uh, last man on earth.' Maybe, if I hadn't been called out of town so suddenly that day, I could have attended the dance and, perhaps, stopped the wholesale slaughter of many, many of our friends and classmates.

"Let us not forget that tragic day this year: Someone with an anti-aircraft battery on top of our beloved Hammer High shot down Delta Flight 666, from Casablanca to Venice, Italy. It crashed into our attendance office, killing everyone. A bright side to this tragic occurrence was that it obliterated the attendance records. Several of us, myself included, were not held back for missing too many days of school after being called out of town, unavoidably, as I was that day.

"So, in retrospect, that plane crash was a blessing in disguise.

"But I come not to bury the graduating class of Hammer High, I come to praise them. I'd like to stand up here and tell you that it's all sunshine, flowers, and marshmallows from here on out, but I'm your friend, not your messiah. I wouldn't mislead you.

"In reality, it's a paint by numbers world out there and every number is thirteen. The future is like a dark, filthy alley that reads like the bottom of a package of Lucky Strikes: LSMFT- Leaches, Scum, Murderers, Fruitcakes, and Thieves.

"You will fight for each desperate inch in this alley of life, as you crawl your way from failing streetlight to sputtering lamppost. Be careful as you seek refuge in the waning pool of light, as it blinds you to the monsters lurking just outside.

"You'll have to watch your step as you trudge through the cesspools between the not-so-dark spots. With one misstep you will slide into the Stygian depths of the foul sewers. You will try vainly to keep your head above the sucking quagmire that has become your life. The pathetic stench of all those who have made the futile attempt before you makes you long for the peaceful sanctuary of death.

"Then, just as you give up and begin your final descent into oblivion, you spot a light at the end of the tunnel. With your last fraction of an ounce of strength and willpower, you crawl toward that shining beacon of hope.

"For eternities, you struggle through the slime and mire, getting ever closer. At long last, you arrive, and, with tears of joy in your eyes, you look up and see a glowing gate. Above this door, carved into the stone, are the words: 'Abandon All Hope, Ye Who Enter Here.'

"The gates of Hell will suddenly burst open and a snarling, slimy, demented spawn of Satan will grab your leg, gnawing on it as he drags you inside.

"Trumpets sound from on High, and a ray of light severs you from the merciless clutch of the Abyss. The angel Gabriel will swoop down from above and take your hand . . . leaving you to stare at the remaining bloody stump of what's left of your arm. As he returns to the Heavens, you hear him say, 'Thanks for the solid-gold graduation ring, sucker!' Trust me, I've met him. Gabriel can be a real jerk like that.

"Anyway, congratulations, fellow students, and have a nice life."

INTERLUDE FOUR

I graduated from unconsciousness and into the land of the living. Looking at the sterile confines of my room, I almost wished that I'd been held back my senior year.

While I was "in class," someone, probably Jay, had brought in a TV. I guessed he got bored watching me and had a television sent up so he wouldn't miss his Soaps. My bed shot to a vertical position—if they hadn't had the foresight to strap me down, I would have launched at the far wall, smearing it with my masculinity. Rather than hurt myself escaping again, I decided to watch a little tube and heal my wounds. The remote control was on the Formica table next to my bed, so I picked it up, pointed it at the tube, and hit the button.

I pressed the lower button and was soon comfortably horizontal again.

I checked the TV Guide. According to my Mickey Mouse wristwatch, I'd already missed the game shows, and still had half an hour to kill before "The Talk Show" came on.

I gnawed through the leather restraint pinning down my chest, which gave me enough play to work myself out of the rest. Free, I walked over to the TV set and turned it on, hoping that they hadn't canceled "The Love Boat."

The picture tube brightened on a cheap replica of someone's

foyer. The prop door opened, and a fragmentation grenade was tossed onto the set. The explosion sent shrapnel and human flesh all over the room. I smiled. This was my type of show. I sat down on the bed to watch.

After the screaming on the set ended, a simple tune began playing offstage. The door opened wider, and a man wearing a white robe came in. His hood was blood-stained, with three holes cut in it; from two, beady eyes stared into the camera, and the third hole revealed a Charlie Chaplin moustache. He took off his hood and wiped his spit-shined jackboots on the welcome mat.

*****SUPPLICATORY AUTHORS' NOTE**: *The following television show, "Herr Lugars' Neighborhood," (which is in no way to be confused with "Mr. Fred Roger's Neighborhood," God Rest his soul) is blatantly offensive to, well, just about everyone, even us. We hope that by having such a foul, evil persona, such as an Adolph Hitler-type character, presenting such foul, evil opinions (that are not ours, really) in this novel, that such will be taken in the humorous light with which they were intended. Besides, we didn't write this part. The ghost of Mickey Spillane, author of the Mike Hammer series, wrote this and inserted it in our novel to ruin book sales and clear his good name.****

The man bore a striking resemblance to Adolph Geshtappo, my elementary school principal, although the actor was much older. His graying hair was wild and flew in random directions. He pushed the bloodied stump of an arm off of a bench, sat down, pulled off his jackboots, and put on some slippers. While he changed clothes, he sang a familiar little ditty:

"It's *ein* beautiful day in *mein* neighborhood,
Ein beautiful day for slave labor.
Would you be white? Not a spade or a kike?

"If the darkies should start to run,
Get in *mein* pickup *und* load up *mein* gun!

Get rid of *der* WOP, *und* make *die* Jew drop.

"I've always wanted to live in *ein* neighborhood
mit you,
I've always wanted to live in *ein* neighborhood
without Jews!

"So, let's make the most of dis beautiful day,
Let's find some darkies *und* blow dem away!
Would you be white? Not *eine* spade, or *eine* kike?
Und, den you can be *mein* neighbor!"

He gave the camera a twisted grin, showing off a mouthful of brownish teeth, and then took off his robes, revealing a khaki uniform underneath.

"Hallo dere, *meine kinder.* Today on Herr Lugars' neighborhood, we are going to give a house warming party to a family of Negroes that just moved in. Can you say 'Molotov Cocktail'?"

Herr Lugars reached into the closet and came out with a bottle of clear liquid. He unscrewed the lid and fed an oily rag into the top. "I knew you could.

"Und after dat, *meine kleine teufelhunde,* we are going to take a field trip to a local convenience store. Do you know what we'll find dere? That's right: we'll find filthy foreigners who are stealing jobs from your Mommies und Daddies."

He walked down the stairs and sat in a comfortable recliner. Herr Lugars picked up a book that had been sitting on the table next to him and held it up to the camera.

"Gather around, *meine kinder,* it's story time. Today's story is not from Nietzsche or from dat *wunderbar* book, Mein Kampf. Today's story is *See Spot Run,* one of *meine* favorite children's books."

He opened the book to the first page and began reading. "See Spot run. Run, Spot, run." Herr Lugars looked up at the camera and added, "Spot is *eine Deutsche* Sheppard. When he is not playink mit Dick und Jane he is running around der Maginot Line to play mit der French poodles."

"See Jane run. Jane is a little colored girl. See Jane chase Spot. Run, Spot, run! See Spot fear for his life. See Jane froth at the mouth. Jane has rabies." Herr Lugars looked up to explain, "Do you know what rabies is, boys and girls? Rabies is a disease that animals get; it makes dem go crazy like a Jew spotting *zwei* euros on *der strasse*!

"See Spot slip. See Spot break a paw. See Jane catch Spot. See Jane bite Spot's leg. Poor Spot. See Spot howl in pain. See Jane take another bite.

"See Dick drive the ASPCA van. See Dick dressed in white. See Dick shoot Jane in the head with a .44 Magnum hollowpoint slug. See Jane's brain scatter in the wind. See Dick put Spot on a stretcher. See Dick drive Spot to the hospital. See Spot happy."

Herr Lugars smiled and closed the book. "What a sad story, boys *und* girls? Poor Spot. Let's watch some television, *ja*?"

He picked up a remote and turned on the TV. Rhythmic sounds filled the air. Herr Lugars drew his Luger and pumped nine rounds into the picture tube. Still smiling, he turned to the camera.

"Dat vas 'Yo! MTV Raps' *und* Barney the Dinosaur performing his new hit song, 'Children, the Other White Meat!' I'm sorry dat Herr Lugars had to turn off der TV so soon, kiddies. *Die dinosauren* were givink Herr Lugars one of his fits."

The ding-dong of the doorbell calmed him down. He jacked back the bolt of his Luger, checked his ammo, and walked up the steps.

"*Vas ist los?*" Herr Lugars asked in his sing-song voice.

A soprano voice replied, "It's Mr. Postal Worker."

Herr Lugars smiled and twisted the doorknob. He brought his gun to waist level and yanked open the door. Michael Jackson, wearing a Postman's uniform and black face, handed Herr Lugars some mail. Michael screamed and spun around, grabbing his crotch.

Lugarson eyed him suspiciously. "*Vas ist* your problem?"

"Crabs," replied Michael.

There was a loud bang, and Michael dropped to the floor. "Filthy, stinking *Schwartzes.*" Herr Lugars, holding a smoking Luger, smiled at the camera.

"That little trick was called a 'gut-shot,' boys *und* girls. It is one of many tricks you can learn by sending away for *Herr Lugars' Tips for a Safer, Cleaner Environment.* It's only $29.95 through this special TV offer. And, if you act now, I will ensure that it is signed by me *und* my co-author, Kim-Jung Un. Green, like der color of Jew blood, is a color Der Commandant likes."

An address flashed on the screen, care of WKKK TV, Dixieland.

When the address disappeared Herr Lugars said, "Now let's open *der* letter. Oh, mine goodness! How exciting! Look, boys and girls, it's an award from *die* Grand Imperial Dragon, himself. *Der* letter says: 'To Herr Lugars, for duties performed above und beyond *die* call of Brotherhood. I present you *mit der* Burning Cross.'"

Lugars held up the letter, "This boys und girls is proof that anyone who lives correctly will be rewarded, both on Earth und in heaven."

As Herr Lugars beamed with pride, the "Toot, toot" of a steam engine could be heard. "Look, boys und girls, here comes der trolley."

As the trolley chugged into view, Herr Lugars noted, "Poor Mr. Conductor, it is *eine* bad day for business, der trolley is almost empty! Dere are fifteen people in the first twelve rows, und thirty-three darkies in the last two. How are you doing today, Mr. Conductor?"

Mr. Conductor spit a huge wad of chewing tobacco on Herr Lugars' carpet and said, "Jus' freakin' peachy," in a southern drawl.

"And what are you doing here today?"

"Nuttin'."

Herr Lugars looked directly at the camera and said, "For those of you who don't speak American, Mr. Conductor said,

'Nothink, I just stopped by to appear on the show and receive a paycheck, because I am union. But, hey, at least I'm not on der welfare.'

"Mr. Conductor is almost as lazy as the colored folks. It makes der Fuhrer vonder how der Vaterland could have lost der *Krieg* to such lazy *Schwartze* lovers. Speaking of *Schwartzes*, boys und girls, Herr Lugars has a special offer for all our Jewish und colored friends. I'm sponsoring a summer camp this year. This camp is free, und people like Herr Lugars will help you focus your mental abilities. A concentration camp, so to speak."

I lit a Lucky and sighed. Looking at my Mickey Mouse, I realized that it was time for "Orcah" the only talk show left on the air. Not long ago, Orcah was thin and had a small talk show that didn't do too well in the ratings. With the Donahue, Geraldo, Montel, Ricki Lake, Jerry Springer, Richard Bey, Jenny Jones, Rolanda, Maury Povitch, Regis and Kathy (or Kelly), Leeza, Anderson Cooper, Rosie O'Donnell, and Sally Jessie Raphael shows, among others, for competition, the ratings war had been intense.

One day, after the near-tragic loss of yet another family member, Sally Jessie disappeared. The same day, Orcah appeared to have gained weight and began sporting red-rimmed glasses. And she lost a very close family member. Orcah captured Sally's market share, if not more.

Then Montel disappeared, and Orcah shaved her head. The very next week, Donahue disappeared, and Orcah started wearing a salt-and-pepper toupee. Now it was obvious that she had put on some pounds. Her ratings soared.

Ricki Lake vanished. Orcah's ratings and dress size continued to increase exponentially. Then Jerry Springer vanished, followed by Rolanda, Jenny Jones, Leeza, and Richard Bey. Regis and Kathy Lee, hip to the trend, relocated their broadcast studio to an underground bunker in Berlin. After discovering that her bouncing baby boy Cody was, in fact, the Anti-Christ and realizing that she could no longer release cheesy, over-done show tunes, Kathy Lee, tragically, blew her brains out on live TV, splattering them all over Regis. Coincidentally, it was sweeps week and their ratings soared. Regis didn't live to enjoy the success as he and his new co-host, Kelly Ripa disappeared soon after. During the funeral, broadcasting live from the services, Orcah broke into a cheesy, over-done rendition of "Some Enchanted Evening." Subsequent exhuming of the graves by Geraldo found, after an hour of primetime television, the coffins empty, of course.

Maury and Geraldo were the only other talk shows left. Geraldo disappeared the same day Orcah grew a cheesy handlebar moustache.

I hit the channel button on my remote control. The TV showed a comfortable soundstage, the set of Orcah's talk show.

It was decorated with tan, bland furniture: soft and inviting chairs waited for guests, while a couch sat behind the host's desk. Warm, earth-tone curtains rose from the polished wood floor and served as a backdrop to the entire set. Behind that pleated cloth, something rustled. The audience held its breath while the very fabric of reality parted. Only the eyes of the insane (or one of the show's regular viewers), could recognize the slowly emerging form.

A dark, unwholesome blob, wearing a thigh-hiding black dress and hideously-malformed black pumps, was propelled onstage. It crept slowly forward, out of the darkness to which it belonged, and into the light.

A salt and pepper toupee sat squarely atop its mass, and the Blob wore large red-rimmed eyeglasses. A grotesque handlebar mustache covered the top of its heavily lipsticked mouth. Although the creature had probably spent hours applying make-up to appear human, it still resembled a sucking chest wound.

A pseudopod painfully extended itself from the Blob, reaching toward and enveloping a microphone. The "arm," now coupled in unholy matrimony with the mic, retracted. The Dark Unwholesome Blob opened its mouth to speak, and a foul wind began to blow. In the distance a wolf howled and a baby cried; a black cat walked under a ladder thirteen times.

It spoke:

"Today, on the Orcah show: the barbeque-slathered bones of actor Marlon Brando and Eddie Shyster: the only lawyer not involved with the O.J. case, law-professor, accountant, and shoeshine boy! Let's give him a hand!"

The audience clapped as Eddie, a tall, good-looking Negro, came onstage from behind the curtains. He wore a gray, tailored suit and shiny Florsheim wingtips. In his left hand he held a fat, juicy steak.

Eddie circled Orcah warily, and It moved to stay between him and the guests' chairs. With a jerk of his arm, Eddie flung the steak behind the host's desk. Orcah looked from steak to Eddie, and then back. After deciding that getting the steak required less physical exertion, she maneuvered behind her desk and began eating the meat. Eddie jumped into the guest chair farthest from the host.

Satisfied for the moment, Orcah turned toward Eddie and asked "So, Eddie, what's it like working with the Son of God? Is it more of a challenge defending an All-Being, than, say, a Kennedy or a Clinton?"

"Well, Orcah," Eddie started, "besides the obvious similarities, the Son of God has the ability to send the jurors to Hell, if a guilty verdict is returned. Something, I believe, the Kennedy's cannot do, outside New England. The Clintons could exile jurors to Arkansas, which may be worse. So it's a toss-up there."

"So you're not concerned about the Son of God being found guilty?"

"No."

"Despite the overwhelming evidence?"

"I'd disagree with that statement. The case against my client is entirely circumcised. I mean circumstantial."

"What about the photos, the six hundred and sixty six eye-witnesses, and all those affidavits?"

Eddie cleared his throat, "It is a well known fact that my client closely resembles Jerry Seinfeld. It is my suggestion here, and to the court, that it was Jerry Seinfeld that committed those heinous crimes. My client is a benevolent, caring deity. Mr. Seinfeld, on the other hand, besides being the real murderer of Nicole Brown Simpson, Ronald Goldman, Tupac, Biggie Smalls, and Smallie Bigs, has had motive to frame my client since the network canceled his latest television endeavor. And it's not the first time my client has been framed. Remember the Pharisees, still upset over the whole 'money-table' thing, trumped up some charges, let the murderer Barrabas go free, and the rest is history."

"Now Eddie," Orcah began, "isn't it true that the Son of God may assume any form he pleases? And isn't it also true that the Son of God, jealous of Jerry's success and in an attempt to frame him, assumed Mr. Seinfeld's form?"

"No, Orcah, it is a fallacy that my client may assume any form he pleases. Given the liberal media bias, only a Democratic Presidential nominee can do that and even then only in an election year between the primaries and the general election. Anything my client or his family does is immediately blown completely out of proportion. Case in point: my client's father, vacationing on Earth some two-thousand years ago, had a one-night fling with some Jewish tramp named Mary something or other;" Eddie paused dramatically, "and look where we are now."

SUPPLICATORY AUTHORS' NOTE: THE SEQUEL: The preceding comments are blatantly offensive to, well, just about everyone, even us. We hope that by having such a foul, evil persona, such as a lawyer, presenting such foul, evil opinions (that are not ours, really) in this novel, that such will be taken in the humorous light with which they were intended. Besides, we didn't write this part. Robert Parker, who hasn't had a hit since the "Spencer" series, wrote this and inserted it in our novel because he is insanely jealous of our talent and universal success.*

Orcah belched as she polished off a case of Twinkies. "I believe you have a film-clip of the trial the time you defended God?"

"Yes."

"Roll the clip, Johnny, and bring me a milk-cow."

A terrified and pleading "Moo" was heard from off-stage.

A courtroom filled the screen, and God sat in the witness stand. His sandaled feet were propped on a stack of Bibles while He sipped a Mint Julep. As naked slave girls fanned Him, He gave testimony.

God coughed politely, ". . . so yes, I am all-powerful. I don't deny that fact because it is, well, a fact: I am all-powerful. But let Me remind the court that with omnipotence and great power comes great responsibility and at least a four-movie deal for the Spiderman franchise. Only I, and I alone, know when to exert My powers. Sometimes, quote-unquote tragedies occur, like Batman Returns with George Clooney, but believe me, it's all for a Greater Good. By the way, I cast Michael Keaton before moving on to the next project; Satan was responsible for Clooney getting the role. I mean Satan's been responsible for some evil of biblical proportions, but what the Hell!? I'm not taking the rap for that one.

"If the jury will open the bags that my lovely assistant Vanna is now passing around"—God pointed at a nubile wench who was handing sacks to the jurors—"you will find many, many hundred dollar bills. Take a few and look at the backs of each bill. Go ahead. It's okay. Now, do they not read, 'In God We Trust'?" He, along with the jury, nodded. "Yes, it does. So trust Me, ladies and gentlemen of the jury. Even though only the good die young, and the rich get richer while the poor get poorer, trust Me. And in return, I'll trust you to find Me innocent.

"Thank you, ladies and gentlemen. The defense rests."

There was a roar of applause, and the screen flashed back to Eddie sitting next to the Dark Unwholesome Blob. Her head was buried inside the bloody carcass of a cow, and she made grunting noises from somewhere inside the bovine ribcage, splashing blood and chunks of flesh and bone onto her couch. Eddie was doubled over, vomiting into a trashcan. Orcah smiled at the camera from between what was left of the cow's ribcage, grabbed the trashcan, and drank from it.

Disgusted, Eddie spat, "How can you (*coff-coff*) drink that!?"

Orcah belched, smiled and said, "If you can swallow Geraldo, you can swallow anything! Ha ha snort, get it?" Orcah wiped her lips and said, "We now pause for a brief com—"

Feeling ill, I looked for my remote control and the off button. To weak to reach salvation, I voluntarily returned to a deep, deep coma. My last conscious sensations were the sound of Orcah's next guest crying out, "The horror. The horror."

THE COLLEGE YEARS

It was a bright and sunny morning and the bluebirds of happiness were gaily singing Wagner's "Flight of the Valkyrie," in C minor; their joyful voices lilted down from the lofty perches in the fragrant elms. The forest had not yet fallen into the tender clutches of autumn, and fluffy bunnies frolicked amongst the tree roots. A brook, which sounded amazingly like William Shatner's legendary James T. Kirk, babbled nearby. Colorful butterflies danced hither and yon about me as I bounded merrily through a field of daisies.

Wait a minute! That's not my life. Hey! Angel of Death! Somebody else's life is flashing by me! This one isn't mine!

The landscape blurred and darkened. Bunnies and birds burst into flame and crumbled to ash. Lightning struck the elms, splintering the branches and igniting the leaves.

It was a wet and miserable day. The kind of day that made you feel like you'd gone through an automatic carwash with your windows down. Cold, biting rain poured from the heavens. Birds of prey perched in the withered branches of the elm trees, singing a hopeful dirge for their dinner. Picked bunny skeletons lay amongst the gnarled roots of the trees. A babbling brook twisted through the elms, cursing like a sailor. Rising beyond the treeline were the Gothic spires of Marlowe University, my alma mater, located outside the town of Merry, Virginia. Gargoyles scowled atop the gray buildings, keeping the sunshine and happiness at bay.

Yeah. This was more like it. There's no place like home.

I pushed my fedora back on my head and stared into the eyes of a cold, gray gargoyle that sat perched atop the colder, grayer student union building. It stared back, determined to make me blink first. I was winning when a clown in a letterman's sweater decided to use it as a diving board.

The letterman screamed, "The platypi are coming! The platypi are coming!" and performed a double somersault, triple gainer into the sidewalk at my feet, forcing me to take a step to my left and, unfortunately, blink.

"No fair," I said to the gargoyle. "You cheat."

The gargoyle winked a bloodshot cement eye at me and resumed glaring.

I crushed out the burning ember of my cigarette and thought of a Viking funeral pyre. I wondered why I thought that. Then I wondered why I even bothered wondering why I thought anything anymore. Then I decided that I still didn't know, fired up another Lucky, and went to register.

The registration hall was like a dress rehearsal for Dante's *The Inferno*. I passed through the portcullis marked "Abandon All Hope Ye Who Enter Here." Inside, the temperature was unbearable, and lost souls wandered endlessly from line to line. There were lines to enroll, lines to drop classes, and lines for information about where to enroll and drop classes; lines for buying books, and lines for selling books; lines for the Coke machine, and lines for the dope machine; lines for people who really enjoyed standing in lines, and lines that appeared not to be for anything.

WITH-IT AUTHORS' NOTE: Did you catch how we remain hip by throwing in subtle drug/college jokes? Dope machines right after Coke machines--get it? Watch for more tragically hip drug jokes because we're not going to point them out any more. Nyah!

I wasn't about to wait behind sniveling, pimple-faced punks, so I whipped out my trusty .45 and squeezed a couple rounds into the air. A dead platypus fell from the rafters to my feet, forcing me to take a step to my left.

A few people turned and looked at me with utter disgust. A guy who looked like he spent the summer as a rock group roadie said, "You must be a freshmen, dude. Let me clue you in, buddy: indiscriminant-firing-of-shots-into-the-air-to-clear-the-line was last semester. And don't try the fire alarm trick. And don't even think about calling in a bomb threat. It's been done and it don't work. People will die before they leave this line."

"What if I have a real bomb?"

"Nope."

I needed another plan quick. What would Plato do in a situation like this? Wait. College students . . . I had it.

Grinning, I ran out side and shot down the first single engine plane that I saw. Then I ran back inside and shouted, at the top of my lungs, that a plane carrying an illegal shipment of drugs had crash-landed in the quad.

I was almost crushed as they stampeded to get outside. The roadie yelled, "Not bad, dude. Don't believe you for a second, but I ain't taking no chances."

Within thirty seconds, the registration hall was a ghost town. I registered, bought books, and got a dorm assignment in eight minutes flat.

I'd been assigned room 1313 in the Doyle House. I'd wanted room 221B, but it was being renovated. I decided to stroll over to my new digs, which would double as my office, and meet my roommate.

I walked out of the registration hall, down the steps, and headed in the dorm's general direction. A white shroud covered the ground, making it look like it had been snowing. Students frolicked in the drifts around a smoldering Cessna, while others lay face down in the stuff, snorting deeply.

This is odd, I thought, *for September*. I scooped up a handful of the powder and tasted it. It wasn't snow, that's for sure. A long-haired friend of Jesus flew by, screaming maniacally between bursts of laughter. I clotheslined him to get his attention.

"Hey, buddy, what's all the hubbub?"

"The Lord, our shepherd, has provided for his flock!"

I put my Florsheim on his throat. "In English, you hippie freak, before I send you to meet your maker!"

"That's a huge pile of cocaine, man! Do you snort?"

"No," I replied casually, "I just like the way it smells."

I released the hippie and thought, *The drug problem is worse than I imagined.* There was only one way to deal with the scum that trucked in addictive substances: Cold, swift violence delivered in neatly wrapped packages of hot lead.

I lit up a Lucky, inhaled, and unholstered Richard.

The carnage was amazing.

I could see the headline now: Drugs Kill.

Continuing across the quad, I bumped into a Girl Scout selling cookies. She had a killer smile so I ordered one of everything she had. She flashed her pearly whites and promised to bring them by later. I gave her my new address and left.

The Linguini's limo was idling in the parking lot behind my dorm. I headed for it, hoping my Dad, Frank, had stopped by to wish me luck.

Frank "The Screwdriver" Linguini had adopted me when I was eight years old. I don't remember a whole lot before that, except Elvis movies — lots of Elvis movies. But Frank saw a little bit of me in his younger self, and decided to take me in. I remember the days when I'd help him out at the office: contract work, loan-repayment, and arranging client entertainment. Frank was a shrewd businessman; with my help, he managed to turn a Mom-and-Pop outfit into a thriving family business. He'd come to America when he was eight years old and had never gotten past the sixth grade. It was his hope that I would get an education. I didn't really want to go, because I thought school was for sissies. But it was Frank who'd pulled me off the streets, and I didn't want to disappoint him.

The limo driver saw me coming and jumped the curb. As he cruised across the lawn, the back window of the car rolled down. A Tommy gun poked out, spitting hot death at an Asian family that was in the way of the vehicle.

I lit a Lucky and watched the Asian bodies crumple to the ground in heaps of blood and flesh. My stomach twisted into knots; the screams and the gunfire reminded me of a place half a world away. Back then, the name on my uniform read "Screwdriver," but everybody knew me as: Blaze O'Glory Steinman!

From somewhere, bass drums pounded a familiar ominous overture.

My first month in the jungle, I was ambushed on a routine patrol and taken prisoner by Charlie. A stray round had struck my combat fedora and knocked me unconscious.

When I came to, I had found myself in a bamboo cage, stripped of my camouflage trenchcoat, cigarettes, and lucky whiskey flask. I was tortured for years in that POW camp, enduring pain that would have broken a lesser man.

I'll never forget the camp commander, Suwit; his cruel face is burned into my brain. The sadistic bastard would smoke in front of me while doing unspeakable things to me with a fork. I'd try desperately to bum a cigarette, but he'd just poke me with the fork and smile.

I accidentally escaped one morning during breakfast. Let's just say it involved crepes and leave it at that. For weeks, I survived in the jungle, eating whatever crawled or slithered past me. Learning to survive on wits and instinct, I wove a trenchcoat and fedora out of jungle vines, enabling me to blend into the background. At times, I would ambush an enemy patrol, killing them all and taking their rations. I heard later that a legend grew out of my exploits. They called me Rambo, which meant "killer forest ghost who wears a trenchcoat and hat but not underwear." Eventually, after years in the jungle, a friendly patrol crossed my path and took me back to an American firebase. Having made it back to friendly lines, I swore that one day I would find my torturer Suwit. Rumor has it that he fled to the States during the fall of Saigon. I swore I'd find him, and when I did, he'd smoke in hell.

Vinnie "The Plumber" Alfredo shook me out of my reverie with a smack from the red-hot barrel of his Tommy gun.

"Hey, Kid, youse o.k.? Youse looked kinda lost there for a moment."

"Yeah, Vinnie, I'm fine. I just need a cigarette."

"Sure, Junior," he said, and fished a butt out of his pack. "Have one of mine."

I took a coffin nail from him and started to stick it in my mouth before realizing what it was. I looked at Vinnie in disgust.

"Vinnie, this is a Virginia Slim. What kind of sissy-fag is this, anyway?"

"I was out Chesterfields, so I took the little woman's," he replied defensively.

"Sure, sure, Vin. Well, I'm out too, so maybe just this once."

Vinnie lit our smokes with the barrel of his gun and said. "Youse know, we really oughta cut down on dese things; they're killers."

"Yeah, yeah," I said, enjoying the feminine caresses of the Virginia Slim in my lungs.

"Remember," Vinnie said, changing the subject, "your new name is Phillip H. Screwdriver. We don't wants anybody to connects youse wit' us. It could be hazardous to everybody's health."

"Sure, Vin. What's the 'H' stand for, by the way?"

Vinnie shrugged. "Nothin', far as I know. Boss figured it was Jesus' middle initial, so it must be a good one. Now, go over youse history one more times."

I cleared my throat and started: "Okay, okay. My father's name is Reg Screwdriver. He was a patrol cop in L.A. and drove car

Adam-12. I became a cop until one day I decided that a cop's law wasn't always man's law and did what needed to be done. I was given the choice of prison or the army and became a master sergeant in 'Nam. Before that I flew a bomber over Japan; and before that I was president of a small Latin American republic.

"If anyone asks, I can't talk about my past because I'm wanted for war crimes. Did I get it all this time?"

"No, youse half-wit vegetable. Youse forgot the part about the security position, the school custodial job, and night watchman at the dump. Youse were also the NBC program executive who canceled *Star Trek*, and towel boy at the YMCA. Gots it now?"

"Sure, Vinnie, I'se gots it." Dammit! Now he had me doing it.

"And remember, Phil," Vinnie said, winking, "nobody, but nobody, can knows whose you really is."

I reached inside my jacket and grabbed Richard. "You know who I am," I said as my finger tightened on the trigger, "don't you, Vinnie?"

His eyes went wide and a neat hole appeared directly above his left nostril.

Knowing he was next, the chauffeur stomped on the gas pedal. I calmly dropped the old magazine from my automatic and inserted tracer rounds. I jacked back the bolt, chambering the first bullet, sighted in, and squeezed off five quick shots.

I watched the tracer trails streak into the gas tank of the limo. It exploded into little-bitty, genuine GM parts. Momentum carried the flaming chassis into the still-smoldering wreckage of the Cessna I'd shot down earlier.

I smiled. Somewhere up there, Vinnie was looking down. And he was real proud of me.

The sky grew dark, and was split by a bolt of lightning. Raindrops began falling like teenaged girls for Elvis Presley or maybe Old Blue Eyes.

Yeah, Vinnie was real proud of me.

Tonight's Episode: Slaughter of the Sacred Herd

Passing the bridge over the babbling brook on my way to the dorm, I heard the voice of James T. Kirk again. Deciding to investigate, I unholstered my gat. I crept quietly along the bridge railing. As I drew closer, I heard other voices.

The regulars of the Starship *Enterprise* were gathering around Kirk, who struck a dramatic and manly pose. He flipped his communicator open, and said, "Beam us up, Scotty!"

The voice on the other end of the line belched and slurred his words, "Aye, aye, Cap'n. But the transporters canna take much more."

"Goddammit, Scotty," Kirk paused dramatically, "We're in syndication," another dramatic pause, "we don't need to be," dramatic pause, "dramatic. Everyone knows we're going to make it eventually." He put his hand over the walkie-talkie and turned to the pointy-eared fellow with the bad haircut. "Spock," dramatic pause, "I think he's plowed again."

"Negative, Captain," the over-sized elf replied deadpan. "If large Terran farm equipment had passed over his body, I highly doubt that his ability to communicate would remain intact."

A thin man with an attitude and a stethoscope spoke up, "Spock, you green blooded, half-breed moron! Jim means that he's plastered to the gills!"

Spock arched an eyebrow, "Negative, Doctor McCoy. First, with the exception of the inhabitants of Rigel IV, no humanoid species still possess gills. Secondly, if Mr. Scott did in fact have gills, and they were covered in plaster, he would be unable to breathe and, thus, not able to verbally communicate. Lastly, there is no plaster aboard the *Enterprise*; the entire ship is constructed of a highly volatile uranium/plutonium compound."

Kirk pulled out a cheap-looking plastic gun, and said, in an annoyed voice, "Set phasers on stun. Let's try this one more time. Spock," dramatic pause, "Scotty's shit faced!"

"Negative, Captain—" Spock began.

Kirk twisted the dial on his phaser and said to the rest of the crew, "Set phasers to 'Violent Death,' and," dramatic pause, "fire at w—"

It was Spock's turn to cut off Kirk. "Oh, you mean inebriated, Captain. I concur; tricorder readings place his blood-alcohol content well above the terminal level for humans."

Kirk's shoulders slumped, and he ran his fingers through his toupee, mumbling to himself. "I knew I'd never make it," dramatic pause, "without losing my mind. I never thought I'd be thankful that Screwdriver canned the show." He lifted his head and looked at the over-grown elf. "Spock," dramatic pause, "or any of you," dramatic pause, "does anybody have any ideas about what we should do," dramatic pause, "next?"

I took this as my cue to make an entrance. I stood up and said, "How about we join Scotty and pass the bottle around?"

The crew turned to look at me, and Kirk whispered something to Spock, who looked at the tape recorder hanging around his neck.

"According to my readings, Captain," Spock said, arching an eyebrow, "it is a Terran male with unusually low levels of testosterone and improbable levels of estrogen. A chemical imbalance in his hypothalamus points toward the possibility of latent homosexuality and recent brain hemorrhaging. He appears to be somewhat autistic, having no concept of reality, but able to interact with it in an indirect fashion. He has violent fits and is armed. I suggest that we set phasers to 'Untimely Demise.'"

As every crewman simultaneously whitened their knuckles on phaser fire buttons, I pulled out Richard...

THE END.

****Just kidding. We apologize for any action you may have missed.****

I holstered my smoking cannon and sauntered over to the carnage. Mangled bodies were twisted in a gory dance of death, and

I smiled. Grabbing a communicator from Spock's lifeless hand and a phaser from Kirk's, I prepared myself to board the *Enterprise*.

I said "One to beam up," dramatic pause, "Scotty."

An unintelligible burr answered me, and at first I felt like a man on a fuzzy tree. And then I felt tingly all over; it was like the cool, refreshing sensation of a York Peppermint Patty. Then I was in the transporter room of the *U.S.S. Enterprise*.

Scotty stared at me in surprise and went for his gun. I threw him my whiskey flask. When he went for it, I set my phaser to "Last Rites" and fired. Scotty glowed a pickled green and then collapsed to the floor.

I scooped up my flask and went over to the control panel. After I'd hit a few random buttons, the voice of Gene Rodenberry's wife said, "Fifteen seconds to self-destruction."

I'd seen the show, so I knew how to get out of here: you pulled down the three red levers and went bye-bye. I put Scotty's limp and lifeless hand over to the controls and stepped onto the transporter. As I'd planned, rigor mortis set in; Scotty's hand stiffened, pulling the control levers down. In a cloud of dust and a flash of light, I was beamed the hearty hi-ho hell out of there.

When the tingling stopped, I was in room 1313, Doyle House. I walked to the window to watch the large explosion in the southern sky. Glass panes rattled for miles around. I smiled. Nobody said that Phillip Screwdriver, *last of the real men private investigators*, had unusually low levels of testosterone and lived to tell about it.

I was still enjoying the view of flaming debris raining from the sky when *she* came strolling up the walkway, and back into my life. When she knocked, it felt like she was pounding my face, not rapping, gently tapping at my door. Like a knock, knock, knocking on Heaven's door.

I crossed the room faster than an Irishman accepts free whiskey. When I opened the door, she was standing impatiently, her smart green outfit hugging every curve of her delicious form; her delicate fist poised in mid-knock.

I hadn't seen her in over an hour, but I'd always known, with all seven ventricles of my heart, that she wouldn't stay gone.

I wished she had.

"Hi, Cookie," I said. "It's been a long time."

She started forward, "Can I...?"

I cut her off, grabbing her and kissing her hard; I wanted her to feel all that time we'd spent apart. She finally pulled away from me, and I noticed the boxes in her hands.

I pulled out a Lucky Strike and headed straight for the scotch I'd seen on the windowsill. It wasn't my bottle, but I guessed the last guy here had been a scotch fan, and left it as a gift. I didn't really give a damn. I claimed it, poured a double for myself and offered the guy silent thanks. I tossed it back and poured another. I looked at Cookie and said, "It's always business first with you, isn't it? I guess that's why I like you." I lifted the bottle, "Drink?"

"Sure, mister. Can I bum a smoke, too?" She grabbed the single malt from my hands and downed it easily. "Smooth," she hacked through a coughing fit. "You may not be much of a kisser, but you're no chintz in the liquor department. Buy me another, sailor?"

I eyed her suspiciously. "How did you know I was in the Navy?"

"Gimme a light."

I lit the cigarette between her red, pouting lips and poured another drink. I guzzled it and stared at her over the rim of my glass. "I knew you'd be back."

She smiled. "Of course I'm back. You said you'd buy everything I had. When I told my Scout leader, she was so excited that she made me Girl Scout of the Year."

"You've got them on you?"

"Yeah, give me the dough, and I'll give you the loot."

I gave her what she needed, and she handed over the boxes. Then she kissed me, and was gone.

I poured myself a double and stared at the thin mints and samoas, and drank. *To hell with her damn cookies*, I thought and kicked them across the room. I started to pour myself another when I noticed that the bottle was empty. I grabbed my hat and decided to go to the liquor store to buy me some memories.

Suddenly, the front door exploded inward and two toughs in black trenchcoats leveled their blue-finished automatics at me.

"Hands up, Screwdriver!" demanded the bigger of the two.

The other guy kicked the door shut with his loafers, his eyes never leaving me. His face was too thin for his body and his lips were too thin for his face. I had no idea who he was, but I knew his type. His overcoat was open just far enough to reveal a pinstriped German suit.

The goon searched me when the thin guy, who was obviously in charge, nodded. He found Richard in my shoulder rig and took her from me. Fortunately, he didn't look under my hat.

The Thinman gave me the standard tough guy speech. I'd heard it so many times, from so many dead men, that I had to laugh.

The big guy didn't like my attitude and smashed his pistol into my jaw. Fortunately, I was a heavy drinker and didn't feel a thing.

"You're almost as tough as Jim, here, Screwdriver. Almost."

I gave the Thinman a metallic smile and spat back, "We all know that Jim and I can take a punch; do you want to try and make the team?"

His pistol roared and pain shot through my right shoulder. The bullet had only grazed me, but I felt it through the scotch.

The Thinman leered at me, and said in mock-apology, "Oh, gee, I'm sorry. I'm not real good with these things."

He let out a booming laugh and tucked his rod under his trenchcoat. "You've made a lot of enemies, Screwdriver," he continued. "Any guess on who I happen to be?"

"Jabba the Hutt's ugly kid brother?" I snapped, ignoring the growing pain in my arm.

His smile flashed beneath cold eyes and he nodded his head. "Yes. Yes, I am. Consider yourself Princess Leia."

The phone rang. The Thinman looked, but Jim's peepers, and his gun, never left me. Beanpole told me to get the phone. I kept my eyes on Jim and lifted the receiver to my ear.

It was her voice.

"Mr. Screwdriver?"

"Yeah, Cookie?"

"I left my hat over there. I'm in Mommy's limo, and we'll be there soon."

"No, now's not a good time," I said slowly. "I've, uh, I've got to . . . leave."

"You'll wait," she replied, and a dial tone replaced her voice.

I looked at Jim and the Thinman. "It was the Girl Scout. I couldn't stop her," I pointed to the green beanie on the floor. "She's coming for her hat."

For professional hoods, they weren't very clever; even Jim looked down. As they stared at the beanie, I pulled the shotgun from its hiding place in my fedora. Neither man noticed.

The Thinman said, "I wonder if she knows she's done her good deed for the day; buying you a few more seconds of life."

"That's the Boy Scouts," I said and pumped the shotgun.

"What?" They both looked up.

"The Boy Scouts do good deeds, the skirts sell cookies."

He stared hard at the business end of my sawed-off Winchester, as if trying to get it to go away." Girl Scouts, Boy Scouts, what's the difference?"

"That's what I say: what's the difference?" I smiled and pulled the trigger just as the door burst in.

The Thinman lost half of his face in a blast of double-ought buck. Jay, who had just kicked in the door, introduced Jim to his .38.

Jim smiled politely at the introduction and charged Jay like an angry bull. Jay emptied his revolver. Two steps before he reached Jay, Jim dropped like a ton of bricks.

I put my Winchester back on the clip in my hat and fired up a Lucky. "It's good to see you, Jay. Do you always kick in doors and come in firing?"

Jay looked puzzled before smiling, "No, just in your room."

"Oh," I acknowledged. "Well then, what are you doing here?"

"My cousin is a building contractor specializing in fire damage remediation. He's working in 221B. He asked me to keep an eye on you. Besides, I'm your new roommate."

"I thought you were dead."

"What?"

"Weren't you in the attendance office when Delta flight 666 crashed into it?"

Jay stared at me quizzically, "What the hell are you babbling about?"

I pushed my hat back on my head far enough to give him the eye. It was obvious that he'd been drinking too many soft drinks laden with Nutrasweet (which is suspected to cause memory loss). I let the matter drop, feeling bad for him. With such deteriorating brain capacity, Jay would probably end up a cop.

"Say, Phil," he asked hopefully, glancing around the room, "you wouldn't happen to have any doughnuts lying around would you?"

I nodded toward the fridge, and Jay made for it, indulging himself in a feeding frenzy that would make Jaws proud.

Through a mouthful of doughnuts, Jay asked, "Have you seen a bottle of 125 year-old scotch around here?"

"No," I said casually, and pushed the empty bottle off the windowsill. "Why?"

"Family heirloom. Every man in the Swell family drinks a single shot on his first day of college, saving the rest of the bottle for the next male child."

"Oh," I said, loud enough to cover the sound of glass shattering on the pavement far, far below. "Well, we're out of booze.

You want to join me for a drink?"

"Maybe later."

I shrugged my shoulders and closed the door behind me.

* * *

After a little snooping around, I discovered that the "Premature Burial" was the hottest speakeasy on the route. Anybody who was nobody came there to drown inhibitions in a deluge of cheap booze.

Walking through the beer-soaked front door, I was assaulted by the grating sounds of Hanson's "Mmm-Bop" as covered by Josh Groban. I opened fire on the DJ booth, hoping he'd understand my request. The needle scratched the record as it was quickly removed.

The bar, like its front door, was wooden and beer-soaked. Stepping down from the dimly lit foyer, my Florsheims landed in a lake of cheap beer. I sloshed past the shelves of sports trophies, heading for the bar. I grabbed a barstool vacated by an underage platypus. The mammal stumbled off, holding his stomach with one webfoot, and covering his bill with the other. I grabbed his beer and made it mine.

I drained the glass and called the barkeep, a rotund man wearing a sequined leisure suit. As he stumbled toward me, my eyes made out the initials "E.P." on his chest, stenciled over with "Norm." His large sideburns looked like rodents stapled to his face.

Norm looked at me through diamond-rim sunglasses and said, "Are you lonesome tonight?"

"No more than usual. Give me a draft."

As the big man pulled me a beer, I thought that he looked vaguely familiar. I shook the feeling off, and caught the mug he had slid down the bar.

I took a pull and asked, "Know anything about two torpedoes and a hit over at Doyle?"

Norm looked the bar over before whispering, "Down at the end of Lonely Street, at Heartbreak Hotel."

"Thanks," I said, and drained my glass.

"Un-hunh-hunh."

I flipped Norm two bits and stood up to leave. The DJ thought about playing a Hannah Montana tune so I shot him. Twice. Then I threw him a double sawbuck.

"Buy something more upbeat, like Sinatra."

There was a 7-Eleven next to the busstop to Lonely Street. Since the bus was scheduled to arrive in two minutes, I knew that I had at least an hour to kill. I ducked into a 7-Eleven to get some smokes. I was down to my last carton.

Behind the counter, a bovine beauty belched, "Howdy, Stranger! Look! I can eat free! All I want! Pizza! Nachos! Anything that falls on the floor is mine! Whoops!"

I watched in horror as she grabbed the pizza machine and toppled it with wanton abandonment. She paused long enough for me to read "Liz" on her nametag before she belly-flopped into the greasy pool of pepperoni and cheese. Fat oozed from around the seams of her Spandex bodysuit as she wallowed orgasmically in the German mire.

"Could I get a carton of Lucky's, if it's not too much trouble?"

She grunted and twisted her hindquarters into the Nacho machine, knocking it to the floor. The fabric of her bodysuit rode further up the crack of her butt than the laws of nature should have allowed. She picked up a fistful of chips and shoved them in my direction. I felt ill and seriously considered vomiting.

I finally shook my head in disgust. "No. Smokes. Can I please have some smokes?"

She nodded, and stopped feeding long enough to toss me a carton.

"Thanks, Kitten. Put it on my tab."

Liz stood, spraying food as she tried to reply. I turned to leave and was blown through the plate-glass window.

When I regained consciousness, I stood up and lit a Lucky.

Standing at the epicenter of the smoking ruins, Liz was stark naked and munching on a Reese's Peanut Butter Cup. Cellulite hung from her ankles like sailors on a Philippine hooker.

I blew a stream of smoke and asked, "What happened?"

"Damn Spandex blew out, again! Third pair today!"

Before she could eat anything else, my bus pulled up to the curb. I jumped on the bus and pulled out a single. As we were driving away, I looked out the window and saw pedestrians fleeing in terror. A handful of wafer thin mints moved closer, ever closer, to the gaping chasm of Liz's mouth . . .

The busdriver said, "That'll be fifty cents, Mac."

I handed him my George Washington, looked him dead in the eye and said, "That'll be fifty cents, Mac."

The driver shoved the single into his cashbox and slammed it shut. "Ha, ha, ha, exact change only. Thanks!"

I mumbled something about overripe watermelons and hollow-point ammunition, and shuffled down the aisle.

The only seat left was at the back of the bus, next to an insurance salesman. Go figure. I sat, and he handed me his card. He offered to sell me term-life at an amazing, one-time-only, special discount for private investigators.

"No thanks, pal," I said through clenched teeth. "This is your only warning: I hate bigots, I hate criminals, I hate televangelists, I hate fifties' TV reruns, I hate heavenly choral music, I hate light beer, I hate peer pressure to date, I hate duck-billed platypi, but more than that, above all else, I hate insurance salesmen!"

"But, sir! This is a great deal! The offer of the cent—"

I shoved Richard down his throat and squeezed off a couple of rounds.

The man across the aisle from us leaned over and said, "Say, buddy, that was an illegal act you just performed. You're going to need a lawyer. Fortunately for you, I'm Harvey Mouthpiece, Attorney-at-"

I grabbed him by the throat and screamed, "Lawyers! I forgot Lawyers! I really, really hate Lawyers!"

I released him, shoving him back into his seat.

"But, sir!—" he sputtered until Richard spat hot death.

Blood spurted onto his double-breasted suit, running down his watch chain and onto the floor.

The man behind me tapped me on the shoulder. I whipped around, gun muzzle raised. "What!"

"Um . . . I sell frozen yogurt, please don't hurt me!"

"Yogurt," I snarled. "I hate yogurt!"

Fifteen minutes later, I parked the bus on Lonely Street, a block from Heartbreak Hotel. I exited through the door, pausing just long to shoot the cashbox and retrieve my fifty cents. I paused for a moment and debated setting the bus on fire. Nah, from the looks of it, property values had already taken a beating around here.

Lonely Street lived up to its name. Broken pavement crumbled beneath my feet with every step. The skeletal remains of a better time glowered at me from either side of the street. Desolation sung a bittersweet song through the twisted and gnarled vines, choking the dreams from the tired souls that had been left behind.

I started moving toward Heartbreak Hotel. A feeling in my guts told me that whoever wanted me dead would be found here. I'd have to stay on my toes, be quick on my feet, cover my ass, cross my fingers, not overplay my hand, keep danger at arms length, get something off my chest, keep my chin up, nose to the grindstone, keep my ear to the ground, and my eyes peeled, um . . . head out of clouds, . . . world from my shoulders, . . . show intestinal fortitude, find something for the rest of my body to do, and then maybe get a bite to eat.

I bumped into a lamppost that had mysteriously appeared in front of the hotel. I shrugged off the blow and shouldered my way into the lobby.

The decor was right out of the McDonald's fast food restaurant interior design manual: ancient red velour clung tentatively to the walls, which were done tastefully in early decay. Dust covered everything, including a lounging bell-boy.

A battered and time-worn oak desk stood in monument to the hotel's long years of loyal service. I rang the bell twice. After two minutes, when no one had showed up, I shot the chandelier from the ceiling. It fell near the bell-boy, who then hopped to and offered to get my bags.

The desk clerk shuffled out of the back room. "Can I help you, sir?"

He looked as run down as the hotel itself; he'd probably seen the neighborhood back when the horses weren't under the hoods of the cars, but out in front of them. He was thin and gaunt, a threadbare tuxedo hanging from his frame like rope from a gallows.

"Say, old timer," I asked, "Do you know anybody who wants me dead?"

"Sure, stranger, but nobody stayin' in a classy joint like this!"

"Yeah, right," I said, dropping four bits onto the counter, "a half buck says there is."

"Ooooooh, Mr. Big Spender! You really shouldn't be flashing a big wad like that around in this neighborhood. A fella could get rolled."

"A fellow might," I said, drawing back the folds of my trenchcoat. "But I have Richard here for a safe deposit box."

The clerk palmed the two quarters and scanned the room nervously. "Watch your back, Screwdriver. The Platypus Liberation Organization is gunning for you. This place is lousy with the little duck-billed bastards. You'd better make tracks."

I tried to grab the clerk but his lapels fell off in my fists. I threw the fabric down and wrapped a paw around his throat.

"Look, pal," I said, my face 3.14 inches from his, "nobody threatens me. Nobody. My great-grandmother threatened me once." I paused dramatically, "Once!"

I crammed his face into the mail slot behind the desk. He

gurgled and I pulled him up.

"Talk, you four-bit punk, or they'll be forwarding your mail to Hell!"

"Two-B! He's in Two-B!"

Was the Platypus in Two-B, or was the clerk lying? Two-B, or not Two-B, that was the question. Whether 'tis nobler in the mind to suffer slings and arrows of outrageous mammals, or to take arms against a pond of troubles, and by opposing, end them.

I unholstered my .45 and headed for the stairwell.

Webbed footprints cluttered the dusty stairs like a dance-step diagram. Moving quietly, my size nine Florsheims replaced the platypus tracks in the dust. Richard's weight became increasingly reassuring as I neared the landing.

As I drew closer, I heard voices chattering twisted mammalian schemes. My name was repeated once or twice, usually following a synonym for murder. Apparently I was the only man alive who could stop them from total world domination.

A shiver raced up my spine as I felt the fate of the entire human race drop onto my broad, masculine shoulders. Without warning, the floorboards gave way, dropping me into the world headquarters of the infamous Platypus Liberation Organization.

I landed in the middle of a room filled with six-foot tall, slavering Platypi. Drool fell from their bills and onto their rented polyester tuxedos. They would have looked sharp if it weren't for the Uzi machine guns pointed at me.

The leader wore a commodore's cap and a navy peacoat. His weather-lined face cracked as he smiled. The Platypus' voice was deep and gravelly. "So, my retooled son, you have at last returned to me. It's taken me years to find you. Tell me, can you forgive an old mammal for what he has done?"

There were eight of them, and one of me. If I was going to get out of here alive, I'd have to play along until the numbers fell my way.

I holstered Richard, "So, Pops, now that you've got me how

you want me, what's your next move?"

"Well, son, I thought we'd throw the ball around, shoot some pool, toss back a couple of drinks, blow up New York. You know, manly things!"

I lit a Lucky to cover the bitter taste of bile rising in my throat and looked at him coolly. "Sure, old man, sure. But what if I'd rather not do manly things? What if I'd rather throw a tea-party for my dollies instead?"

His face darkened with storm clouds and he struggled to contain the thunder of his rage. "You pathetic little worm! If you could only appreciate what I've done for you!"

"Done?!" I snapped. "You haven't done anything but take me prisoner! And tried to brainwash me into being your little boy! Well, Pops, it's not going to work! I've gotten out of tougher scrapes than this and I'll be damned if I play patsy to overdressed freaks of nature!"

Richard appeared in my hand and permanently closed the eyes of two of them before anyone could blink. I dove for one of the bodies, and grabbed his Uzi.

Bullets slammed into the dead platypus I was using for a shield. In return, my commandeered Uzi sang them the chartbuster on the Grim Reaper's Top Forty.

As the Platypus escaped into a dumb waiter, thirty-six men dressed as Ronald McDonald burst into the room. The clowns' guns blazed, chopping the remaining PLO into platypus McNuggets.

After the gunsmoke cleared, Frank Linguini entered the room dressed as the Hamburglar. He spotted me behind the platypus corpse and motioned me over.

"Phillip, my son, are youse alright?"

"Fine," I said, looking myself over. "I was just nicked by a few bullets; it's nothing serious."

"Good, good! We thoughts we might have been too late!"

"No, I was doing alright. The Platypus wanted me to rule the world by his side. I refused; the day I join forces with a sick, psycho thug like him is the day they can hang up my hat and plant me six feet under."

"As your Godfather, I am always concerned for youse health," he smiled. "Youse hungry, Phillip?"

"Sure, Frank, nobody makes linguine like you do."

Outside the hotel, Frank and I got into his limo and the thirty-six clowns piled into a polka-dot VW Bug. Knowing that I had class tomorrow, Frank offered to drop me off at "The Premature Burial."

"Philip, though youse is in college, there is a few things youse still needs to learn. One: pink flamingos represent all that is good and pure in this transient existence. I know for a fact that there are flamingos outside the Pearly Gates, on God's lawn."

I lit up a Lucky, sighed, and sank back into the plush leather seat of the limo. "Sure, Frank, nobody makes linguine like you do."

Not hearing me, Frank continued to ramble, "Two: Shakespeare, though not of the caliber of your Authors, wrote his own shit. This Sir Francis Bacon thing is a crock."

<u>GRATUITOUS AUTHORS' NOTE</u>**: *We had nothing to do with Mr. Linguini's literary views. It is entirely coincidental that he, a man of power and prestige, is chauffeured in a model-year limousine, while Phil is forced to resort to public transportation.*

I turned to Frank and quickly agreed, "Yeah, my Authors are the greatest literary minds to ever grace the face of this planet. I truly believe that the earth will never see the likes of such prosemen again."

Frank turned to me and smiled, "Phillip, I wish to give youse a limousine, as a friend would give another friend a limousine. I'll have Carmine drop it off."

"Sure, Frank," I said, heading for the front door of the bar, "nobody makes linguine like you do."

* * *

The Premature Burial, or "Preemie" as it was commonly referred to, was packed with nubile, voluptuous, vibrant, writhing, sensually succulent, bite-sized furry rodents who weren't too quick on their feet. I ran my tongue across my fangs and smiled.

<u>EXPLANATORY AUTHORS' NOTE</u>: *Our humblest apologies, dear reader, for that last paragraph. It was written by a cat named Ted Turner, while we went out for beer. This is not a celebrity endorsement for drinking and writing, nor is it an aggrandizement of Ted Turner. On the contrary, we wholeheartedly disapprove of his colorization of classic black-and-white films. We also disapprove of his marriage to traitor bitch queen-whore, "Hanoi" Jane "Look At My Butt" Fonda. Oh, they got divorced? Well, maybe he ain't so bad then...****

The "Preemie" was dead tonight. Frank Sinatra's "One For my Baby," crooned from the speakers and a lone figure sat at the bar, telling Norm a joke.

"What," dramatic pause, "is the difference," dramatic pause, "between a green chick and a toilet?"

Norm shook his head and pulled me a beer.

"The toilet," William Shatner continued and paused dramatically, "doesn't follow you around the galaxy for six months after you use it! Ha, ha ha. That joke slays me every time I tell it!"

I broke in, "Speaking of slaying, pal, didn't I kill you a few pages back?"

Turning to me, he said, "No, you cretin." Dramatic pause. "You killed my stunt-double, and," dramatic pause, "four hundred and thirty two of my loyal crewmembers whose," dramatic pause, "lives for which I was formerly responsible!"

"Shut up, Shatner. You know the rules: point a heater at me, 432 people are bound to get killed. Do it again, and I'll waste every stunt-double and toupée for miles around."

"You fiend! Why I ought to—"

I set the phaser I'd confiscated earlier on "Out of Sight, Out of Mind," and fired. I don't remember what happened next, but I woke up the next morning with a terrible headache; the kind you get after watching a *Glee* marathon.

I looked around and noticed that I was under the sheets of my bed in the Doyle dormitory. My hand darted out of the covers, grabbed my cigarettes and lighter, and retreated back in. I jammed a Lucky into my unshaven face and spun the wheel on the lighter. The wheel struck a flint and caused a spark. The spark ignited the butane escaping from the stove.

With a violent roar, flames engulfed the room. Fighting through the smoke, Jay leapt out of bed and grabbed the fire extinguisher from the wall. I watched as he put out the fire.

When he was done, Jay looked at me, snug in my asbestos sheets, and said, "Dammit, can't you make coffee like everybody else?"

"You're upset," I said.

"Yes, I'm upset! Nobody else I know leaves the gas on all night to flashheat their coffee!"

I blew a few smoke rings that went unnoticed in the hazy air. "You know I'm not worth a damn in the mornings without my first cup."

Jay looked at me quizzically, sighed, and grabbed the oven mitts. He poured two steaming cups of java. He gave me mine, and added a few lumps to his.

"Today's the first day of classes, you know that, right?" he said.

"Oh, yeah? You know I think I'm late for my first class?"

Jay smiled slyly. "Go figure."

The classroom was dark when I arrived, except for a single beam of light shining on the movie screen. I took the first seat inside the door, sat down, and struck a match.

The flame arced through the air, briefly illuminating my features and the room in front of me. I cupped the match to the cigarette hanging from my lips and breathed deep. The tip of my Lucky glowed warm red as the smoke gently nestled into my lungs. It sat in my chest for a moment until I kicked it out like company that had overstayed its welcome. I shook the match out and flicked the burnt remains across the room.

PROSE-CONSCIOUS AUTHORS' NOTE:* *The above paragraph may be read: "I lit a Lucky." The verbosity inherent herein should in no way indicate, to the quality minded reader, that we are being paid by the word. Unless, of course, this is an excerpt for a magazine. In that case, the rag's editor would probably cut out these last two paragraphs because periodicals DO pay by the word. So if you're not reading this, please buy the book.

The classroom lights lit up in a far less dramatic fashion than my cigarette. A middle-aged man, who looked like he took jogging far too seriously, stormed up the aisle toward me.

He stopped in front of desk and started to yell, "Monsieur Screwdriver! Put out that cig—"

I stood up, sending books flying. Richard belched flame and the slide projector exploded with lead.

He tried to look calm, but I knew he was terrified; the eyes are the windows to the soul, and his panes were smeared with terror. So that, and the fact that a yellow pool was forming at his feet, tipped me off.

"I'm through playing games, pal," I barked. "Ever since I got to this stinking joint, I've had nothing but corpses following me around, someone's tried to kill me more often than I can count, and *you* want me to put out my cigarette?"

A dame who had taken cover two rows in front of me broke into the conversation with, "Excuse me, Phil. I think Mr. Embolism wasn't objecting to your smoking in class, but merely attempting to enforce University policy!"

She stood as she spoke, rising like the flag in all her glory. She threw her shoulders back, and her breasts leapt forward faster than a sailor volunteering for shore leave. I was hard pressed to keep my eyes and rod on Embolism, so I made my play while I still had half a mind to.

My fists grabbed the lapels of the teacher's tweed jacket and shoved Richard up underneath his chin. My voice dropped to a menacing whisper, "I smoke where and when I want to. We need to talk about my grade this semester, and," I paused for breath, "what's her name?"

"Yes, yes, fine!" he stammered.

"Her name is 'Yesyes Fine?' Is that Chinese?"

"I don't know her name, but you don't have to come to class anymore. You're obviously an 'A' student. I'm just a waste of your time! Relax, go outside and smoke, throw yourself in front of a bus, have a good time!"

I released him and looked around the room. The whole class, except for the chick, was looking at me with adoration from under their desks. I walked toward the nameless beauty, holstering Richard.

I cupped her chin in my hand, and she lifted her head slightly. Her lips, wet and glistening with desire, rose to meet mine. I kissed her hard and long, leaving her wanting more.

I stepped away, holding her at arm's length, and she breathed, "I'm going with you!"

"Crazy kid, I don't even know your name."

"It's Joyce, Joyce Sisters. I'm studying for a doctorate in psychology, and I'm very interested in you. I've got a new couch I'd like to break in. Maybe you can lie down while I go get—"

"More comfortable?" I said, finishing her sentence. "Thanks but I don't have time right now. I've got to find the plot."

So, in pursuit of that oh-so elusive plotline, I left Joyce and headed to my next class, which was across campus at Parker stadium. As I left the building, I was slammed into a brick wall.

Buick-sized fists grabbed the lapels of my trenchcoat and flattened me. Then they repeatedly backed up and crashed forward into my stomach like a demonic demolition derby.

I decided it was time to make my move. I head-butted his fist until we were both drenched in my blood. The A-negative plasma lubricated my face enough that his next punch slipped off. Momentum took him forward to the ground; just like I'd planned.

I dropped on top of his massive form. Hard. The over-muscled mountain didn't even grunt. An over-sized paw swiped me off his back like a fly, and into the wall. He heaved himself upright, rising like a wrecking ball, poised to strike.

Muscle-boy grunted, "I'm gonna use you like toilet paper."

"Oh, yeah," I replied, "what if I cry like a baby and run like a scared jackrabbit?"

This seemed to puzzle him. "You a sissy?" he said and cocked his head to the right.

"No. You?"

This seemed to perplex him even more and he cocked his head to the left.

"No . . . I don't . . ." he trailed off. "Hey, quit changin' the subject! I'm supposed to be poundin' you now!"

I wiped the blood from my face and decided to get this over with.

"Alright, country-boy, but a quick question first: you do this for kicks, or do you get paid to beat up freshman?"

"Oh, I gots a full scholarship doin' this. Nuttin' personal, but I gots to pay the rent this month. Can we get this over with?" he asked, assuming a fighting stance.

I reached inside my suit jacket and unsnapped my holster. Yeah, we were going to get this over with quick.

"So who's paying you to work me over?"

"Dean Ma . . . uh, um, I can't tell you. Sorry. He wants you hurt bad, though."

"Dean Martin, singer, lush, denture wearer?"

"I ain't sayin' nuthin'!"

All right, we'd have to do this the hard way.

Like lightning, my fist shot from my side and into his groin. He belched and smiled again.

"Christ," I said, totally amazed, "I hit you in the nuts with everything I had, and you smile at me?"

His smile widened and he pulled back the fist I was getting to know so well. "Steroids. Breakfast of champions," he whinnied.

From the ground, I looked up at him through rapidly swelling eyes and decided to end this before I had to really hurt him. Richard appeared in my hand and I stood up.

"Alright, Kong, I'm going to feed you lead until you tell me what I want to know. Then maybe I'll feed you more. Spill the beans: who's paying you?"

His eyes went past my left shoulder and he said, "Look out behind you."

"Yeah, right. Do you think I'm as stupid as you are?"

"Okay, buddy, but don't say I didn't warn you. This ain't nothin' personal, you know."

I laughed and pulled the hammer back. I heard a whooshing noise and my head snapped forward. The stars came out as the sun dimmed; my head was pounding "Taps" and I wanted to vomit.

Two bleary forms hovered over me. The larger one drawled, "Not bad for a second-string punter. You get him in one shot next time, you might make first-string."

"So what do we do now?" said the little splotch.

The bigger splotch shook from side to side and said, "Hit 'em again, dumb-ass!"

I heard "Okay," and the lights went out.

* * *

My vision swam out of the deep end of the pool and into the shallow, where I could stand with my head above water.

"Are you okay?" a sweet voice asked.

"Yeah, just let me towel off."

"What?"

"Sorry. Metaphor."

"What happened to you?"

"Boating accident."

"Boating accident?"

"I got sapped by a Buick and knocked into a lake."

My vision cleared, but was still a little foggy and when I noticed Joyce Sisters was leaning over me. Her low-cut blouse gave me ample view of her scenic landscape, and I noted that mini-skirts were in fashion this semester.

"Are you sure you wouldn't like to come back and rest on my new couch?" Joyce asked. "You look like a frog with its guts exposed and baking in the sun, lying dead by the side of the road."

"What?"

"Sorry. Simile."

"Look, Dollface, I've got to get to law class, and then find out who had me sapped by the second-string punter. After that I think I'll have a long, cold shower."

"Are we still on for tonight?" she asked, a lustful glimmer like waves in her sea green eyes.

I must have been hit on the head damn hard to have forgotten a date with this angel. I decided to play it off as coolly as possible.

"Uh . . . yeah, uh, why . . . why, did you think I"d forgotten? I wouldn't forget. No, not me! No way, not me, nope! I remembered!" I paused. "Where and when are we meeting again? Simile practice, right?"

My fingers shook as I lit a cigarette. I inhaled the nicotine and my hands steadied. I guessed I'd played it off successfully because her smile shone on me, warming my soul and giving me an even, all over body tan.

"I'll meet you tonight at the Preemie, anytime you can get there is fine; I'll be there until closing!"

"I'll be there around twelve, kid. Like I said before, I've got to take care of some rough business first."

"You will be careful, won't you, Phil? I'd hate to lose you

before I'd written my doctoral thesis!"

I took the butt from my lips and blew an unconcerned stream of smoke into the cool morning air. I watched as charred tobacco wisps danced lazily to earth and the smoke spread thin, disappearing slow and smooth, like the sunset of a hot summer day. I returned my attention to Joyce.

"I'm always careful, kitten. I have to be. If I lower my guard for one second, I could end up dead; buried in cement or sapped by the second-string punter. Dammit!" I cursed, shaking my head. "That hurt!"

"Oh, I'm sorry. Maybe we should get you some ice!"

"I meant being taken out by a second-stringer. I'm the *last of the real men private investigators* and Mr. Big sends cut-rate cutthroats to rough me up. I'm insulted, and I'm not going to take it lying down! Second string punter! Sheesh!"

Her face did a double take and then a triple gainer with a twist. She looked worried and was shaking.

"You can't mean Akbar Mjolnir, Marlowe University's second-string punter!"

My lips spread tight over my teeth and I gave her my best death's head grin.

"Sweetheart, I don't stutter. You got something on this clown," I said, my finger stressing the "you's," "you spill it, sister!"

"He's my ex-boyfriend! Akbar is so sweet and so gentle! He can't be the man you're looking for!"

"Do you have a picture of this creep?"

"Sure, in my wallet."

Joyce reached into her purse and came up with one of those basic black, platypus-skin deals. She flipped it open to the plastic picture section. Next to the Sears standard family photo was a picture of a little splotch in a football uniform, with a blackjack poised dramatically.

"This is Akbar, Phil. He wouldn't hurt a fly! Look how cute he is! He's got a pet bunny named Snuggles, and when he's cold, he says 'Brrrrzzy, brrrrzzy, brrrrzzy; I'm cold!'; it's so cute!"

"So why'd you give him his walking papers?"

"He wanted to marry me," Joyce replied, "so he could stay here after his green card expired."

"Alright, the punter's in the clear. Anybody who says 'Brrrzzy, brrrzzy, brrrzzy; I'm cold!,' can't be a ruthless malefactor. In fact, with a kindly face like that, I'll bet he's a volunteer down at the old folk's home. Yeah, some guys are just swell that way. I bet he even helps handicapped people carry groceries to their car. One-in-a-million, that Akbar. I mean, how many guys stop to smell the roses, or give their life-savings to Jerry's Kids? I can't even make it through a Jerry Lewis film, let alone, that damn telethon without feeling homicidal! What a pillar of the community! Salt of the earth, cream of the crop, top of the heap, A-number-one, top of the list. Start spreading the news, I'm leaving today. Gonna make a brand new start of it, in old—"

"Phil?"

"Huh? What?"

"You're rambling. Or was that supposed to be a cheap segue into a musical number for the screenplay?"

"Real Men don't sing."

"I thought Real Men did anything they wanted to."

I nodded in agreement, "Yes, but there are basic guidelines. No singing, no diaper changing, no quiche, and no flatulating on first dates, although it's inevitable. You can't excuse yourself to the bathroom fifteen-twenty times a night, so you try to make them silent. But they smell the worst, so you try to let loose while on the move or fake a loud cough to cover the sound. Play innocent and hope for the best, that's my plan."

"Phil," she said, pen and pad in hand, "tell me about your mother."

I lit a new Lucky from the dying embers of the old one, and looked into her innocent baby-blues.

"Why do you want to know about Mom?"

"No reason, just your normal, everyday conversation. How's the weather, tell me about your mother, that kind of thing. So, tell me about her."

I tipped my fedora back past my hairline and trailed my hand down the side of my face. The hand continued, unbidden, down my torso, and into the inseam of my trousers.

"Uh, Phil?"

"Huh, what?" I said.

"Did you know that you are displaying masturbatory tendencies in public?"

"Uh, I gotta go."

***<u>FACE-SAVING AUTHORS' NOTE</u>:* *The above material is not happening. Remember, Phil is in a flashback and he has been rendered unconscious. Everything after "I heard 'Okay,' and the lights went out," is imaginary and never occurred. Phil is just working out a couple of sexual fantasies while he's unconscious. No last of the real men private investigators would ever masturbate in public. By the way, according to the Catholic Church, "touching oneself" is a cardinal sin. This is not to be construed as a holy circle jerk with bishops, popes, and cardinals spanking their little altar boys at every opportunity. Quite the opposite, we're sure that the Pope rarely beats off, and certainly never in public. But if he does, we're sure he forgives himself, does a few "Hail Marys," a couple of "Our Fathers," and maybe one or two, "Oh God, Oh God yes, Oh Lord it's the second comings."*

Phil's about to wake up, so consider the rest of the story you're about to read true. Only the names have been changed to protect the innocent. Besides, the cat, Ted Turner (see previous explanatory authors' note), wrote the masturbation scene while we, your devout Authors, were at church, donating huge gobs of cash to L. Ron Hubbard, and sacrificing virgin goats. ***

I felt woozy as I tried to stand, leaning against the brick wall for support. Whoever had sapped me sure as hell knew his business.

Christ, now I had fourteen loose ends to tie up before I could come out of this flashback. As near as I could figure, only three of those loose ends had any basis in reality. I could pretty much discount the crashing planes, Vietnam, ever getting a limo, the *U.S.S. Enterprise*, and the girl scout as irrelevant manifestations of my subconscious. And what the hell were duck-billed, web-footed mammals doing in my flashback?

I had to get to the bottom of this, quick, before the chapter got too long. All the ends had to tie up, just like it says in *The Private Investigator's Handbook*, chapter 11, section 8.

That left me with the two creeps that tried to take me in my office, the guys who sapped me, and the Platypus Liberation Organization. It seemed pretty obvious: The P.L.O. wanted me dead for some unknown reason. Fortunately, Frank Linguini, my step-father, wanted the P.L.O. dead. I wondered if there was a connection. Nah.

The clock tower struck seven of the hour, so I hurried off to law class.

I walked through the battered doors and into the Parker Stadium where they were holding class. The place was packed. *Damn*, I thought, *I hate these over-subscribed classes; they're so large and impersonal.*

A few minutes before class, I'd overheard some Casper Milquetoast-types fearfully whispering about the professor. It was rumored that he was related to Genghis Kahn, and lived up to his heritage: he was trained in divorce work.

I shuddered.

The geeks had said that the professor's policy was: you did things his way, or you'd wasted your tuition money. No ifs, no ands, no buts, no conjunctions whatsoever.

I laughed in the face of this new danger, just like I laughed at all dangers. I wasn't going to let any vulture pick my bones. I felt Richard's reassuring weight and smiled.

I made my way to the front row and parked myself next to

Spock and Captain Kirk. I leaned over to Kirk and asked "What are you doing here?"

"Studying for roles on TJ Hooker and Boston Legal. Shh. Look at the teacher's aide!"

Spock was busy checking out the voluptuous teacher's aide, who was bent over, sharpening a piece of chalk. He was staring at a cheap plastic tape recorder again while Kirk waited intently.

The long-eared freak said, "Captain, tricorder readings indicate that her phone number is 555-1212. She is five foot six inches tall, and weighs 117.4 pounds. Vital signs indicate 38DD-24-36. Turn-ons include pointed ears, logical minds, and directing ability. Turn-offs, Captain, include men with toupees, melodrama, and men formerly responsible for the lives of 432 crewmembers."

"Spock," dramatic pause, "are you out of your," dramatic pause, "Vulcan mind? Everyone," dramatic pause, "knows that 555 exchanges are fake, and used only for," dramatic pause, "the movies!"

"Negative, Captain, I am in full possession of my intellectual facilities."

"Then what, Spock," dramatic pause, "are you doing?" Dramatic pause, "I always get the babes."

"Vulcans cannot lie, *mon capitan*, I accurately read the tricorder."

"Gimme that damn thing!"

As Kirk grabbed the tape recorder and flipped it over, a panel flew off the back. He peered inside and shook his head.

"Oh, Spock," dramatic pause, "this thing's been tampered with!"

Spock was whistling loudly and studying the back of his outstretched hand. He flipped it over and casually studied his palm. "Really, Captain? I had no idea."

"I'll just turn a couple of screws and . . . hah! Now read it."

Spock took the tricorder from Kirk and read "Turn-on's include bulging, over-dramatic, toupee wearing actors with no directing ability."

Kirk jumped from his seat, "I knew it! I'm in! Score!"

I pulled a butt from my deck and tapped it a couple of times on the desk to pack the tobacco. I thumbnailed my last match into flame. But before I could light my cigarette, Kirk blew wind and my match went out. Annoyed, I tapped Spock on his padded shoulder.

"Hey buddy, got a light?" I paused, "Didn't I rub you out, too, or was that another damn stunt double?"

Spock raised his left eyebrow and pulled out his cheap plastic toy gun.

"It would be illogical to kill off a regular. We all have doubles. However, if our writers did script such an onerous boner, those Rigellian whores wouldn't be able to write sequels. They tried in *The Wrath of Khan*, and it just didn't work. Do you think a two-bit punk like you could succeed where so many others have failed?"

"Look, you overgrown elf, could you save the patter and just give me a light? I'm tired of speeches from actors who couldn't get a better gig than *In Search Of*."

Spock set his phaser to "Zippo," and lit my cigarette.

Kirk jumped onstage to hit on the teacher's aide. He dramatically ripped off his shirt, revealing a leather-boy combat harness that handily hid his bulging girth. A furry alien materialized by the chalkboard and tossed Kirk a battle-axe. The two began battling over the blonde as cheap sixties soundtrack music filtered in over the loudspeakers.

Mr. Spock leaned over and asked "Pardon me, but could I procure a Lucky Strike from you?"

"Sure," I said and handed him one.

We had just settled back to watch the show when a three-piece pinstriped suit stepped in front of us, blocking our view.

I heard, "Hey, boss, I heard you was in town. Welcome to my class!"

I looked up to see Eddie's face sticking out above an Arrow collar and silk tie. I exhaled a plume of disbelief and said, "Hi, Eddie.

You mean you were straight with me about all that lawyer stuff?"

"Sho'nuff, boss." He pulled out a Swiss pocket watch from his vest. He smiled and peered at me over the dial. "I gots a class to teach, but you had best be gettin' out of town, boss. Dean Manicotti has teamed up wit De Platypus to git you kilt!" Eddie shrugged. "Sees you round, boss!"

Eddie had said more than a mouthful. That explained the hotel and the sapping. They each had tried to take me and failed. If either Dean Manicotti or The Platypus thought they could take me, they were dead wrong. Now the deck was stacked in my favor and it was my turn to deal.

I bared my teeth like a rabid gerbil in a silk purse being delivered to Richard Gere. It was only the first day of classes and already I'd made the Dean's list. Now Manicotti had made mine.

Before I went to the Dean's stronghold, I decided to pick up a pack of smokes from 7-Eleven. Lord knew, I was going to need them.

Overnight, the store had been rebuilt by Canadian migrant farm workers, but now a sign out front read: "Under New Management — Green Card, Inc." Construction had just finished when I arrived, and the Canadians were spreading out in the aisles. They started picking up things nonchalantly, examining them and then putting them back on the shelves.

I sauntered up to the register and eyed the tabloid headlines. *The Inquisitor* read: "Geraldo Disappears, Orcah Gains More Weight!" *The New York Com-Post* said: "Elvis Alive, Bartending!"

What crap. Who believes that stuff?

A North Vietnamese man, wearing an orange and green smock, was behind the counter, jumping up and down, pointing at the Canadians by the magazine rack.

"I saw roo!" he screamed, his lips not moving in sync with his words. "I saw roo put magazine in jacket! Roo a teef!"

He reached behind the counter and came up with a Soviet

bloc automatic rifle. His smock fell to the floor, revealing black pajamas underneath. A coolie hat fell from a heating duct and landed squarely on his round head.

"Grab sky, round eye!"

The Canadians compliantly put their hands up; several copies of *Soldier of Fortune* fell out of their jackets, and onto the floor.

"Get out of my store! Nevah come back!"

The migrant farmworkers left the store, mumbling about Cheez Whiz and its explosive properties.

The clerk looked at me, dropped his rifle, and adjusted his straw hat. "May I help roo, sir?"

I fished in the glass bowl on the counter for some matches and replied, "Yeah, sell me a pack . . ."

My words trailed off as motion caught the corner of my eye. A migrant farmworker had lit the fuse on a can of "3 Mile Island Cheez Whiz" and chucked it through the plate glass window. The clerk and I had just enough time to stare at the can before it exploded.

As the debris settled around us, the Asian again asked, "May I hep roo, sir?"

"Yeah," I replied, unshaken. "Could I have a pack of Lucky Strikes?"

His eyes squinted further, as if that were possible, and he looked me up and down.

"No," the clerk said, shaking his head, "Roo too young to smokie-smokie."

My eyes widened as I remembered the last time an Oriental had refused to give me cigarettes: it was in a hell-hole that geographers called Vietnam. The P.O.W. camp commander, Suwit, had taunted me with cigarettes for six—no, eight—eight long years. Pain washed over me in waves as the memory surfed its way into a wipe-out.

I opened my eyes and stared at the clerk's nametag. It read: Vic Charlie, Manager.

But I suddenly knew it was him. I'd found Suwit! After all those long nights, sweating in the darkness, afraid to sleep because of the nightmares I knew would greet me: Lucky's just out of reach; Zippo lighters flaring in the darkness; the smell of butane and tobacco lashing at my olfactory nerves; a fork dancing before my eyes.

I started to shake and my palms became clammy. I knew it was him! Sure, he'd changed his name, shrunk four inches, dyed his hair blond, and had his teeth surgically lengthened, but I knew it was him.

I pulled Richard out and put her barrel to his left nostril. I snarled, "Ever since hearing you'd escaped, I've dreamed of this moment."

His eyes opened and he quaked in fear. "What roo talking 'bout? What war? I born in Salt Rake City! I Mormon! I have free wives! Want one?"

"Yeah, right," I snarled, shoving the barrel further in his nose. "No Wife is free. I remember it all as if it were yesterday: it was me, Boo-boo, Yogi, and the Ranger. We were on a break from patrol, sitting on a picnic blanket, and eating C-rats. Suddenly, gunshots split the foul night air."

I inhaled deeply on my Lucky and spat a little piece of tobacco at Suwit. He had a terrified look on his little Asian face. A single tear welled up in his eye, pleading for mercy where he knew he would find none. He might as well be arm-wrestling with the Venus de Milo.

"A firefight followed, but we had been caught with our pants down. The Ranger had told Boo-boo to go around to the right and try to outflank them. As the last words of the Ranger's career left his mouth, a stray round from Yogi's M-60 ended the life of a good soldier.

"With our leadership lying dead on the jungle floor, Yogi suggested that we surrender and make a statement about this so-called conflict. Boo-boo raised his little paws in the air and muttered, 'The Ranger wouldn't have liked this, Yogi.' Then a bullet ricocheted off of my combat fedora and knocked me unconscious.

"The next thing I saw was your smiling face, leisurely smoking one of my Lucky's and prodding me with a fork. When I tried to get one from you, I discovered that I was chained like a dog.

"Years this continued, until I accidentally escaped. Now," I growled and pulled back the bolt on my trusty .45, "it's pay-back time!"

"No! Prease don't kill me! I give you flee carton of cigalettes! Prease! Take anything in store!"

I began to feel a little sympathy for my former captor. Would I be just as bad as he was if I killed him? Did revenge really do any good in the long run? Did two wrongs make a right?

After a few seconds of mental debate, I decided that at the very least it would make me feel better. I brought my gun to bear and noticed that I was staring down the barrel of an automatic rifle. Damn the Authors and their stupid soliloquies.

"Now sandal is on other foot, round-eye!"

Before the two of us could attempt to stare the other one down, Officer Sean Mahatma O'Strasser, a retired Mexican detective, came into the store.

Early in his career, Sean had dedicated his life to combating the scourge that was drugs. He'd put in twenty-seven days on the Tiajuana police farce before realizing that there were more drugs on the average college campus than in all of Mexico. Sean had been assigned here two days when he'd crashlanded a Cessna, coked to the gills. The college promoted him to Police Chief and he and his career began to fly high.

Sean flatulated loudly and in a deep bass as his girth crossed the rubbled threshold of the convenience store. "Top of the marnin' to ye, Suwit, Phil. Sure'en as me dead, sainted mother be feedin' worms, it be a beautiful day for free coffee and powdered donuts! Too Ra Loo Ra Ay!"

Suwit's eyes darted to what used to be the door and I made

Tonight's Episode: Slaughter of the Sacred Herd

my break. Seconds later, after grabbing a carton of smokes and stuffing it into my trenchcoat, I rolled behind the charred ruins of the candy aisle. I furiously fired my automatic until the hammer fell on an empty chamber (Which is impossible, but much more dramatic than the slide locking back). Suwit's rifle slugs pummeled the KitKat's beside me. I grabbed some peanut M&M's to return his fire while I reloaded. Unfortunately, they melted in my hand, leaving a gooey, chocolaty mess. I decided to cut my losses and make my escape.

Officer O'Strasser provided an easy out for me when he waddled between me and Suwit, rooting about for Bavarian Creams. I ducked out of the rubbled store and behind the Dempsey dumpster, slamming into a gargoyle.

The gargoyle was smoking a clove cigarette and was wearing a black beret. Ray-Ban number fives perched atop his snout, glaring at me like he used to on the Student Union building. His mouth opened and he exhaled a plume of noxious green smoke, clearing his throat.

"Dig me: the Grim Reaper plays shuffleboard with his scythe. McDonald's opens a nuclear power-plant in any neighborhood but mine and it's okay. Jesus places an 'Out of Order' sign on the bathroom door. I enter, defiant, and discover that his works are good. A tapeworm begs for alms on a street corner, while Jerry Seinfeld eats a TV dinner and watches the dryer spin. Koo-koo Voodoo, Baby. Grok?"

The bridge of his sunglasses shattered as .45 slugs entered his stony skull.

Officer O'Strasser tapped me on the shoulder, "Y'know, laddie, it be a wee illegal to discharge firearms within the fine limits of this fair city. As sure'en as me sainted mother be sippin' whiskey with the angels, I'll have to be runnin' ye in."

Before I could defend myself, the gargoyle coughed blood and said, "God farts and blames it on Saint Peter . . . the Lord is my plumber, I shall fear no crack—"

The gargoyle's teeth splintered in a snowy mist as .38 slugs from Sean's service revolver lobotomized his green skull. "Sorry, Phil. 'Twas a mercy killin' ye be performin'."

Suwit walked up behind us, rifle raised. He laughed, "Ro-ro-ro! I have you now, round-eye! Roo escape my crutches before, but not dis time!"

He'd just jacked back the bolt of his rifle when the gargoyle raised his Swiss cheese-like head and said, "Pets are our friends, but they won't pick us up at the airport . . . Ten bucks, same as in town . . . Grandpa bought a rubber for an underage inflate-a-date-"

Suwit's tiny frame shook as his rifle took the lead in the gargoyle's dance of death.

"Shrit!" he exclaimed after a few frenzied seconds. "I'm outta bullets." He looked at us and shrugged, "Same time tomorrow, guys?"

Sean and I looked at each other and then started beating the snot out of him. When the truck of Canadians pulled up with videocams running, Sean threw his hands over his face. He quickly waddled over to his squad car and left the scene. I dropped Suwit and smiled. I knew that the Unions could do more damage to him than I ever could.

Suwit staggered over to the pickup, screaming, "Why you come back?"

The foreman oozed out of his seat and slid to the ground. He lit a Cuban cigar, pulled up his pants, and said, "Union rules, bub. We do all repairs and construction until the end of time, eh."

The Union workers who'd bombed the store snickered and started singing, "Look for the Union label!"

I hummed that tune all the way back to Doyle.

I'd just found my room key and put it to the lock when a menacing figure stepped from the shadows. His duckbill quivered as he motioned me inside with the barrel of his gun. Kicking the door shut behind him, The Platypus told me to fork over my piece. I dropped Richard and parked myself on the sofa by the window.

"Alright, Manicotti, you can come out now. I saw your car out front," I said.

Dean Manicotti strolled out of the kitchen carrying three glasses. He handed me and The Platypus a drink before sipping his own. They situated themselves across from me in the over-stuffed recliners.

Manicotti eyed me over the rim of his glass and said, "If you saw my car, why did you allow yourself to be so easily taken by surprise?"

I reached into my jacket for smokes, and The Platypus tightened his grip on the chopper. I gingerly pulled the pack out by two fingers and offered one to them. Both declined.

I lit mine and inhaled deeply before replying, "I wanted to know, Dean, why a man of your power and prestige would throw in with this," I pointed at The Platypus, "twisted thing."

With a smirk on his face, Manicotti replied, "I've seen your track record: Parker Preschool, Spillane Elementary, Chandler Middle School, and then Hammer High. I didn't want Marlowe University to be next."

The Platypus smiled a wan little smile and sipped his drink.

I nodded. "Okay, point taken. No hard feelings. I really hadn't planned on burning your school down. But, then again, I never planned the others either."

Manicotti's face brightened, "Really?"

I nodded.

"Well," he said and stood up, "I guess I'll be going then."

One down, one to go. I smiled, "And you, Platypus? What do you have in mind?"

"A person of your obviously limited intellect could not possibly comprehend the magnitude of what I . . . have in mind —"

Tires screeched to a halt outside, cutting off his self-righteous monologue. That was my cue. I grabbed the edge of the coffee table and flipped it up, diving behind it.

Bullets pounded the table futilely, shielding me as I crashed through the window. Fortunately, I'd had the table constructed of depleted uranium, like the walls of the starship *Enterprise*. I didn't have a stunt-double to do my dying for me. Besides, in my line of work, you never knew when you might need a bulletproof table.

When I'd seen Manicotti's car in front of my building, I'd called Guido and told him what to do. His timing was perfect, and so was my swan dive.

Thirteen floors later, I fell onto the air cushion set up by Guido's boys. Everything was going according to plan: Manicotti was out of the picture, and The Platypus was trapped on the thirteenth floor. What I hadn't counted on was the entire Platypus Liberation Organization showing up seconds after I landed. Damn my luck.

The PLO Volkswagen microbus plowed into the Guido-mobile, machine guns blazing from their windows. Vinnie, one of Guido's boys, threw me a pistol and I joined the firefight.

The battle was going our way; I'd nailed two of them in their left nostrils. Platypi dropped, littering the ground until only one was left standing. I sighted in and my finger tensed on the trigger.

The remaining freak shouted something in platypese and detonated the satchel charge strapped to his chest. Shrapnel from the explosion shredded the remaining mobsters and knocked me to the ground.

I lay dazed and helpless on the brick sidewalk. The Platypus towered over me at a grotesque film-noir angle, cold blue steel projecting from the right sleeve of his black Navy trenchcoat. My head swam; my body, not knowing how to swim, dog-paddled behind it, just doing what came natural to keep the head above water. With the sickening sound a cockroach makes when you crush it, his gloved thumb pulled the hammer of his pistol back.

"I am your father, Luke. Join me and together we shall rule the galaxy," he rasped from beneath his obsidian facemask.

"Luke? If you expect me to believe that you're my father, let alone rule the galaxy with you, you're going to have to get my name right!"

"Luke? Did I say Luke? Oh Christ! I meant Phil, really. It's just that I've been busy, kid. You gotta believe me! Can we take it from the top?"

"I don't know," I said, mostly directing my reply to the Authors, "can he? Or are you going to whore your literary mistakes and get a few extra dollars for the additional type?"

***INDIGNANT AUTHORS' RETORT:** We resemble, uh, resent that comment and any inference that any symbol we scribe is extraneous. If we say supercalifragilistic, we meant to say supercalifragilistic, and our use of the word supercalifragilistic has a deep connection to the plot and its myriad themes. So, nyah.* ***

My plan was working. I'd used the supercalifragilistic Authors to distract The Platypus and give my head a chance to clear.

Looking around, I saw dead Mafiosos and platypi littering the surrounding area. Students stepped over the corpses like they weren't there, following their daily routine. One astronomy geek, holding a slide-rule and a telescope, was marking a large 'X' on the ground.

What the hell? Even students couldn't be so uncaring and cold-hearted as to not help wounded men. Maybe the bodies weren't there after all, maybe this was just another crazy part of my flashback. I had to find out.

"You'll never get away with this, webfoot, there's too many witnesses! Look at all the bodies!"

The Platypus shrugged a careless shoulder and disagreed. "It's New York."

Damn. He was right. Next time, I'd have to remember to go to a school in a more attentive state. If there was a next time.

The Platypus leafed through a book he was holding. I couldn't make out anything on the cover except, "No.1 Best Seller, 523 Weeks on the New York Best Sellers List!"

"What are you doing?" I demanded. "Are you going to kill me or what?"

He waved his gun at me impatiently. "Hold your damn horses, I gotta find my place in this Novel. If it says kill you, I kill you. If it doesn't, you live. It's that simple. However chances are you live. It really sucks to be the villain when there's almost another hundred pages left to go in the book. Remember you still have to come out of your flashback."

I nodded. "Thanks for being so candid with me, Platypus."

He smiled, and I kind of liked his smile; it was like we were old chums.

"Hey, think nothing of it, Phil. I'm sorry I've been shooting at you and having my goons trash your buddies, but it's in the plot. Blame the Authors! Wait! Here it is, I'd dog-eared the page. Yep, I kill you, but only after you and I trade a couple of macho, anal-retentive phrases back and forth."

My fedora shook angrily. "Anal retentive?" I stood up and grabbed the book. "Let me see that."

I scanned the next couple of paragraphs. I was getting angry. My character was obviously oral fixative and the bozo Authors had me as anal. I mean, I could see how a six-foot tall genetic mutation like The Platypus could be anal-retentive—but me?

"What are you trying to pull, Screwdriver? Get back on the ground, dazed and helpless."

"Okay," I muttered and did what he said, "but I'm getting grass stains all over my trenchcoat."

"That's not the only stains you're going to have all over your jacket, bub. If you don't join me to rule the literary world, I'll shove this gun so far up your—"

I cut him off. "Okay, okay, cut the crap. I don't know what the Authors were thinking, but you can't say 'I'm going to shove a gun up your ass,' in a family book. It's just not done. We're thinking Disney for the movie adaptation."

"Well, you just did it, moron!"

"Who you calling a moron, duckbreath?"

"Duckbreath!? Nobody calls me Duckbreath! I don't care if you *are* my son! I brought you into this world, and I'm going to take you out! Say your prayers, Phil!"

His webbed fingers had begun squeezing the trigger when I stopped him.

"Wait!" I yelled. "You haven't given me time to say my prayers!"

He looked exasperated and his bill quivered with impatience. "All right, all right, but hurry. I got a limo to catch."

"You get a limo, too?"

"Yeah, it's in the contract. Every character in the book gets a limo, didn't you?"

"No! No I didn't. The Authors make me take the bus!"

"Well I'm sorry, but it doesn't matter anymore. I'm going to kill you, so say your prayers."

I thought hard for a minute. "Umm, Dad?"

"What?"

"I'm agnostic; I don't know any prayers."

"Oh come on, everybody knows a prayer."

I shook my head. "Nope, not me. I don't remember any."

"Try saying grace. I know you know how to say grace."

I smiled. "Yeah, I know a couple of Graces! I could do one of them for you!"

"That's my boy!"

I knelt on the ground, and my palms were together in prayer. The Platypus put the pistol to my left nostril, and I began. "Rub-a-dub-dub, thanks for the grub, Yaaaay God!"

I stopped and The Platypus didn't pull the trigger. I looked up at him and asked "What are you waiting for?"

"You call that a grace? Didn't your mother ever teach you better than that?"

"No."

"Okay, well then, see you next flashback. Good night,

Gracie."

His fingers began squeezing the trigger when an arrow pierced the shoulder of his gun arm. It was the same spot that every villain is hit when he's thwarted, but lives to threaten another day. The Platypus dropped his pistol on the ground beside me and staggered back; he was clutching his wounded shoulder. I grabbed the pistol and pumped six rounds into his chest. I didn't care if the Authors wanted to let him live and give themselves an easy path to a sequel. It was my life they were toying with.

The Platypus rolled around in agony for a dramatic while and then lay still, face down, bleeding.

I looked around to see who had come to my rescue. It was her! My second love had come back to save me. She was radiant in her green tunic and brilliant colored merit-badge sash. It was my Girl Scout!

"Thank's, Cookie. I owe you for saving my life again. Put me down for another box of mints."

She took my order down, and I handed her the bills.

I gazed longingly at her maiden form and wistfully asked, "Let's you and me take a vacation, go somewhere far away. What do you say?"

"Can it, geek," she lovingly replied. "I just came back for my hat. Make with it on the double; Mom's waiting in my limo."

"You got a limo, too?"

"Yeah," she said distractedly. "My agent got one for my Scout Leader, too. It's in my contract." She was looking at herself in a compact and applying blood-red lipstick. "C'mon, snap to it!"

"But I love you, Cookie! I always have. If you won't love me back, it would have been better to have died at the webbed, gnarled, blood-soaked hands of the Platypus!"

She stuck a Camel unfiltered cigarette between her pouted lips and puffed. "Look, Phil, I'll level with you: I'm not really a dame or a Girl Scout. I'm just a cross-dressing Cub Scout Leader. The den mother puts up with me because nobody sells cookies like I do. So fall in love elsewhere. I'd be bad for you."

Tears were welling in my eyes when Cookie cupped my chin, closing off the floodgates. "I know it'll be tough; I feel what you feel. But it would just never work out. If it'll make you feel better, take my limo."

I snuffled, "R-Really? I can have your limo?"

"Sure, Phil, it's yours. It's even got a bar."

We hugged for a long time until it was obvious both of us were getting five o'clock shadow. Wordlessly, we left each other's arms, and he walked away.

He didn't look back. I know he didn't. I watched him walk away for a few seconds, and then put six slugs into his back. Only when he had flopped to the ground like a rag doll did I turn away. This time, I didn't look back.

My new limo (I'd wondered how the Authors were going to write it in; after all they had promised me one) was parked by the curb. I limped my aching body toward the car, ready for a rest, and hungry for home.

The unmistakable sound of a shotgun being cocked shot through my soul. I turned around. The Platypus was standing, but just barely; an evil force kept him on his feet. I knew if I could delay him a few seconds, he'd pass out, and I'd be safe.

"I won't let you delay me for a few seconds until I pass out, Screwdriver. You're dead *now*!"

I wasn't worried. He was standing on the "X" that the astronomy geek had marked on the ground a few pages back. Time slowed as his fingers jerked on the trigger. Before he could finish his pull, the *U.S.S. Enterprise*, which had been burning as its orbit decayed, smashed down on top of the "X", and The Platypus. The dying ship then slid forward, destroying everything, including the entirety of Marlowe University, in its path.

Well that was good. The flashback had to be over now that I'd burned down the school. My keen deductive mind began to sense a pattern in these flashbacks.

An unperturbed chauffeur—he was English—had exited the limousine and come around to the back door. He opened the door, which swung the wrong way, and motioned me inside. I climbed in.

Unbeknownst to me, The Platypus had survived the crashing of the starship. He had crawled to the limo and placed a small thermonuclear device in the trunk.

Fortunately, the bar in the limo was a gay bar. Not into that alternate scene, I had the driver drop me off at the Airport. I caught the red-eye out. My flight took off just in time for us to fly a survivable distance from the ensuing explosion and firestorm that turned the Big Apple into the Big Smoking, Radioactive Pit. Of course, none of the citizens noticed.

And I, as usual, was out of town during a tragedy.

The explosion rocked the plane violently. I thought I was going to die (or worse, continue with this literary travesty) until I heard someone yell, "Get the doctor! He's convulsing!"

I'd come out of my flashback.

CHAPTER ONE

The time finally came for me to leave the hospital, and it was with no remorse that I closed the door to my antiseptic jail behind me. Jay had shown up to help me with my suitcases, but I grabbed them myself. The weight against my long-inert muscles felt as nice as French-kissing a lemming.

I asked a nurse where I had to go to pay my tab.

Her directions were: "Follow the red line until you reach the Booth/Mudd Memorial Osteopathy wing, and there you'll switch to the blue. Once you reach the Elisha G. Otis Memorial elevator, go down to the twelfth floor and continue on the blue until you see the lime polka-dot line, just past the Dr. Nick Rivers Memorial Preteen Maternity Ward . . ."

She continued babbling for some time, mentioning things like ". . . give a herring to the German shepherd . . . ," and ". . . thrashing water in the shark tank generates hydroelectric power in the elevator." She finished a full half an hour later.

"You got all that?" the nurse asked.

Jay's eyes were glazed and his jaw hung loosely on its hinges. I was watching the shadow of my hat brim violate the pristine white walls, casting an imposing silhouette. The nurse repeated her question.

"Christ, sister," I sneered. "I've been plugged so many times,

I know this place like the back of my hand. In case you forgot, I blew this place three weeks ago with only half as much blood as I have now. And it's a Siberian husky; the shepherd died two years ago." *Besides,* I thought to myself, *I know a few shortcuts.* I didn't mention that I'd escaped before by a parachute I'd purchased from a vending machine on the forty-fifth floor.

I grabbed a suitcase with my left hand and threw the other one under my left arm, and then grabbed Jay by the back of his collar and pulled him along like a tow truck.

Jay wanted to know who'd shot me and why. Actually, the why wasn't important, except that the flatfeet down at the station had a pool going. As we walked along the hallway, he asked me about it.

"So, Phil, what was it? I've got a hundred big ones on an outraged client not finding you with his wife."

"You forget, Jay. I don't make it a habit to sleep around. I take this safe sex crap seriously. Very seriously."

Jay looked at me and chuckled. "Well, then, just to satisfy my curiosity," he paused and snorted, "have you ever actually . . . uh, you know?"

I gazed at him, perplexed at his line of questioning. "Have I ever what?"

"Have you ever kissed a girl before?" He emphasized the "kissed."

"Like on the lips?"

"Yeah, on the lips." He stressed "lips" that time.

"Of course I have. Her name was Katy. And I liked it. So there. Sheesh. Have you?"

Jay stared at me with wide eyes. "I have three kids."

"So? That doesn't answer my question, copper. Quit ducking me. I always took you for a certified bachelor."

He was silent for a moment, apparently staring at the pink elephant that had landed on the ceiling in front of us. I dropped my eyes and fished for a butt from the complimentary deck of Lucky's the hospital had given me. I contemplated the elephant while lighting up.

Jay stared at me. "What are you doing? You can't smoke in here. They haven't allowed smoking indoors since Clinton and the whole cigar thing."

I smiled. "Yeah."

Jay shook his head.

"Is Dumbo with you?" I asked from around my cigarette.

"What?"

I pointed to the pachyderm and repeated the question. For a cop, Jay wasn't very observant.

Jay looked where I had indicated and then back at me. "Phil, are you on . . . Oh, never mind. First answer my questions, then I'll answer yours."

I nodded and tipped my hat to a passing candy-striper. She smiled and her long, blond hair waved hello. Turning to Jay, I noticed him staring at the girl and absently fingering his wedding band.

I inhaled on my cigarette and blew some smoke at the elephant. Dumbo coughed and swished at the smoke with his trunk. I wished the damn thing would go away. It followed us out of the hospital, and waved bye-bye as we climbed in Jay's squadcar. His last words to me were something about blah-blah protect the Queen, blah-blah. I flipped him a nut for his troubles. Nobody does anything for free anymore.

Jay smiled and turned on the sirens as he pulled away from the curb, ignoring the parking tickets under his windshield. "The job doesn't pay much, but God I love the perks!" He punched the accelerator and the cruiser lurched forward. The tires screamed as they spun on the asphalt. Most of the paid-for-by-your-hard-earned-tax-money tires were left smoking at the curb. That's what I liked about Jay.

He narrowly avoided slamming into a black Toyota 4x4 as he forced his way into traffic. I turned around and looked at the two suspicious-looking men riding in the cab of the truck. The driver was wearing a smart black fedora and a government-issue trenchcoat. The guy riding shotgun wore the same style trenchcoat and a pair of MacArthur Ray-Bans. The two glared at us and flipped the bird in our direction. I started to return the salute, but paused. The two men looked hauntingly familiar. Where had I seen them before? Where, dammit?

A half-empty Michelob bottle crashed against the trunk of Jay's Ford Caprice, and I thought about insidious forms of product placement. The guy wearing shades was hanging out of the window and shouting obscenities that would have made Amsterdam pet-store worker who moonlighted as a crack whore blush.

I drew Richard when Jay and the driver of the Toyota, still following us, both signaled right. We'd only driven thirty-six feet from the hospital and already Death was on safari for me again. I slapped a magazine into my personal game warden and sneered. No one was mounting the head of this *last of the real men private investigators* on the wall of their trophy room! And if they did, they better make sure the fedora was properly blocked and displayed at a jaunty angle. And, for the love of God, don't forget the Lucky hanging with disdain from my lips, letting everyone know I didn't go out easy! Attention to detail was what really sold it. Nobody takes the time to do it right these days. It's just stuff it, shellac it, and throw it up there without any regard for craftsmanship. I mean, that's fine for a squirrel or a platypus, but for a human head? Please! In my day…. What's that? I'm sorry, on advice of counsel, I need to say, Never mind.

No one was going to mount my head in their trophy room!

Jay turned into the parking lot behind my favorite bar, the Twenty-First Amendment, fishtailing into the last parking space. Large rats scattered like scared large rats.

My door whipped open, and I combat-rolled into a pair of large rats feasting on a familiar-looking pit bull and swilling Bud Light. One of the rats wore a spiked collar and sported a neon-green

Mohawk. The other rat wore a leather aviator jacket emblazoned with a Vargas-girl Mother Theresa French-kissing the Pope. The second rat pulled a switchblade. The metal hissed from its sheath like an adder on LSD.

These were obviously rodents to be reckoned with.

I tipped my hat to them and combat-rolled back to the car. Obviously, there was nothing going on here. Just another Friday night in the Nation's Capital. The necrotic gas escaping from the bloated pit bull's body skirled "America the Beautiful." A solitary tear welled up in my eye, but I brushed it away before Jay could see. A guy like him would never understand.

Richard was clenched in my fist as I stood behind the shield of the open squad car door. I steadied my gat with my other hand as I traversed the parking lot. I sighted in on a pair of lovers holding hands and urinating on the building next door.

Sigh, how romantic! The pit bull's necrotic gas segued seamlessly into "Some Enchanted Evening."

Without taking my eyes from Richard's gunsights, I called over to Jay.

"Jay," I said, "do you see them?"

"See who?"

"The goons in the black pick-up! They're trying to kill me!"

"What?" he demanded, pulling a piece of folded paper from his pocket. He looked at his watch. "Dammit! I had nine o'clock in the office pool. Are you sure they were trying to kill you? Maybe they just wanted to merge."

Once again, for a cop, Jay wasn't too observant.

"M is for murder, not merge."

With a wary glance, I holstered my rod. The rats were busy gnawing on the bare bones of what used to be a star of beer commercials.

The half-light of the alley parking lot flickered across Jay's dumbfounded face. He took his hat off and scratched his head, muttering under his breath. Sweat had begun to bead on his brow like a pearl necklace on a moonlighting crack whore.

"I need that beer you're going to buy me, Phil."

"No! The goons in the Toyota! We've got to get them first!"

"Why? They're just a couple of punk kids with nothing better to do."

I stared hard at Jay. "Sure, let them off, Jay. Today, they're innocently throwing beer bottles at police cruisers. Tomorrow, it's writing deeply misunderstood novels about private detectives. It's a gateway drug, Jay! Don't you see?"

Jay grabbed me by the sleeve and started dragging me out of the alley. I pulled back hard, fearing Jay hadn't seen the rats.

"Those rats are killers! Look what they did to that dog!"

"So, a couple of vermin eat a 7-Eleven hotdog. Big deal. Better them than me."

"Jay, they're killers! One of them has a knife!"

Jay threw his head back and silently pleaded to the heavens. They say that some prayers go unanswered. Jay's prayer was answered by the blessing of a passing pigeon. After a few seconds, he tiredly dropped his gaze to meet mine.

"Phil," he said, shaking his head, "can't you go thirty-six feet without suffering a paranoid delusion?"

"No," I replied. "Can you?"

"Forget about them. Let's get some beers," he sighed.

"Consider them forgotten," I answered, a rare smile crossing my lips.

Nobody tried to kill me as I walked around to the front of the bar.

Since it was Friday, Happy Hour, and within walking distance to three colleges, the line to get in was longer than usual. We took our places behind two big guys wearing government-issue black trenchcoats. The shorter, stockier one had a smart-looking black fedora perched atop his head. The taller one wore MacArthur Ray-Bans and was holding a half-empty Michelob bottle in his hand. They looked familiar, but I couldn't remember from where.

Jay accidentally bumped into the taller of the two, causing him to turn and eye Jay menacingly from behind his shades. Apparently he recognized Jay as an officer of the law because he did a double-take, and turned back to his cohort and mumbled something.

Jay must have recognized them, too. He nudged me and then tapped the tall guy on the shoulder.

"Excuse me, buddy. Don't you drive a black Toyota 4x4 with an extra cab?" Jay grilled.

"Uh, no," the tall, shaded one replied, "but he does." He pointed to the one wearing a fedora.

The fedora wearer did his best cherub impression and looked quizzically at his friend. "I do?" he asked as if perplexed.

"You do," the shaded-one replied.

"Oh, yeah, I do. But my friend certainly didn't wing a half-empty Michelob bottle at your shiny Ford Caprice patrol car mere moments ago."

The tall guy looked back at his friend and asked, "I didn't?"

"You didn't."

They both turned toward us and flashed charming, blinding smiles.

"Are you sure?" Jay inquired. I don't think he was buying what they were selling. But I don't know why. They looked like solid citizens to me. I mean, how can you not trust someone wearing a fedora and a government-issue trenchcoat. Not too mention someone willing to pay homage to one of America's greatest generals!

"We're sure," they said in unison.

The tall, shaded one said, "We are writers—"

"Nay, artists!" chimed the fedora wearer.

"—and we tread gently upon the land—" continued Shades.

"—bringing happiness and joy to all we survey—"

"—much unlike the giant, flatulent lizard kings that once strode the earth—"

I wagged a knowing finger at Jay. "That's true. Man, those lizards loved their chili!"

" — in an era, long since past," finished the Hatman.

"Amen to that, brother," I agreed.

Jay glanced heavenward with a "why me" look on his face. A second pigeon blessed his other shoulder. Then, from somewhere a 1920's ragtime piano banged out "Play'em off-stage music" and the two trenchcoated wonders did a soft-shoe number out of line, passing the rats, who had cut in line, around the overweight bouncer, who waved to them, and into the bar.

After wiping the epaulets of his jacket, Jay whipped out his badge and flashed it to the bouncer. As we were waved passed the zit-laden college crowd, I nodded to the rats to follow and then chuckled to myself. Phillip Screwdriver, *last of the real men private investigators*, had triumphed over the cow-like masses.

Again.

I sparked up a Lucky as Jay and I entered the bar. As usual, the joint was packed like a Rastafarian's victory garden. I knew the bar was sixty feet from front to back and maybe twenty wide, but the haze of medical marijuana made it difficult to see the No Smoking signs. A couple of ceiling fans spun lazily above the thoroughly intoxicated crowd, doing little to circulate the air but giving me a hankering for brownies.

Early twentieth-century advertisements hung on the walls, arranged from an interior decorator's nightmare. Large mirrors behind the bar allowed a real-man-private-investigator to casually watch his back; or check out kilts. An uncountable number of spilled drinks had long ago dissolved any varnish on the old oak bar, staining it many shades of brown. People were crowded at the split wooden rail, screaming at the tapsters over the loud sounds of a fast dance tune. The old television in the corner showed even older Orcah reruns — back from when she looked almost human.

Norm and John at the bar were friends of mine; John gave me my drinks for free. He was quick with a joke or to light up my smoke but man, there was some place that he'd rather be. The pair sweated into the drinks, doing their soldier best to fill everyone's order. Norm looked up and saw Jay and I shouldering our way through the crowd. He waved and flashed a quick smile. I signaled him for a pitcher of the best house beer. I'm sure the bar owner had hooked a garden hose from the sink to the tap; house beer was like having sex in a canoe: it was fucking close to water.

Jay and I had just made it to the rail when Norm finished drawing our pitcher. He signed the canvas, handed it to Jay, and then filled a pitcher from the tap. He pulled two frosted mugs from the freezer beneath the register and set them down in front of us.

There were no stools empty, so Jay flashed his badge at an obviously underage student who quickly left. The nervous kid was holding one hand over his mouth while the other clutched his stomach. Yeah, to be young.

I pulled my London Fog back a little and showed another punk my gat. He released his stool and faded into the crowd.

We sat down and grabbed our frosty mugs. I took a pull on mine; giving birth was easier than drinking *Twenty-First Amendment* beer.

Jay wiped the foam from his lips as he placed his empty mug on the bar. He hoisted the pitcher and quickly poured himself another. A disgusted look dawned on my face as Jay pulled a stale jelly donut from the hip-pocket of his trenchcoat. I watched in horror as he dipped the donut into his beer. He turned to me and smiled the smile of the damned.

"Donuts and beer! Nothing better!"

My stomach churned and performed a Ringling Brothers' act as he pulled the donut from his mug. He popped the entire sopping mess into his maw and washed it down with the beer.

I held my nose and finished my mug. If Jay could down that slop, this real man could handle straight brew. I drank deep. The hops got caught in my throat like dolphins in a tuna net. I turned my head quickly to avoid spitting up all over Norm and choked back the ale. Before I could decide whether or not to let the beer fly, I saw the kid on his phone, and time stopped in the bar.

It was the same kid who'd conveniently gotten sick when Jay flashed his badge. He was eying us now and talking nervously to someone on the other end. My eyes grabbed his, and he stopped breathing; he knew that he'd been made.

Norm was tugging on my sleeve, asking if he could talk to me alone. Without saying goodbye, the kid pocketed his phone and made for the front door. I stood up and grinned; the kid stopped and frowned. His face looked like he had suffered a Dirty Sanchez.

We both knew he wasn't going to make it.

Norm held my sleeve and said, "My friend, I'll state my case, of which I'm certain..."

I waved him off and took a step toward the punk. The kid, looking resigned, turned, wiped his nose, and walked toward me, pushing my trench aside to show them the hard steel of Richard's shaft.

"You win, gnarly gun-toting dude! My name's Amro. Can I buy you a drink?"

Before I could respond, Jay placed a hand on my shoulder and spun me around.

"What's going on, Phil? One: you don't pull your gun in a crowded bar; this isn't Dodge City. Two: Who's your pal?"

Amro ordered three whiskey sours, and Norm started pouring.

Jay shook me and repeated, "Who's your pal?"

"No pal of mine, Jay. His name's Amro, he works for The Platypus, and he just dropped a dime on me. He's hoping that I'm going to let him live long enough for his buddies to get here." I turned my head toward Amro. "Isn't that right, friend?"

He smirked and shoved the whiskeys down the bar toward Jay and me.

"I can see why you're a Dick. I must be a pussy, then," he paused, "cause I'm fucked! Where do we go from here?"

He seemed like too nice a guy to kill outright, especially with all these witnesses.

Jay asked, "Who's The Platypus, Phil? Is he the one who shot you?"

"I gotta get out of here, Jay. Arrest Amro for disturbing the peace or something." I turned to Norm, "Buddy, show me the back door, and quick!"

He stammered "I can't help . . .," and I cut him off.

"Now! Dammit, this is my life!"

John, the head bartender, gave me my chance. He said "Norm, take your dinner break, get the hell outta here! I'll cover the bar!"

Norm grinned and shouted "Now's the chance to make a break!"

I hopped the bar, and we made for the back room. Norm moved surprisingly fast and graceful for a man of his girth. His rhinestone-studded half-cape flapped behind him, giving the illusion of a man in flight. I hoped the flight wasn't one-way, but I was sure there was going to be some heavy turbulence.

When I looked back to wave to Jay, I saw him shaking his head and finishing the shots Amro had bought. Christ, let a cop get off duty . . .

AUTHORITY RESPECTING AUTHORS' NOTE : *Phil is quite mistaken in his assumption that all police officers are booze guzzlers. Jay drinks because he's married, with children.* ***

In the back room, Norm grabbed his car keys from his spare cape. His key chain was a shining gold "TCB" logo, with a lightning bolt design. There was one key on the chain, and it went to a shiny, pink 1959 Cadillac convertible.

"Let's go for a ride," he said in his usual southern drawl.

The back door opened to reveal a ledge six feet above the parking lot. Norm's Caddy shone brightly beneath us in the waning moonlight, glowing as if it were the sun. The fins on the back of the car thrust suggestively into the air, like some obscene phallic symbol; like a piranha-fish on wheels. The sound of the engine surrounded us in Dolby stereo.

The whitewall tires seemed to glisten with expectation, and the chrome glimmered with preternatural radiance. The pink and white velvet tones of the body were soft and willing, inviting us inside, pleading for us to take it for a ride.

As if by magic, the convertible top began purring as it slowly slid back, revealing its warm and silky interior.

Norm's slurred words snapped me out of my reverie. It was out of character for him. "She kinda makes ya wanna slip your hands down the front o' yer trousers, don't she? It's okay, boy, I felt the same way myself when I first saw her."

I was still dazed when he slapped me on the back.

"Hop in, Phil, we're going fer a ride!"

We jumped from the ledge and into the front bench seat, the leather upholstery squeaking happily as the car's shocks bounced us up and down.

The key slid into the ignition slot, and Norm turned it, ever so gently. The car's engine came to life, growling and demanding that Norm pump the gas pedal, and accelerate until all four carburetor barrels were flung wide in wanton abandonment, greedily sucking precious fluids.

Norm neutral-dropped into drive, and we shot from the parking lot like a televangelist from an Amsterdam petstore.

We both lit up Luckys. I rolled over, and went to sleep until Norm gently pummeled me about the head and shoulders, screaming, "I want to talk, I want to talk!"

I rolled back over and grimaced. "You always want to talk. I need my shut-eye; go to sleep."

Norm sneered, reached out, and viciously grabbed my ears.

"I gotta keep my eyes on the road and my hands upon the wheel . . ." He seemed to think about something for a minute. "Never mind, dammit, just wake up. I gotta talk to you."

"Okay, okay. Spill your guts, just don't let it run all over your upholstery. This car's too pretty for that."

I could tell by the look on his face that he wasn't going to let up until I'd heard him through. I fished out a trout, uh, smoke from my pack. I punched the cigarette lighter on my door's armrest and waited.

"For reasons I'm not at liberty to disclose, my past must remain . . . clouded in mystery. What I can tell you is that I, uh, a woman I knew gave birth to a little girl about twenty-three years ago. Seven years later, she gave the child to a man named Spillane. A few months after that, the two of them disappeared."

He paused, juggling his thoughts. He dropped a few of them, gave it up, collected his thoughts and said, "The woman, Richard Steinman, asked me to track them down. I finally found Spillane six months later, face down in a gutter with a bellyful of whiskey. Wait a minute, sorry; that was me. Anyway, I found Spillane.

"He told me that the girl had run away shortly after they'd returned from overseas. Together, we searched for almost two years. He slowed me down. I didn't like his style, so I broke away from him and kept lookin' on my own. Years went by and I still couldn't find her. My career, my life, everything, was on the skids. I finally had to give up."

The lighter in the armrest popped out, and I touched it to the end of my cigarette, inhaling deeply.

"That's a long time to look for someone, Norm," I said, even though I'd been trying to find The Platypus for quite a while myself. Or, rather, we were both trying to find each other. "What kept you going?"

He looked at me with sad, serious eyes. "That little girl was my daughter. And I want you to find her for me."

CHAPTER TWO

The radio-alarm blared *Some Enchanted Evening*, grating my eardrums like cheese and forcing me to slam an angry fist on the snooze button. But it was too late; I was awake.

I rubbed my eyes open enough to see that I was dressed like a bi-curious circus clown. I was wearing a sequined, red and yellow terrycloth bathrobe, and yesterday's underwear. Sitting up on the bed, I rubbed my eyes again. I stood slowly and contemplated the cheese doodles my feet crushed into the leather carpet.

There was a fifth of Jack Daniels on the dresser, so I grabbed it. I was about to pour myself a shot when I caught a glimpse of myself in the vanity. The corners of my mouth turned down in response. Muscles hung from my tired frame like meat on a butcher's rack: red, fatty, and dead looking. My chest sagged like the breasts of a ninety-year-old stripper, and I felt bloated with cramps that rocked my body like a satanic hobby-horse ride. Well, at least I wasn't bleeding.

I sat back down on the bed. The Jack swung lazily between my legs, dangling from my fingertips and a swig shy of empty. Since I didn't plan on getting pregnant or operating heavy machinery today, I raised the bottle and let the last few drops of the snake oil slide down my throat. The feeling spread warm and nice through my body, like a bullet burrowing through my brain. It was quiet in

Norm's condo, too quiet. I pulled back the slide on Richard just to hear the reassuring sound of the *ka-chunk* as a round chambered.

The bottle dropped and I stood, shrugging off the robe. Norm may have been a lousy dresser, but he saved my life that night, getting me out of the bar and hiding me here like he did. He said no one else except us knew about this condo, that it was his once-in-a-while escape from life. I would have preferred Club Med, Sandals, or Gitmo, but beggars can't be choosers.

I opened a dresser drawer and found a pint of Bacardi 151. I started sipping and toasted to Norm's health. It wasn't often that I raised a glass to a dead man; usually I just smiled at a job well done.

After telling Norm that he should get another detective to find his little girl, like a dick without a contract on his head for example, he'd dropped me here and asked me to sleep on it. He also suggested that it might be a good way for me to get out of town until this blew over. I had shaken my head and he'd taken off in that damn Cadillac of his, leaving me little choice.

When I woke up the next afternoon, I had called Judy to let her know that I was peachy-keen. Jay had answered the phone and demanded to know where I was. I told him to stuff it, and he told me to stuff it myself because Norm was dead. The police had found his body in his car, both shot to death behind the Twenty-First Amendment.

I'd slammed the receiver before he could order me downtown.

Then I started drinking; before I passed out, I'd set the alarm clock for a few hours so I could get up and drink some more. I'd sworn that after I emptied his liquor cabinet, I'd find Norm's killer, and his little girl. I wanted both of them to know the man that neither had really known, but had so greatly affected his life.

My mouth opened, and I put the rum to my lips. My pipes opened wide and the 151 ran down my throat. The liquor burned bright and clean, like the alabaster coffee mug Charlie Sheen drinks his Tiger Blood from – when he's winning, duh. Then the light exploded. I collapsed, falling forward into the dark.

When I regained consciousness, it was still dark and my skull hurt worse than before. I was sprawled on the rug, my hair matted with Brill-cream, blood, and Bacardi. My head must have hit the dresser: a dried brown trail ran from drawer to drawer, mapping my fall to the floor.

I used the walls and furniture to help me wobble to the bathroom. Death snickered at me from a mirror for the second time today. I stuck out my tongue and then turned the faucets on warm and began wiping blood from my face.

I was looking better, even though I felt like I'd been shot again. For the hell of it, I checked my body for new bullet holes. There were no new ones, but the one I had was bleeding again. *Christ*, I thought, *it seems like every twenty-eight days or so . . .*

I stopped messing around with the washcloth and hauled my butt into the shower. The water felt good enough for me to consider the possibility of not dying, if I got some breakfast. I needed eggs, toast, A-negative blood plasma, and a side order of bacon. And some Scotch, of course.

Dawn's early light shouldered past me as I opened the front door of the condo. It came in, made itself at home, rummaged through the pantry, and made a few long-distance calls to someone named Tony in Orlando on Norm's princess phone. Then it started screaming at me, bellowing something about having to get up so damn early. I agreed. I would have shot it but that would only have added to the noise which was already more painful than a Ke$ha music mash-up on Glee.

I stumbled out and slammed the door behind me, then really wished I hadn't. My eyes sang hosannas to my name as I fished Norm's diamond-studded sunglasses out of my trenchcoat. With a flick of the wrist, I unfolded the arms and donned the dark specs. I don't know how they got in there, but I was grateful.

I made it down the steps and into the parking lot.

This was my first time here, so I didn't know where the Metro buses ran. I headed left, deciding to keep going until I hit a major road.

I noticed that the parking lot had tremendous speed bumps every four or five feet. The mounds of asphalt were hideous and evil, fiendishly disproportionate to the clearance space of most cars. The slumlord who ran this cheeseball place must have a brother in the towing and repair business.

As I was leaving the parking lot, a demonic black Toyota 4x4 truck jumped the curb of the median strip. It was driven across the lawn as if possessed; the exhaust spit fire and tires spun rich, black sod high into the heavens. The truck drove over the grass and into the parking lot, bypassing twenty or so of the speed bumps.

Two large men jumped out as the truck screeched to a halt. One of them wore a smart, black fedora and a black government-issue trenchcoat. The other, taller one, wore an identical trenchcoat and a pair of dark RayBan's. The two looked around quickly, scanning the parking lot for potential authority figures. Satisfied, they whipped jackhammers out from inside their trenchcoats and went to work. Budapow, budapow, bang-bang-bang-bang-bang.

I stood there, smoking. I knew these hellspawn hoodlums. They were the same two who I had seen at the Twenty-First Amendment. They laughed maniacally as they reduced the speed bumps to specks of basaltic waste, their trenchcoats billowing in the air like batwings. Then, for some reason, they paused.

MOLTEN AUTHORS' NOTE: *We're using a plethora of satanic words because it is morning, which is evil, and should be destroyed. Or at least outlawed. Maybe morning should be kept in a museum, so people can see it, and learn from past mistakes. As for the basaltic material, if you don't know what it means, look it up. We used it because it sounded real neat.* ***

As they resumed, I watched calmly as people came out onto their balconies angry at their rude awakening. They started to shout, but as recognition lit upon them, they began cheering riotously and screaming their approval.

Hatman and Shades looked up and saw me. The three of us stared at each other for a long second before I went for Richard and they put on toothy grins. I smiled back as I felt Richard's warm steel caress my palm.

The two stowed their jackhammers back into their voluminous coats. Hatman tipped his hat to me and Shades curtsied with his trenchcoat. I heard that damn piano music again. Then they did a softshoe number back into the truck, and sped off.

One of these days, I'd have to find out who the hell they were and why they kept popping up all over the place. And why a piano always played them off stage. Hell if we could get their piano player together with my trumpeter maybe they'd form a band and leave me the hell alone. They had a look about them that I didn't like, like they knew something I didn't. While he was stowing his jack-hammer, the shaded one had dropped a sheaf of papers. I walked over and nonchalantly picked them up, stuffing them in my pocket. I'd read the pages later, but right now I needed breakfast. I started walking.

After a hundred yards, the road dead-ended; I could go either right or left. Since there seemed to be traffic sounds on my left, I pointed my size nines in that direction and resumed walking.

During my stroll, I took some time to look around at the area. The neighborhood seemed nice enough: kids playing catch with their pets; black limousines parked in two-car garages; local youths enjoying the free enterprise system and selling dope at a corner stand; strung-out junkies knocking on doors, looking for a fix; a nondescript body decoratively splayed about the occasional lawn. I could have been anywhere in America. I walked through without so much as a second glance from anyone.

There was a King Burger just ahead, and my stomach informed my feet that that was where we were going. Not in the mood to argue, I acquiesced and soon found myself ordering most of the breakfast menu.

"That'll take some time, mister; the grill is down," the pimply-faced kid behind the register said. "But we can get you something from the deep fat fryer. Do you want to wait?"

"Do I want to wait?" I snarled. "DO-I-WANT-TO-WAIT? No, I don't want to wait, you fast-food Nazi! But I can wait for breakfast if I have to. I know how to wait; I've done it before. I waited for days in The 'Nam, crouched in one spot, afraid to breathe! Too damn scared to move, almost afraid to breathe!" I paused for a moment. "Wait, I said 'too afraid to breathe' already. Where was I?"

The punk stammered, "Uh . . . uh, you were saying you'd wait for breakfast, right?"

"Yeah, yeah. Just make it snappy, will you?"

He handed me a cup of Java and said he'd bring my food out to me when it was ready. I grabbed the early edition of the *Washington City Paper* and parked myself in the corner farthest from the window, where it was nice and dark.

The headline on the paper was bold and designed to hook the reader like a hungry trout: **DAN SNYDER STILL SUCKS**! Below the fold the paper read: **ELVIS FOUND DEAD BEHIND DC BAR**. The article read like something out the movie of the week:

> (AP-Washington) Elvis Presley, the King of Rock and Roll, was found shot to death behind a popular bar on Pennsylvania Avenue, NW.
>
> His body was found early this morning in a convertible pink Cadillac by police officers on routine patrol and identified by fingerprints and dental records.
>
> In 1977, the King had been reported dead on his toilet at his estate, Graceland. Since that day, Elvis sightings and Rock-a-Billy cults had sprung up like weeds in a garden. There was even one cult that purported that Elvis had purged himself for our sins and wore tiny rhinestone studded toilets around their necks in reverent memory. Even that asshole Dan Snyder,

while not sodomizing Redskins' fans, thought Elvis was still alive and offered to trade draft picks to the Titans for his rights. It looks like they were correct—even Snyder: Elvis had faked his death. However, this recent turn of events put an end to any hopes for the second coming of the King . . .

Sheesh, what a rag. Some people will print anything for a quick buck.

There was something striking about the photograph that accompanied the article, though. A bloated face with diamond-studded glasses, a pompadour, and thick sideburns, Elvis' dead, lifeless face bore a remarkable resemblance to Norm's. He wasn't a dead ringer, if you'll pardon the pun, but he was damn close—like Miley Cyrus and Hannah Montana. Someone had it in for guys with diamond-studded glasses, pompadours, and thick sideburns, like this Elvis guy and Norm. Maybe it was this Dan Snyder guy the *City Paper* kept mentioning. I made a note to look him up.

I pulled my trusty flask from my pocket and used its whiskey to sweeten the coffee and lit a Lucky and started trading drags of nicotine with shots of alcohol as I waited for my breakfast.

Around 11 o'clock, Mr. Acne tapped me on the shoulder.

"Uh, sir?" he said, voice quavering.

I turned and stared at him with the flaming bloody orbs that my eyes had become. "What?!" I answered finally.

"Um . . . Your breakfast, well . . . it's . . . it's not done. Yet. We're . . . we're all out of breakfast stuff, really. And it's after 10:30, so the breakfast vat is sealed. So we wanted to know if you wanted a burger or something. Compliments of the house . . . Urk!"

The barrel of my .45 replaced the teeth in his mouth. I cocked the hammer back and growled, "Listen, kid, I've had a really rough night. One of my best friends has been gunned down, there's been an attempt on my life, I'm hung over, and, to top it all off, my underwear is too small. Now," I shoved my gun further down his throat, "are you telling me that I can't have breakfast?"

He nodded.

"Not too bright, kid. Take me to your manager. *Now*!!"

The kid fouled himself, and then slumped to the floor as if his spine had suddenly skipped town. I looked up and noticed that the whole place was staring at me. Thinking quick, I fired a round into the ceiling tiles; plaster chunks fell on to the no-wax floor at my feet and people screamed.

I reached into my jacket and pulled out my P.I. ticket. Flashing it around, I shouted, "Nothing to worry about, folks! I'm from the Health Department! There's been complaints about abnormally high amounts of rodent feces in the coffee, and I've been sent here to check it out. I think it would be best if everyone left the establishment as quietly and quickly as possible so that I can sort this out."

A thunderous raspberry arose from the diners as they spewed fountains of coffee into the air. Then, the cow-like masses calmly stood up and stampeded for the door. The staff held their ground behind the counter. I smiled a death's head grin, turned, and leveled Richard at what appeared to be the manager-in-training.

"You, too," I ordered. "Everybody goes." The creepy, plastic-faced King Burger mascot didn't move. He just stared at me with his short eyes and that unchanging leer as if I were a six-and-a-half year old boy.

"Okay, your Highness. Have it your way." I pulled the trigger twice.

The management trainee wisely chose not to play hero and ushered the staff out the side door.

As soon as everyone was out, I vaulted the counter and shot the lock off the breakfast vat. Then I rummaged around until I found some eggs. I cracked thirty-seven of them onto the grill, where bacon was already sizzling. I stepped on some hash browns, next to some mushrooms growing out of the cracks in the breakfast vat. I used a spatula to scrape them from my shoe and onto the grill.

In a few short minutes, I had done what it took the whole staff hours to do. It just went to show that if you wanted something done right, you have to do it yourself. And except for the burnt toast and the taste of those weird mushrooms, the feast was fit for a god.

I was on my second helping of hash browns when breakfast was interrupted by approaching sirens. Always willing to help out the boys in blue, I slipped out the back door to see if I could be of assistance.

Out back was a grimy, fly-infested alley. I drew my gun and eased the door shut behind me. The barrel had barely cleared leather when I noticed flies swarming into a classic V-formation. Once assembled, the phalanx of flying filth hovered, buzzing quietly and waiting.

The alley walls sounded with blasting trumpets and bugles that would have made Satchmo jealous. When the top of the dumpster flipped open, I thumbed off the safety and sling shot the slide of my .45. A horde of flies, dressed in royal blue coats piped with gold, flew toward me. The well-clad insects unrolled a red carpet and held it aloft with their bodies.

I reached into my pocket and drew out a Lucky from the crumpled pack. I lit it and stood there watching patiently.

A hog-head palanquin was lifted out of the dumpster by four burly horse flies. One of them said, "Kneel before your King! Supplicate yourselves before the Master of All Flies! Behold! The Lord High Drosophila!"

After a moment, the same voice spoke again, "You, fly! Yes, you; the black one with the transparent wings. Why are you not kneeling?"

The questioned fly answered, "We don't have knees. How do you expect us to kneel, huh, Bob?"

"Oh. Well then fly upside down, or something."

"Look, Bob, we've gone over this before. It was cool when we scared the crap out of those British schoolkids back on the island, but this is America! The land of the free, home of the brave, greatest democracy in the world. We've had a taste of representative government, and I think I buzz for all of us when I say: We're sick and tired of your bloody power trips! Right, guys? Who's with me? Unite! Overthrow the Lord of the Flies!"

The fly turned and looked at his comrades who were all very busy flying upside down and looking casual.

"Yeah, well . . . I'm sick of you!" he continued, apparently unfazed by his lack of support. "Lord High Drosophila, my thorax! You're just a fly like the rest of us! Rise, flies! Rise against the evil fist of tyrannical power! No longer will we kowtow to the whim of some maggot whose parents were conquerors of Sani-Flushes and dumpsters everywhere! The time is now, fly brethren! We have buzzed! No longer will we be kept silent by the stormtroopers and strong-wing tactics of Drosophila! The revolution is now! Down with tyranny! Death to-*Urk!*"

A flyswatter, engraved with the Latin words: "*Mal fistus powerus tyrannosaurus rexus, lovus Mom*" slammed down on the rebel fly, bringing an abrupt end to his existence and the dream of drosophilan democracy.

I stood there, puffing on my Lucky and thinking about what the fly had said. Should man be subject to the mere whim of anyone who happens to be in a power position? Even in America, this shining beacon of democracy, the whims of the President are nearly law. Should we speak out for what we believe is true and right? Against what we see as evil? Is the soul but a black and twisted thing that feeds on the subjugation and oppression of his fellow man? Should we listen to and consider the voices of the anti-establishment, or should such minority dissent be silenced with swift and mindless violence?

My fingers tightened on the trigger of the answer: the cold, hard steel of my trusty .45.

The palanquin halted in front of me, snapping me out of my reverie. Lord Drosophila pulled a fly-sized Lucky from his pack and stuck it in a tiny cigarette holder. Eight thousand thorax-kissers swarmed around him with little lighters.

After the flies resumed their supplicatory positions, the Lord of the Flies said, "Friend Phillip, join with us. You are pursued, nay, hunted by those inferior to you because you are different than they. Your experiences have proven, time and again, that homo sapiens, mankind, are inherently evil.

"I offer you the chance to lose yourself in the world of the Fly; to become one with the collective unconscious. Flies are all that is pure and good, whilst human ilk are bad seed. The Brotherhood of the Fly is the greater good. You will be one of many; one of the few, yet still one. Six legs and translucent gossamer wings, good. Two legs and flyswatters, bad. It is not only my law, but God's as well, as I am sure you are aware."

Drosophila paused, puffed on his Lucky, and then added, "What say you, Friend Phillip?"

I inhaled on my own cigarette and blew a plume of second-hand smoke into the Lord of the Flies' face. Raising Richard, I hoped that the Authors weren't going to make me spew out another long, pointless soliloquy before I pulled the trigger.

My lips didn't move, but my trigger finger did. Bullets struck the hog-head palanquin, exploding it into a red mist, like an over-ripe watermelon dropped from thirty-seven stories onto the pavement.

Silence hung in the air like laundry on a clothesline as the mist and gore floated to the ground. Then a low buzzing began, quickly gaining volume as more voices joined in the chorus. The flies were cheering and singing. I strained my ears to make out what they were saying.

"Ding-dong, the witch is dead! The wicked witch! The wicked witch! *Ad nauseum.* All hail! Phillip Screwdriver, last-of-the-real-Lords-of-the-Flies!"

Not wanting to be the lord of anything, much less followed around by a swarm of flies, I resolved to start using soap when I bathed. Thinking quickly, I kicked the backdoor of the King Burger open and yelled "Breakfast's on me Boys!" There was a buzzing cheer as they swarmed inside.

I made a break for the street. Fortunately, a bus labeled "Washington, DC" pulled up, and, after a quick twenty-yard dash, I was on.

The driver eyed me, smiled, and asked for fifty cents. I handed him a bill and said, "That'll be fifty cents, Mac."

He smirked, and replied in halting English, "Exact change only. Sorry!"

I whipped Richard out of my shoulder rig and struck the business end in his left nostril. "Look, pal," I snarled, "you and your buddies have been pulling this crap on me for years. This is the end of it, right here, right now! Enough people give you exact change that it won't be too much trouble for you to give me my goddamn fifty cents!"

He whimpered and started to complain, "But—"

"No, on second thought, I think I'll ride for free this time. Give me back my dollar."

He grudgingly handed over my bill and then pulled the handle to shut the door. With a hiss, the bus lurched forward into traffic. As we pulled away, I saw the SWAT team and several cops standing around the King Burger parking lot, looking confused. Whoever they were after must have gotten away.

It suddenly occurred to me that the guy they wanted might be on this bus. I looked around and saw that it was just the driver and me on board; the guy probably wasn't here. I sat back in my chair and sampled spirits from my colossal flask collection.

The driver screamed frantically into a CB as he weaved in and out of traffic. I tried to catch what he was saying but he wasn't speaking any language I knew; it wasn't English, Spanish, French, German, Swahili, Russian, Serbo-Croatian, Swedish, Japanese, Latin, Vietnamese, Aztec, Klingon, Arabic, Mandarin Chinese, Esperanto, Tagalog, binary, or any other of the seventy-four languages in which I was fluent. Given my suspicion that they are paid by the word, I was surprised that The Authors didn't have the pecuniary gall to print the whole list.

During the ride downtown, people of all shapes and sizes entered and exited the bus. The Authors, again, didn't take the time to have me describe them as they were feeling rather drained and lifeless at the moment. *Actually*, I thought, *so am I*. I realized that I was only insulting The Authors so that they'd defend themselves in an Authors' Note and give me a chance to get some shut-eye.

I waited for a few minutes, but The Authors didn't bite. I should have known: they worked the night and hated to get up early. Needing some way to pass the time, I decided to test my .45. I randomly shot out thirty-seven or so windows, and blew apart a fat lady's Carmen Miranda hat.

The next stop was the police station. I got up and walked down the aisle, toward the front of the bus. The passengers, (when did they get on?) probably in awe of my marksmanship ability, parted willingly, like the legs of a two-bit hooker receiving a C-note.

As the bus neared the station, a crowd of cops rushed toward the bus stop. Knowing that it would be impossible to get off the bus with that mob pushing to get on, I jerked the emergency stop cable. The bus slammed to a screeching halt, the door flew open, and I jumped out into the Washington work crowd. About thirty-seven officers boarded the bus as I walked into the station house.

Inside the building, uniforms were running around in various stages of riot gear. I made my way through them and up to the front desk. I found Officer Sean "Hershey's" O'Strasser hiding behind a wall of donut boxes. He was the desk sergeant.

"Hey, Sean, where's Jay? He's been looking for me all morning."

O'Strasser scraped some chocolate residue from beneath his walrus moustache with a fudge-encrusted finger and flung it at the wall disdainfully before replying.

He directed me down the hall and to the right for the men's room and down the hallway on the left to Jay's office, and then went back to licking fudge from under his fingernails. I guessed up the stairs and to the right and found Jay staked out by the water cooler. He was holding a map in one hand and a two-way radio in his other.

"Hi, Jay. I heard you wanted to talk to me. Spill it. I don't have much time to blow. I've got to find a killer or two."

Jay looked up and I could see the adrenalin in his eyes. "I want to talk to you about Elvis' death, but it'll have to wait. Right now, I've got to coordinate with the mayor. Osama Bin Laden's been shooting up buses all over the city!"

"Isn't he dead?"

Jay gave me the stink eye. "Don't leave town."

AUTHORS' BLATANT SEQUEL TIE-IN NOTE: *After the mayor mobilized the National Guard to help search for the ruthless terrorists—who were, in all actuality, a non-English speaking bus driver's excited description of our protagonist, Phillip H. Screwdriver—SGT. Steve Manson, Jr. had to miss his son's championship pee-wee league T-ball game. The boy, Li'l Chuckie, always relied on his Dad's presence at the game to give him confidence. He was the star hitter for the team, and everyone was counting on him to win. Without Sergeant Manson there to bolster his son's confidence, Li'l Chuckie was having a terrible game. His teammates played valiantly, and in the bottom of the ninth, with three men on, two outs, his team down by one run, Li'l Chuckie came up to bat.*

He swung and missed: strike one. The Manson boy looked desperately into the stands, hoping for just one glimpse of the father he knew was not there. Strike two, and all eyes were upon him. The umpire placed the ball upon the tee and then patted young Charles on the back. Chuckie heard the Ump's reassuring words, but couldn't see the tee through the tears falling from his seven-and-a-half year old eyes. He swung blindly and hard; as his bat contacted the ball, he heard his father's voice inside his heart: Just do it, son. Run like Helter-Skelter for first base! Don't let the little piggies get to you!

Little Charles Manson popped the ball straight up into the air, where the catcher easily made the play. Li'l Chuckie, and his team, had lost the championship.

From that day forward, Charles was an outcast from his peers. He underwent years of therapy, but to no avail. The words of the Beatles screamed out to him that Phillip Screwdriver was the walrus, and must be killed. Fortunately for Phil, Chuck misunderstood the screams of John, Paul, George, and Ringo. History records Charles' misunderstanding and subsequent incarceration. In prison, he had time to mull over the message until he realized his mistake, but that is another story, coming to a book store near you, if this one gets us on the "Orcah Windfull Show." So buy at least three copies and rave to your friends about it. Write letters to the Pope. No, better yet, send the Pope a copy so he'll abdicate and canonize Phil. Why? Because we told you to do it. It's common knowledge that the cow-like masses will do anything they're told.

So, shove a banana up your nose, empty a can of Spam on your head, go buy thirty-seven more copies of the expensive hard back addition, drain your savings account, and send your money to L. Ron Hubbard, even though he's dead, because Scientology is something even we consider deranged.

"Hey, Deus?"
"Yes, Ex Machina?"
"That last paragraph is a little bizarre, even for us."
"So?"
"Okay. Just checking."
"Is that the door?"
"Yeah. See who it is but try not to invite anyone in, this time."
"But they said it was a candygram."
"Oh, in that case…" ***

Jay left me to ponder. Why did he want to talk to me about Elvis' death? What did I care about an over-sideburned ex-King of

Rock and Roll?

I went into Jay's office and found the file that I wanted. Inside the folder was a photograph of Elvis lying in parking lot, chalk outlining his massive girth. I flipped through the coroner's report and discovered that he'd died of thirty-two caliber lead poisoning. From the way he was dressed, he and Norm must have shopped for clothes at the same place.

Norm! Call it a hunch, call it a gut feeling, call it women's intuition: somehow Norm, Elvis, and the Platypus were all wrapped up together. And it was up to me to tie the bow around this little package.

I shoved the file under my trenchcoat, next to that sheaf of papers Hatman and Shades had dropped, and left the station. Nobody bothered me as I exited the building.

I felt sorry for the bus-terrorists when the full force of D.C.'s Finest came to bear.

CHAPTER THREE

I left the police station and hailed a cab. I wanted to put in an appearance at the office for Judy's sake. The poor kid was probably out of her mind worrying about me. With visions of the world's most competent secretary floating before my eyes, I got in the cab.

"Nineteenth and K, northwest. An extra fin if you don't stop for any red lights."

The cabby replied, "Sure, dude. Like, we're there," but I wasn't so sure. Looking at his clean, long, blond hair, and hearing the American-born accent in his voice, I knew I'd been set-up to take a fall. The only real cab drivers in D.C. were Pakistani, spoke three words of English badly, and smelled like IEDs. I loosened the folds of my jacket, making it easy to reach Richard when I needed her.

And I would.

He wanted to talk with me about my line of work, an obvious ploy. I grabbed his ponytail and yanked his head back against the seat. The cabby arched his back in pain and lost control of the wheel. The car screeched across traffic and ramped onto the sidewalk.

In rebellion against the sidewalk-driving genre, there were no pedestrians to jump out of our way, or fruit stands for the cab to smash. Frustrated, I used my driver's hair like the reins of a yak until we found a sidewalk with a fruit stand. It took us a while; they're not as common as they used to be. The driver kept wanting to drive through a federal building but I told him I was no tourist and I wasn't going to pay him to drive through offices sightseeing. I knew there was a fruit stand up the street from my office because it was mine. I don't sell fruit. I just like having a fruit stand to drive through when the mood strikes. When we got close, I yanked his hair again and the cab went careening across traffic, finally smashing through my fruit-stand and forcing pedestrians to leap out of our Chevrolet's careening path.

Finally satisfied, and munching on kumquat, I released the cabbie's hair. He grumbled and stuffed his ponytail up underneath a Nationals cap. I got out in front of the Connections Building, where I kept a corner office. He had the gall to ask me for the fare, so I shot his meter, tipped my hat to him, and bid him a fond farewell.

"Same time tomorrow, sir?" he asked.

"Yeah. And the ponytail was a nice touch. Almost had me fooled." I took a step toward the building. "Oh, and see if you can get better kumquats. These taste like crap."

"Will do, sir."

As the hack pulled away, I stared up at the marble-and-glass mosaic that was the Connections Building. Hard white marble gleamed heavenward, and the building stood tall and proud, like a guardian of the city. The Connections Building was not just a phallic symbol designed by an architect who couldn't get it up; it was also my pride and joy, a monument to justice. As I walked beneath the world globes suspended above the entrance, I spit out the sub-par kumquat. "T'ain't like they used to be."

The lobby teemed with forensics experts, hovering over the body of a scantily clad dame like lawyers outside an asbestos factory. My heart was in my throat as I pushed those circling buzzards out of my way, and my thirty-seventh worst nightmare came true. Judy lay on the tiled floor, chalk-lines drawn around her motionless form; two bullet wounds decorating her heaving bosom.

I dropped to my knees beside her, blood thundering in my ears. I watched her on the stage. My hands were clenched in fists of rage. I knew no angel born in hell could break Satan's spell. And for some reason, I thought of pie.

As I recited the "I will avenge your death" soliloquy found on the dedication page of the *Private Investigator's Handbook*, Judy's bosoms heaved again and her eyelids fluttered open.

"I'm not dead, Phil. I'm just helping out these nice forensics boys! They're having a convention and needed a model!"

"Let them buy an hourglass, kitten, you only model for me. Get your shapely buns upstairs before I paddle them!"

Judy pulled up her bra, tee-hee'd, and sashayed to the elevator. I gave the Shriner-wannabees the eye.

"Take some air, fellows, no dead bodies here. Not yet. But don't go too far, I got a feeling that tonight's going to be . . . kind of right."

Suddenly bored, the conventioneers descended on the building's receptionist. By the time I headed for the elevator, Judy had already gone up. I hit the "up" button, and fired up a gasper.

When the elevator door opened, I joined two men in the car, crushing out my butt on the elevator wall. I flicked the remains into a corner and lit another one.

There were two men: one was tall, thin, and looked constipated; the other was Italian, looked stupid, and proved it by wearing a pin-striped tweed suit. The taller one pulled a shiny, nickel-plated pistol and smiled.

"My name," he started, "is Oberleutnant Elisha Otis, Commandant of the Elevator Enforcers Reich, Nation's Capital division. At long last, you, friend, are busted."

I shook my head, "Kind of a long name; is that Mexican?"

Otis pulled out a fat ticket book and a pen. "What's your name, gringo?"

I blew a stream of smoke in his non-smoking, self-righteous, anal-retentive, former president of the chess club, Nazi weasel face. I would have bet that he was even a hall monitor back when he was a kid.

"Well, rodent-penis, it's Screwdriver, Phillip Screwdriver, *last of the real men private investigators.*" As I finished reciting my name, the elevator Muzak was replaced by the sounds of heraldic trumpets. I hate heraldic trumpet music.

The air was thick with second-hand smoke and tension until he smiled. I didn't like his smile. It was a nasty leer. He was obviously getting his jollies scribbling my name in his book. "I'm giving you a twenty-five-dollar ticket, Ferret-phallus!"

"I hope it's to a Sinatra concert, Swine-schwantz. If it is, I'll take two. I've got a date. You know, with a girl? You do know what a girl is," I paused, looking briefly at my feet before locking eyes with him, "don't you?"

His face reddened, and he squinted his eyes until he looked like a Viet Cong. "No, rooster-rod, not for Sinatra. This ticket's for the judge!"

I moaned, "The Judds?" I shook my head, "I hate country music. It's so depressing. Someone's grandmother is always getting pistol-whipped by a wife who's run off with the crops and taken the dog!"

I'd smoked my Lucky to the fingers so I ground the butt out on the plush carpeting of the elevator. It was a truly lovely shag, except for all the ash burns. I lit another.

"I'm glad you did that," Otis said, "because that's another twenty-five dollars that you owe the Reich."

I finished that cigarette and shook out two more pills, offering one to the quiet Italian, who shook his head. If not for the tweed, and enough greasy kid's stuff in his hair to lube an engine block, he'd have been on the cover of "Hoboken GQ." Since he didn't want to join me in a smoke, I shoved both Luckys into my mouth. Agent Otis wrote two more tickets.

Even two at a time, it took the two of us three hours to work through my carton of smokes. He finished off his last ticket book as I crumpled the remains of my last pack of cigarettes. I tossed the cellophane and paper wad onto the mountain of over two hundred butts and ten plus packages.

Otis smiled victoriously as he signed the last ticket. "Screwdriver, you are the scum of the earth, a foul, evil thing, and a poopy pants!"

I pulled a spare Lucky from my hatband and smiled. "Funny," I thought out loud, "I always considered myself a swarthy rogue."

Otis smiled tightly and pulled a spare ticket from behind his bowtie.

The Italian, still waiting silently, began tapping a foot.

MERCIFULLY EDITED AUTHORS' NOTE: In the original edit, this scene went on ad nauseum, so we cut out a few pages. We decided to insert this text instead: The hot wind raged around me as my mighty sword slashed through Oberleutnant Otis' neck. My gigantic thews, hardened by years of battle, rippled with exertion, and blood spewed from his wounds as I hacked the corpse. The skins of a saber-tooth tiger I had slain myself as a child hung loosely from my steroid-laden frame as I thrust Otis's skull into the air. A scantily-clad blonde was wrapped around my leg, nipples conveniently hidden by flaxen locks.

The smoking ruins of Otis' body were slumped against the far wall of the elevator, directly opposite the door. The quiet Italian, who had watched my epic battle with the forces of retentiveness, had finally pulled out a nine millimeter Beretta automatic pistol and introduced himself to Otis. Holstering his smoking gun (I wonder if Otis would have given him a ticket for it), the Italian turned toward me.

"The Platypus says it's coytans for youse!"

"Thanks," I said, "but tell him that Catamite Draperies put new curtains in my office last week. It's nice of him to offer, but . . ."

The Italian looked confused. "Well, duh, okay, I'll tell him. But I don't thinks he's going to likes it. Youse gets off easy dis time, Screwdriver. But if The Platypus still says it's coytans for you, then Rocco 'Dumbass' Barbelli's gonna makes sure youse gets coytans."

"Alright," I said, "fair enough. Will you hit seven for me?"

"Sure."

While the elevator moved, I tore down the "No Smoking" sign and placed it on Oberleutnant Otis' chest. The elevator stopped, and I got off.

Rocco said, "Be seeing you, Screwdriver."

I stepped out of the elevator, drawing Richard, "Oh, Dumbass?"

"What?"

I pulled the trigger and ventilated his chest. As Rocco bled on the pile of cigarette butts and packages, I shook my head dejectedly, coughed up a glob of lung, and holstered Richard. I didn't know where The Platypus was getting his goons these days, but he sure didn't make 'em like he used to.

Still mourning the loss of challenge in my life, I headed into my office. Judy bounced up to meet me; her smiles were all sunshine and happiness.

"Oh, Phil," she said breathlessly, "I though you were never coming up!"

"Hi, Kitten, how's tricks?"

"I don't do that anymore, Phil."

I heard a rimshot somewhere outside.

"Then what were you doing downstairs with the necrophiliacs?"

"Wha—? You have a real nerve questioning my moral fiber! You, you who can't go a day without kill—" I tapped Judy lightly on the chin with one of those "I got you, Babe" gestures.

She shut up, and decided to lie on the floor, recreating her pose for the forensics boys downstairs.

"Maybe later, Judy, but I've got a lot on my mind right now."

Too bad, I loved that kid, and she loved me. I also knew that I could never show her my love, or let her show me hers. It would put her in too much danger. I headed for the back room, and decided against telling her to "Stop lying down on the job." I opened the door and began whistling a casual, aimless tune.

I could just hear a bottle of twelve-year-old scotch calling me over the Muzak. Bruce Springsteen was performing "I Am Woman," so I shot the speakers and poured myself a drink.

Since it was a dark and stormy night wherever I went, my clothes were wet, and I decided to change. Unfortunately, the only thing clean in the office was my television detectives' softball team uniform. I put it on and fished inside the striped pocket for a deck of Lucky Strikes. I always had one while I was at bat.

AUTHORS' CURTIOUS EXPLANATORY NOTE:** The following section has been patched in from something written earlier. The tone, you will note, is less ludicrous than it has been. Much like the Batman skit in the first few pages, we just liked it and wanted to shove it in somewhere. Rest assured, there will be more lunacy and high jinx after this brief dabble into actual genre literary techniques. And door prizes, too. Speaking of the door, can you go check it? I think someone's knocking.*

Fully dressed, warm and comfortable, I sank into my beaten-leather chair and propped my cleats on the oak desk. I leaned back, puffing on a cigarette, and looked out the window.

The view from my corner office never changed. The city stretched out beneath me like some gigantic concrete cemetery; soot-black buildings served as headstones to the funeral procession of traffic. I spit.

Unfortunately, the window was closed. I made a mental note

to have Judy clean all the glass. As if on cue, I heard her knock and the door opened. She stuck her pretty head halfway through, far enough for me to see the ice-pack she held to her chin.

Her jaw twitched, and she winced before saying, "There's a gentleman with a package for you. He says he has to give it only to you, says it's important. Should I let him in?"

I leaned forward in the chair, unholstered Richard and placed her on my desk, within easy reach. The memory of Rocco swam across my vision.

"Sure," I nodded, "show him in."

The door to my office opened slowly, as if the guy holding the knob wasn't quite sure of himself. A small, mousy man, appropriately dressed in a gray suit, stepped inside. He held a box neatly wrapped in brown paper under his thin arm. Coke-bottle glasses perched on his face; his eyes were black and fluid, looking as if they'd overflow the confines of the rims at the first hint of tears.

"M-Mr. Screwdriver?" he stammered, extending his unoccupied hand, "I've got a package for you from Norm. He told me to give this to you if he . . . if he . . . ever died!"

I spit some tobacco flakes from my mouth and took the package from his outstretched hands. "Thanks, kid. What's your name?"

"I'm Jerry, and I've been delivering Norm his pizza from my place since 1977. I guess I'm out of a job, huh?"

"I guess so, Jerry. Does this box mean I've got one?"

"I don't know, Mr. Screwdriver, I . . . I just knew to deliver the box to you."

"Why me?" I asked.

Jerry squirmed around like a fish on a hook. My eyes chased his like a coyote does a roadrunner.

He cleared his throat. "I shouldn't be telling you this, but I guess it doesn't matter anymore, not really."

Jerry kicked an imaginary can and scuffed what was left of my two-year old wax job. I'd have to remind Judy to buff the floor again. I waited patiently while Jerry found his voice. When he spoke, his words stuck in my throat like fishhooks.

"Norm's not his real name; I don't know what it is, but Norm it ain't. Since late '77 he's been under some sort of government Jehovah's Witness protection program. He . . . he said that whoever was after him might find him and put him on ice. Norm, or whatever his name really is, said if he hadn't found his daughter by the time they got to him, to give this box to you. He said you'd know what to do."

I crushed out my Lucky and lit another, inhaling the smoke like a drowning man does tequila. Why was there always a worm?

Dammit, Norm! How can I turn down the dying wish of a good friend? You knew I couldn't, didn't you? Bastard! I hope you're getting a good laugh out of all this!

Jerry was backing toward the door. "I'm sorry, but I can't afford to stay any longer. I've got pizzas to deliver. Then I've got to start managing Norm's estate. He left me in charge of it for my years of loyal service." He wiped tears from his eyes and finished, "He really was a king among men, wasn't he?"

I nodded an affirmative and pulled a smoke from its hiding place in the pack. Jerry was looking at me with quizzical eyes. "Did you win?" he asked.

"Win what?"

"The game," he said, pointing to my T-ball uniform.

"Uh, we didn't play; the game was rained out." I puffed on my Lucky.

"But you're uniform isn't wet!"

"We're detectives," I said. "We investigated the weather, discovered that it was going to rain, and called the game."

"What did you call it?"

"Canceled." Another rimshot.

"Oh," he said, a knowing look on his face. "Well good luck, Mr. Screwdriver. I hope you do as well for Norm as you did for your teammates."

I nodded solemnly and watched as he left; spinning on his heels, and quiet, he disappeared like a shadow at noon.

I opened the bottom drawer of my desk and pulled out the bottle of Southern Comfort that I reserved for the deaths of best friends. There was only half a shot left in the bottle, so I emptied it into my glass. I tossed off the half-shot in half a second and then tossed the half-shot halfway across the room as I gagged at the strength of the liquor.

I let the empty bottle fall into the circular file. It landed with a thud before singing a dirge as it rolled around the trashcan. Like Norm, the bottle came to a stop.

I stared at the package, and then at the bottle. I knew that no matter how much I drank, Norm wouldn't come back and his box wouldn't go away. I pulled my old combat knife from the same drawer that had held the bottle of Comfort. The wicked blade had tasted blood in The Big One, but now fed on a steady diet of paper envelopes.

The knife went through the brown wrapper of the package like a kid at Christmas . . .

I stood behind my desk and stared into the box, stared at the hopes and dreams of a dead pal, all wrapped up in paper and tears.

Judy poked her face in, holding a T-bone to her chin. "You've got a call on line two."

I looked over and saw the soft lighting of the lobby caressing her shapely thighs under her sheer skirt. Her heaving breasts were barely restrained by the thin fabric of her white blouse. Trails of blood ran from the meat down her delicate neck and into the soft valley between the rising swells of her bosom.

I felt an uncomfortable tightness in the muscles of my throat. I struggled to swallow. A bottle of A-1 sauce swam before my mind's eye and I had a craving for a baked potato and a side salad.

"Line two, Judy? I only have one line."

"I know," she replied, "and it's lousy; that's why you're still single." She left the room cackling and shut the door. I grimaced and lifted the receiver to my ear.

"Yeah?"

The voice on the other end of the line spoke, and I listened carefully. Her directions took me to The Gelded Retriever, a haunt for confirmed bachelors that had been a social fixture in the District for over twenty years. The appletinis and appetizers were some of the best around, and the owner, Rod, a Pisces, was a straight shooter. Oh wait, that must have been somewhere else. I'd never heard of this place before.

I told the caller that I'd be there in an hour, that I had a few things to do first.

The line went dead, and I put the receiver back in its cradle. I tapped a fresh deck of smokes against my palm before tearing the wrapper off. I lit a Lucky, and inhaled deeply. I wished the bottle in the can wasn't empty. I opened the other drawer, fished past the collection of empties, and pulled out a fresh bottle. Then I pulled Norm's box to me and dumped the contents onto my desk . . .

CHAPTER FOUR

I walked into *The Gelded Retriever*, giving a nod to Rod as I walked past, ordering my usual appletini. A quick once-over didn't turn up the dame I was supposed to meet. I had to give Rod credit for the new decor of the bar: it was spacious and tasteful. Fresh floral arrangements gaily covered the wood and glass counters, giving the "Retriever" a casual atmosphere. I sipped my drink (it was fabulous, as usual) and focused on an episode of "Orcah" showing on the television above the bar. The other TV was showing "Ellen."

A woman's hand tapped me on the shoulder and the voice from the phone suggested we get a table. The hand belonged to an elderly woman, and a ring on the second finger said she was married.

"Sorry I'm late, Mr. Screwdriver. My name is Stephanie and the traffic getting here was simply murder!" Her voice was strong for her age, and sounded as stiff as her spine. She carried herself like a granddame, the last of the Southern aristocrats. I was sure I'd seen her at the Twenty-First Amendment, sitting there so refined, drinking herself half-blind.

I parked myself in a booth by the window and she followed. "What's your name again? And what's so damn urgent that I had to meet you now, here?"

Before she could reply, our waiter sashayed over to the table and asked, "May I take your orders?"

I glanced at the menu, not really in the mood for food. Walking in this joint made me lose my appetite, and I said so. But I ordered a footlong and another appletini anyway.

The waiter, ignoring me but, not to be put off, suggested to my lunch-date, "Try the open-face ham and cheese bagel. I think you'll find it's wonderful!"

Stephanie shook her head and the waiter looked at me.

"No thanks," I growled. "I said I'm not hungry. Just bring me the footlong and something stiff."

The waiter giggled, "You're such a Samantha, Phil."

I slammed a hand down on the table and snarled, "Keep your chaps on, Bruce. I meant a highball . . ." I caught myself before he made another dumb joke and forced me to gag him. "Just bring me an appletini, and make it a double!"

The waiter, obviously amused at my discomfort, gave me a patronizing smile, tittered gaily, and left. The woman who'd become my lunch companion looked like she wanted to laugh. I didn't give her the chance.

"I don't have a lot of time, dollface. I'm busy, and I think that this is a pretty queer place to meet." I kept back a smile, sat back in the booth, plucked a Lucky from its place of residence, and waited for a reply. The woman shifted in her seat, looking sad and uncomfortable.

"My name is Stephanie Streeter, of the Priest's Bridge Streeters. I . . . I . . . well, I was so close to Norm, I'm all shook up; I don't know what to do anymore. Not to mention his poor," and she emphasized her last word, "daughter!"

Coincidence smacked me in the face with a Rainbow Trout. I tried to look disinterested in what she had to say. I touched my lighter to the end of my cigarette, inhaling deeply. Smoke blew from my lips.

"I guess that makes us pals. You're friends with the daughter, too?"

"Land sake's, yes!" she exclaimed. "We used to be so close, she was like a daughter to me! Of course," she said, her voice calming down. "I haven't seen hide nor hair of her in nigh on a quarter century now."

"Long time. Any idea where she is?"

"My word, no! That's why I called you: I want you to find her. She probably doesn't even know that Norm has gone to his Great Reward. I want to be the one that tells her . . . I want . . . I want to be there for her! I want . . ."

"You want what a lot of people around here suddenly want. You're just one in a long line of people who wants to find her, and think that I'm the best man for the job. What's so special about this chick? And what's your angle?"

She looked horrified that I would question her motives. "I told you," she said with rising indignation, "I want to . . ."

"Save it, sister," I cut her off. "You haven't seen her for twenty-five years. A father she doesn't know dies, and suddenly you're the only one who can help her through the tragedy. No, I don't think so. I think you want to put the bite on her for whatever inheritance there might be. But, that's your business, and I'm not making it mine. So put away your checkbook. Besides," I slowed, wanting to find out what she was up to, "someone's already footing the bill for me to find her. What do you think about that?"

She lost the starch in her backbone and slumped to the table, face first, trying to hide her eyes. She shouldn't have bothered; I'd seen the tears.

"You . . . don't understand, Mr. Screwdriver. I . . . I . . . oh, let me start at the beginning." She grabbed my hand. "Promise me you'll listen to me! Promise! If you still think me a charlatan when I'm done, I'll leave. But promise you'll at least listen!"

I shook my hand free and leaned back. "All right, it's your dime, don't waste it."

She straightened herself to her former position, upright, and began. "I became Mrs. Mickey Spillame going on thirty years ago. I divorced him, which, of course, was scandalous, a few years after we were married."

"Why the break-up?"

"He was obsessed with having children; male children to be specific. Unfortunately, we couldn't have a child together. I don't know why, we've both had children since. I had two boys and a girl, and he sired Glory."

Bells went off in my head. "Hold it. Glory is Norm's kid."

Stephanie regained her matriarchal composure and began speaking slowly, as if to a child. "Glory was a girl. I told you that Mickey was obsessed with having a male heir to his family line. When Glory was born, he refused to raise the child and divorced Richard."

"Richard?"

"Richard Steinman Spillame, Glory's mother. Allow me to continue, please. Richard left the Sunbelt and came here, to the more acceptable environs of D.C., to raise the child. Here she met your friend Norm, and the two raised Glory for about seven years."

She paused when Bruce brought us our drinks; I was looking forward to my appletini. He had changed outfits. Now he was dressed in a kilt. I scowled at him and sniffed my drink suspiciously. It was a Diet Coke. Real fucking funny. The waiter left in a huff, looking for someone to give him a tip.

I sipped my drink before prodding, "So, then what made the story interesting?"

"Mickey became a famous author! He writes religious mystery texts! Perhaps you've read one?"

I shook my head.

She'd gotten the answer she expected from someone in my line of work and smiled, "Oh, well, you should; they're fantastic works. Anyway, Richard and Norm did just well enough to support themselves and their little girl, but no better. Richard knew that having a bastard child would ruin Mickey's career. She blackmailed him for money and then forced him to take the child. Richard wanted Glory to be raised in a wealthy environment. She disappeared with her money and no one knew where she'd gone; not even Norm. Or if he did, he wouldn't say.

"Mickey only had Glory for six months before the child ran away. During that time, I had baby-sat her often and came to care for her as if she were my own. I continued to see Mickey after our divorce. I still love him, Mr. Screwdriver. I never loved anyone else."

Before I could sort out the truth, Bruce returned, this time in a matador's uniform, pushing a cart of hors d'oeuvres. "Your Hog Spheres Flambé, sir," he lisped, saying "sir" with a hint of frosting. "Compliments of the gentleman in red, sitting at the bar."

The waiter touched a match to the dish, igniting the food and sending flames toward the ceiling. "Enjoy, sir, but remember: Hog Spheres Flambé is a powerful aphrodisiac!" He winked and left.

The man in red sitting at the bar was a paunchy, middle-aged man, balding and pale. He waved a hanky at me. Christ, I thought, it must be my aftershave: Brut by Faberge. No one can resist the stuff. I guess that's why Dad's all over the world get a little green bottle wrapped up in a tie every Father's Day.

The man was still waving at me so I used a napkin to pick up a flaming hog ball and pitch it across the room. My admirer ducked, and the flaming ball crashed into the back wall, where the hard liquor was displayed. Flames erupted from the Vodka and raced up the wood paneling, igniting the ceiling tiles.

I heard feminine screams of terror from all corners as the sprinkler system came to life. The water merely whet the appetite of a fire already out of control, and the restaurant was soon engulfed in flames.

Fortunately for Miss Streeter and me, we were sitting at the front window and made the door quickly, leading a pack of terrified, flaming patrons.

As the crowd poured out the entrance, a black Prius

swerved from the street and onto the sidewalk, bearing down on us. Bullets from a Tommy-gun shattered the window behind us, sending a hurricane of glass and lead into the crowd.

I grabbed Miss Streeter and rolled the two of us behind one of the outside tables. Richard came out like lightning and began pounding the fleeing econo-car with forty-five caliber slugs. The car careened as holes dug into the side, and the rear window exploded in a million pieces. The car slalomed back into the street and its engine screamed as the driver accelerated, jamming gears and screeching tires.

I stood and continued pounding the tail-end of the Prius with lead. To be modest, I'm a good shot: the car spun out of control and smashed into an outdoor cafe. I smiled when a large figure emerged from the passenger side of the vehicle. I couldn't make out any features, but as far as I was concerned, there was a bull's-eye painted on his back.

For fun, I tracked the man for a couple of feet before squeezing the trigger, almost laughing at myself, enjoying a private joke.

The hammer fell on an empty chamber, and the joke was on me. I dropped the empty magazine and slammed in another, but it was too late. He'd made his escape behind a wall of metermaids who'd assembled to ticket the Prius for "parking within five feet, four and a half inches of an alley."

Frustrated, I slammed Richard back into my shoulder rig and turned to look for Stephanie. I spotted her. Patrons lay around her in various stages of dying, and, except for a sucking head wound, she seemed fine.

Satisfied, I dashed across the street to the smoldering carcass of the Prius. Shouldering aside the metermaids, I tore open the driver's door and looked inside. The driver slumped out onto the street, dead. Richard had given him his good night kiss.

Until now, the smart money was that this was The Platypus' latest attempt on my life. Now I didn't think so. Taped to the dashboard, a group of photos that rang bells in my head like an epileptic Quasimodo having a grand mal seizure in the bell tower of Notre Dame. I made a note to use that simile again; it was solid.

The photos were of Norm, Stephanie, Jay, and myself. Norm had been x'd out. It looked as if someone had tried to rub Stephanie out of the picture, too, until I'd stopped them. That left Jay and yours truly.

I rolled the dead driver over to take a look at his mug. It didn't look familiar. Except in the way that all bullet-riddled skulls resembled each other. But I was pretty sure I'd never seen this guy before. Other than suffering from elephantism, having a trunk and being a dwarf, he had your average face and build. Until I'd plugged him, he'd also dressed in a gray suit and kept himself clean-shaven. I rifled through his wallet, which I'd found in his vest pocket, until I found his driver's license. The poor sap's name was Maurice Pierson; another victim of senseless violence.

I was about to stuff the wallet into my jacket when a strong hand and vaguely familiar voice stopped me.

"I can't let you do that; you're no cop," the deep female voice explained, "ans' I knows your not a cop 'cuz I hauled your lily-white butt into the emergency room 'bout a month ago. So gits yo hands off da man!"

Wallet in hand, I straightened my back, turning slowly as I caught her eyes and held them. "Look, Thelma, someone killed Norm, my bartender. According to page 3.14 of the *Private Investigator's Handbook* that means I'm obligated to avenge his death. When a man's bartender is killed, he's supposed to do something about it. It doesn't make any difference what you thought of him or his appletinis or his house cabernet. He was your bartender and you're supposed to do something about it. And it happens we're in the detective business. We drink a lot. Well, when one of your favorite bartenders gets killed, it's-it's bad business to let the killer get away with it, bad all around, bad for every detective everywhere. Plus, someone just tried to put me on ice like a wine cooler or Luca

Braga and I've got to know who. Thanks for saving my life last month, but if you don't let me find out who's gunning for me and my pals, I'll be dead inside of a week and Norm's death will go unavenged. That'd be a waste of all your time and effort and a damn shame for me. Cops haven't stopped them, which you know better than anyone else, but maybe I can. Maybe I have to. So thanks again for sticking my lily-white butt into a peek-a-boo hospital gown, which you put on backwards, so you've seen my 'private dick.' I say we're jake."

She laughed loud. "Wasn't so private when I saw your dick. And as for bein' jake, that little white thing wouldn't get you a stick of gum out of my bubble-gum machine. Looked like a stubbed out Virginia Slim to me! You go right on ahead, honey. Any man with your problems deserves a 'little slack'—get it? Little white raisenettes dangling on a Christmas tree," she said, rocking with laughter.

There was nothing more for me to do here so I grabbed the photos, stuffed the wallet in my London Fog, and hailed my cab. Several TV news crews had already arrived on the scene, effectively blocking the police cruisers from getting through. My cabbie used a little effort and some disregard for the laws of physics to navigate our way through the scene.

"Where are we going, Sahib?" asked the hack.

I pondered his question for a moment, and my eyes briefly scanned his license. The ink was still wet.

Where was I going? I wondered. There was a puzzle piece missing. The letter I'd found in Norm's box said that he'd lost Glory's trail when she and Spillame went to Sweden. Why would a successful author take his new daughter to Sweden? Sure chicks go for men with kids, but going to Sweden to pick up dames was going a little too far. There had to be a reason.

"The airport," I said finally.

"Oh, many apologies, sir, but I am not allowed to take fares out of the city."

I pulled out a Lucky and sparked the lighter. The flame licked the tip of my cigarette seductively and brought it to life. I inhaled the sweet smoke and sat back in my chair.

Gandhi glared at me in his rear-view mirror.

"No, no, no," he shouted. "No smoking in my cab!"

"Why, not?" I asked, getting irate. I hoped that Gandhi here pushed the issue. I'd been stewing for a fight since Norm's death.

"Tobacco is grown in cow manure. Cow is sacred. It is dead ancestor returned to life. My uncle Mahatma no empty bowels so you can pollute the air! Uncle Mahatma no like American much!"

He had me there. I tossed the butt out the window where it landed in an open convertible. "We either go to the airport, bub," I said, "or we go to a McDonald's drive-thru and I order three all-beef quarter pounders and eat them right here in your cab."

"Which one, please, Sahib: the one named for the CIA director or the one named for the actor turned president?"

"Whichever airport is closest."

He nodded, thought about it for a moment, and then took the fastest route out of the city.

CHAPTER FIVE

I paid the cabbie and disappointed the skycaps as I strolled past them and through the automatic glass doors. The destinations board was hiding above the reservations desk, which was hiding in front of a cute blonde. The next flight to Sweden was Disckad-air flight 666, the midnight redeye. I kicked a maze of velour ropes out of my way and strode up to the chick behind the desk.

She was a pert blonde with perky breasts and doe eyes. I lit a Lucky and blew a smoke stream to get her attention. She tried too hard not to look at me, which let me know that she was. Her eyes refused to leave the keyboard as she typed in numbers, asking "Which flight?"

"Disckad-air 666."

"Passport."

I handed her my ticket out of the country. "Here it is, doll, but it's a lousy picture of me."

She stamped my passport, still not raising her eyes past the counter. In a bored voice she asked "Smoking or non-smoking?"

I blew another stream of second-hand smoke in her face, answering the question and increasing her risk of contracting cancer and dying a painful, early death.

"Okay, what class?"

"First."

"Aisle or window?"

"Aisle."

"Any luggage?"

"No."

"Mono- or Polysyllabic speech?"

"Mono."

"Graduate high school?"

"Uh, yeah. Technically."

"Shoe size?"

"Nine E, webbed."

"Married?"

"No."

"Sexual Preference?"

"Umm, listen, I'm in a rush; can I just have my ticket."

Fire flashed in her eyes. I know because it reflected off the polished counter and singed the stubble on my unshaven face.

"I'm going as fast as I can. Sexual preference?"

"Yes," I sighed, starting to get a little hot under the Arrow collar.

"Thank you, Mrs. Namkuntabootikinte, enjoy your flight. Come fly the friendly skies with us again. We'll get you there, we care, we love to fly and it shows, something special in the air, less fare, more care, our spirit will lift you, absolutely, the proud bird with the golden tail, the wings of Kilimanjaro, exclusive service to exotic gems, we really move our tails for you, up, up, and away, you'll love our hypoallergenic nuts, positively guaranteed to get you there over night. Trust us. Buh-bye. Next please."

She handed me my ticket and motioned me aside. My flight wasn't leaving for another five minutes, so I didn't have time to grab a watered-down, "sale-priced" fifty-dollar airport beer. Apparently Dan Snyder had his hooks in the food-services industry, too.

I hurried along to the security counter. The turban and robed TSA agent's nametag was obscured by his long beard, but I could tell it read "bin-Laden." He smiled, asked for papers, and wanted me to carry a duffle bag aboard for him.

"I thought Seal Team 6 got you in Pakistan?"

"Too obvious. Who would think to find me hiding out in an airport allowing dangerous individuals to slip on flights with firearms?"

"Good point. What's in that bag?"

"What bag?"

I pointed to the heavy duffle that clearly wouldn't fit in the overhead compartment. "That one. With the ticking sound and wafts of smoke coming from inside."

Bin Laden shook his bearded head. "Sir, did you pack that bag yourself or has anyone unknown to you handled it?"

"Just you."

He smiled and stamped my passport. "Very good, sir. You may continue on. Enjoy your seventy-two virgins."

"What?"

"I meant, Have a wonderful flight and come back and see us again. Or at least rest soundly in the arms of Allah."

With my right hand, I shoved my PI ticket into Bin Laden's face.

"Who do you think you're dealing with?"

While he studied the badge, I walked past him and used my left hand to flip Richard up and over the metal detector. My bowels let fly with a thunderous, evil wind, further distracting the al-Qaeda mastermind while I caught Richard and discretely holstered her.

"I'm a cop," I said.

"Boy, are you ever!" he coughed, waving me and the noxious gas through.

I was about to congratulate myself when I heard him say, "Wait!"

I froze.

"You forgot your bag."

"Sorry, but it's been out of my possession too long. If I took it now, that would be suspicious. Rules are rules."

The stewardess at my gate was locking the door as I approached.

"Hold on, sister; I'm on that flight!"

"Not anymore," she replied in a snide, whining voice.

I shot her without breaking stride and duckwalked down the gangplank. When I had gone halfway, I executed a daring mid-air spin/half-twist and moon-walked the rest of the way onto the plane.

I handed my ticket to the shapely stewardess and said, "First-class, toots."

She looked at my ticket and shut the door behind me.

It was a big plane: very roomy, comfortable seats that I could stretch out in. And except for the kid sitting next to me, I had the row to myself. A couple of times during the flight, I went forward and mingled with the riffraff, trying to get a feel for how the other half lives, and, of course, checking for suspicious faces that might have been following me.

There was only one thing that I liked about airplanes: those little bottles of booze that they sell. I bought about a fifth of scotch in single-shot bottles and leaned my seat back to enjoy the flight.

Fate, that bitch, had other plans for me. This flight was going to be a disaster. The in-flight movie was a double feature, starting with "Battlefield Earth, the Scientology cut." I tried to be open-minded about religion. I could buy thunder gods and the universe being the root system of the One-Tree, Ygdassil, or even crackers and wine turning into flesh and blood, but I had my limits. Scientology, sheesh.

As the lights dimmed for the in-flight movie, that rogue TSA agent decided that we all could use a vacation in the Middle East. He stood up in front of the screen and grabbed a stewardess, putting one of those cute new plastic pistols to her head.

Somehow, he'd gotten a gun past Security. I can't believe

that airport security was so lax that any maniac could get a gun onto a plane full of innocent civilians. What was the world coming to? I unsnapped Richard.

His plans would have been jake with me since I'd never been to the Middle East before, but the in-flight movie had begun, and he was standing between me and the screen.

"Hey, Osama," I said, getting his attention. "Could you please sit down? The in-flight movie's about to start. I bet you'd like it." It was a lie. Except for Dan Snyder, who never met a disaster he didn't like, nobody liked that movie, not even Helen Travolta, Kelly Preston, or Tom Cruise. But I was stalling for time. "The first one is a thinly veiled metaphor about the inherent flaws of imperial capitalism and its corruption of the soul. The second one is even better. It's *Rambo: Thirst for Blood part 7-Eleven*. It's like this: Rambo goes into a convenience store to buy cigarettes and the Vietnamese behind the counter is the former commander of the POW camp–"

"Shut up, drooling Yankee Satan dog! The People's Democratic Resistance Front for Unified Terrorism, Al-Qaeda Local number 201, is commandeering this plane in the name of Allah! You are now all my hostages! If you stay quiet and obey my every whim, your soft, corrupt governments will give in to our simple demands to get you back, and you will be returned to your homelands safe and sound, albeit returned by crashing into a building. If you do not cooperate, you will face the wrath of Allah!"

I was beginning to get annoyed. The lights had come back on and this bozo was standing in the way of me seeing, for the fortieth time, the best Rambo movie ever made. I fished a Lucky out of my deck and lit it up.

"Hey, pal," I said, exhaling a plume of light blue smoke, "could you take your act up to the coach section?"

He snarled, and waved the business end of his piece in my direction. "Silence, Yankee transsexual dipped in camel dung! Your President has oppressed my people for too long! We will—"

Richard slugged him in the face and cut off his soliloquy

before he could go any further. It was kind of a shame though, I wouldn't mind seeing the Middle East, maybe visiting the remains of the Berlin Wall while I was there. After I solve this case, I thought, I'll take that much-needed vacation.

Since 9-11, dealing with in-flight hijacking was becoming routine. Nobody was the least bit fazed by the body of a dead terrorist. The flight crew even had "Let's Roll" T-shirts ready to hand out and a quick clean-up system; the body was out of the cabin within thirty seconds of Richard's polite "down-in-front." I heard the toilet flush and wondered what they did with the terrorist. Then I wondered if they were planning on patching the bullet hole on the screen.

I was about to give the stewardess that I'd freed from the terrorist a fin for some earphones but decided not to; I knew all seven lines of dialogue in the movie by heart. The plane darkened again.

Exactly one hour and forty-seven minutes later, the lights came back on. By this time, with thirty-seven little bottles of scotch under my belt, I was feeling pretty good. I tried to hail the stewardess for another round, but my arm refused orders. I made a mental note to bring it up on insubordination charges, after I finished a short recess. My brain banged a gavel and retired to its chambers.

I awoke to the sudden jolt of the wheels touching down on the runway. The stewardess had kindly cleared out the thirty-seven bottles of scotch at some point during the flight. I patted my rig, making sure she hadn't helped herself to anything else while I was in less-offensive state. I looked past the kid next to me and out the circular window. Everything was the soft, dreamy white of fresh-fallen snow, with only the occasional swath of color to give it contrast. The *Mama Mia!* soundtrack clawed its way out of the cabin speakers. Either we were on Broadway, back at the *Gelded Retriever*, or the plane had landed in Sweden. My head swam as I peered through that little glass portal at the land outside. Memories assailed my hung-over brain; waves of déjà vu crashed over me again. I looked around; it was only me and the kid next to me left on the plane. And he looked like he had somewhere to be.

I crawled out of my seat and strode down the aisle to the front hatch. As I was about to step out onto the gangplank, a bored-looking stewardess handed me a "Welcome to Sweden" kit. In it was a bottle of massage oil, a blond wig, a Super-8 reel of adult movies, coupons for a free meatball dinner, and a six-pack of Viking lager at Sven Svensen's Smorgasbord.

I could tell that Sweden was going to be a fun town. Except that everyone talked like a damn Muppet here.

After she handed the kid behind me a kit, I tapped the blonde tourist attraction on her padded shoulders.

"How come that sniveling seven-and-a-half-year-old punk behind me gets a DVD and I get stuck with this lousy Super 8? Who has reel-to-reel anymore?"

She gave me a standard shining, inviting, plastic smile, and ran her glistening tongue across her lips. "Dis ka dier, bork! Bork!" she said in a soft, lilting Lauren Bacall voice.

I curled my lips back in disgust. "Save it, sister. I've been around the block enough to hear that rap more times than you've been born. I want answers, dammit! And I want them now! Everybody knows you can't even rent Beta tapes any more."

Any set of eyes less trained than my private pair would have missed her fleeting moment of confusion. She was good; I was better. Still, I almost believed her when she dejectedly said, "Fruzen glaje."

"Alright, Inga, you've made you're point. I know that I don't have a popsicle's chance in Hell of breaking through you're cold, yet professional facade; I know I can't get to the real you, trapped behind that stick-on smile, but think! Think of how much we've meant to each other. The pain we've shared, the love we've endured that's lifted us, transcending lines arbitrarily drawn on the map. "

I grabbed her and pulled her close enough to smell her strawberry lipstick and raw desire. I crushed her heaving bosoms into the lapels of my jacket.

"I'm talking about us, dammit! I can't believe that of all the crummy 'see-or-be-seen' airports in this world that you could've worked in, you had to work at mine. Play it again, Hans. We'll always have Stockholm. This could be the end of a beautiful friendship. If I don't leave now, I'll regret it. Maybe not today, maybe not tomorrow, but somewhere down that washed-out road of life, I will. I have to . . . I have to go."

I shoved her aside, and she rolled down the aisle on what may have been thirty-seven little bottles of scotch. I left her, any chance of deep, meaningful love in this crazy, mixed-up world, and airport security, bewildered and gawking behind me as I exited the gate and headed for the nearest men's room.

The seven-and-a-half-year-old kid with the DVD was just ahead in the gift shop, and I managed to trade him my Swedish Erotica Super 8s for his lager and meatball coupons. I was hungry and parched so I hailed a cab to Sven Svenson's, figuring that that was as good a spot as anywhere to pick up Glory's trail.

Besides, I had coupons.

I turned my collar to the cold and damp, when my eyes were stabbed by the flash of a neon light that split the night, and touched the sound of silence. And in the naked light I saw snowflakes that sizzled as they struck the neon sign hanging out front, warning away tourists. But I was no tourist. Tourists had cameras and wore loud, tasteless shirts. I preferred to keep a low profile.

As my eyes adjusted to the neon, I could make out the Antlers framing the Olde Flagsheims sign. It was called Sven Svensen's Smorgasbord now, but I knew I had come home.

A big lady wrapped in fur, wearing a horned helmet, and performing operatic vocal warm-ups bumped into me, disturbing my reverie.

"Diska?" she inquired, raising a blonde eyebrow.

I shook my head. "No. Not yet."

She shrugged, and hummed something by Simon and Garfunkle as she went inside.

I propped up the collar of my London Fog against the raging blizzard, pulled my fedora down low over my eyes, and kicked the Norwegian pine door down with my size-nine Florsheims.

Sven's was a quaint little dive located at the outskirts of the wrong side of whatever passed for tracks in Sweden. Could've been reindeer tracks or eight-legged horse tracks for all I know. The joint was a wooden, two-level number that G.I.'s probably saw a lot of action in during Ragnarök, back when it was called Flagsheim's and served a better class of pillager.

With a creak, cables lifted the front door off of the ground and settled it back into place on the frame. I knew then that this was my kind of place.

I parked myself at the rail and peered at the barkeep. Sven was a burly, blond, dark-beer-drinking giant. He returned my stare, polished beer mugs, and laughed. His jovial, good-natured greeting, "Fruzen Bork!" sounded oddly familiar. I could hear echoes from my past as the undertow of déjà vu tried to pull me in. Again. It was getting a little annoying.

"Scotch and soda with the special," I said, and handed him my coupons.

"Dis ka glaje!" he smiled, reaching under the counter for a cellophane-wrapped plate. He stuck it into the microwave and sang while he got my drink. It was a catchy tune, hauntingly familiar. I found myself humming along.

Sven sang: "Bork, bork, bork, bork, bork, bork, bork, bork, bork, bork, bork!"

All the patron's in the establishment joined in, eclipsing their worries and woes with happiness, if just for a few brief moments while they sang. Their voices raised in harmony and brotherhood; men who had been bitter enemies threw their arms about each other, shamelessly hugging and choking back sweet tears of joy.

From out of the back, a fat lady in a Viking suit waddled in and cleared her throat. I bounced a .45 slug off her breastplate to get her attention.

"I said, 'Not yet.'"

She dropped her shield and spear on the muddy floor, turned, and slunk into the back.

Sven tried to look casual as he pressed the silent alarm button under the bar where the elkhorn used to be. Not casual enough, though.

I held my bottle of lager by the neck and smashed it on the rail. I grabbed Sven by his thick, wool sweater and shoved the razor-sharp broken glass under his broad, classically cleft chin, just barely breaking skin. A single trickle of blood rolled down from his throat to my fist, leaving a rosy trail along the bottle.

"You know more than you're saying," I said accusingly, our faces 3.14 inches apart. "Spill your guts, before I do."

"Dis ka dier, bork! Bork! Bork! Fruzen glaje! Dis ka bork! Fruzen dier! Bork ka bork glaje, fruzen bork; bork ka dier, dis ka glaje fruzen dis bork bork! Glaje bork fruzen bork, bork dier ka dis, b-bork," he stammered, his eyes flickering with the light of fear.

There was a different light shining from my eyes: a light of primeval fury raged within my optic nerves. I pressed the bottle to his throat a little harder. Blood was staining his sweater now. There was no way he was going to Shout that out; he'd have to take it to Thrymm's Drycleaning, a few blocks from here.

Wait! How did I know that?

"Don't hand me that crap! I want the truth and plenty of it," I snarled.

"Ka ka? Bork ka dier, fruzen," he said, spreading his arms and innocent eyes wide.

"Where in the States?" I demanded.

"Dis ka dier, fruzen bork!"

"Alright. But if I find out that you're lying, I'll be back. And I'll be angry. Trust me: you wouldn't like me when I'm angry!" I said and shoved him back against the bottle cabinet. My eyes glowed a pale green in the mirror next to the moose head.

The door was kicked in and in walked the local constabulary. His badge said Beowulf on it, and he was holding a steaming bag of doughnuts. Fudge, by the smell of them.

He eyed the room, reached into the bag, extracted a warm doughnut, and took a big bite.

"Fruzen?" he said, looking at Sven and spitting some fudgy crumbs.

My eyes flicked to Sven. Sven's eyes flicked to me. Beowulf's eyes followed Sven's to mine. From the back, I heard the fat lady whistling the theme from *The Good, The Bad, and The Ugly*. I blinked. Beowulf's eyes flicked to the blood flowing down Sven's throat, sweater, and onto the bar. My eyes narrowed. Sven's eyes widened and he flicked them, trying to direct Beowulf's eyes toward the shield and spear lying on the ground. I arched an eyebrow and flicked my eyes toward Richard. Beowulf's eyes followed but stopped at the fudgy crumbs he'd spit on the floor.

I said, "Gimme three steps, Mister Beowulf. Give me three steps toward the door and you'll never see me no more."

Beowulf turned and screamed at the fat lady who was diving for the fudgy crumbs on the floor. That was the break I was looking for. You could hear them screaming a mile away as I was headed out the door.

Sweden had coughed up all that I needed. It was time for me to fly.

I made my way back to the airport, needing to leave a country where the sick, twisted things that Sven had told me were possible. Nausea attacked me and a sick, wounded feeling wormed itself into the core of my being. P.I. work makes you jaded to a lot of things, but this latest atrocity of gender against gender damn sure wasn't one of them. I had been wrong. This wasn't my home. At least, not any more.

I cut to the front of the line at the ticket counter, past a group of Canadian migrant farm tourists. An African-Scandinavian chick with doe eyes and perky breasts was parked behind the counter, tapping away at her keyboard and refusing to look up. Some things were the same all over.

"Give me a ticket on the next flight out to the U.S.A.," I said.

"Borking ka dis-borking?" she asked in a bored voice.

I blew a long stream of second-hand smoke into her face, answering the question and increasing her risk of cancer.

" Fruzen, dis ka bork bork? "

"Aisle."

"Dis glaje bork?"

"No."

"Ka fruzen glaje? "

"No."

"Glaje bork dier?"

"Uh . . . yeah."

"Dier bork dier fruzen?"

"Nine triple E, webbed."

"Bork?"

"No."

"Dis ka fruzen?"

"Umm, listen, I'm in a rush. Can I just have my ticket?"

Fire flashed from her dark eyes. I know because it reflected off of the polished counter and singed the stubble on my unshaven face. Some things were the same all over.

"Bork ka dis ka! Dis ka fruzen?"

"Yes," I sighed, starting to get hot under the Arrow collar.

"Bork-bork," she said and held out her hand.

I gave her my passport and ticket out of the country. She gave it a cursory glance, and then furrowed her brows, staring intently at the picture.

She looked up at me with a cat-that-ate-the-canary smile.

"Bork ka dis fruzen dier bork glaje?" she asked, suspiciously.

"Of course I'm Mrs. Namkuntabootikinte; who else would I be?" I replied, calmly reaching into my trenchcoat.

"Fruzen glaje bork ka ka."

"What do you mean, you're Mrs. Namkuntabootikinte? Look at the picture; it looks nothing like you." I looked at the picture. In fact, it *was* a picture of her. I made a mental note to have a talk with my fake passport supplier when I got back. I thought quickly. "It can't be you, you're much thinner and prettier than the troll, I mean me, in that picture. Plus, you have a natural beauty and don't need the kind of make-up that whore—I mean me—is wearing in this picture. Right, toots?"

She looked at the photo again and apologized for the mistake, saying something about her needing to get glasses. Then she pressed the silent security alarm, smiled, and handed me my things. I took off like O.J. Simpson in a Hertz commercial running for Gate 37. I thought about renting a white Ford Bronco, but there was a line at the counter. After I jumped over some luggage, grabbed a drink in the lounge, and stabbed some chick and her boyfriend in the necks, I rounded a corner and stared down a long, dark corridor. About halfway down, a lone figure stood beneath a streetlamp.

A match flared; hot fire arched across the sky and burned a path into my eyes. The shadow cupped the matchstick to its cigarette and stepped forward into the light.

I knew him.

Dashiel Hammett blew smoke from between his lips. "Hi, Phil. I always knew it would come down to just the two of us and our guns."

I threw my trenchcoat back behind me, making it easier to get at my Peacemaker when the time came. And it would.

Hammett slowly reached inside his vest. Just as slowly, I reached inside mine. He pulled out a whiskey flask, I pulled out a Coors Party Ball.

Hammett asked, "Drink first?"

I nodded. "Of course. No need to be uncivilized."

He threw me his flask, and I rolled him my Party Ball.

Hammett flicked his butt into the shadows and calmly said, "We can avoid all this if you'll pay up."

"Pay up what?"

"Your power bill. You owe Conned-Edison thirty-seven million and four dollars and seventy-two cents. That's the original four-seventy-two charge plus late fees and my tip."

"Your Mama," I sneered.

Before we could draw our irons, a maniacally-depressed horde of semi-rabid lemmings did the lambada past us. Their tiny bodies whirled and grinded around our legs, carrying a screaming William Shatner on their furry little shoulders.

Shatner yelled "Call," dramatic pause, "911," dramatic pause, "How was I to know," dramatic pause, "that 'Star Trek XXXVII: Green Chicks Gone Wild,'" dramatic pause, "which I wrote, starred in, and directed," dramatic pause, "would get such bad reviews among rodents." Thoughtful dramatic pause, "No! Vermin, you're vermin! Hey! Watch the wig!" Dramatic pause, "Aaaaaaaaaaa," dramatic pause, "aagh! Agh!"

Hammett and I stood there, watching the scene pass before us. After they had disappeared into the Ladies' room, Hammett looked at me from behind blood-shot eyes.

Without missing a beat, he dead-panned, "So, you have the money?"

"Your Grandmama," I leered.

His hands and trenchcoat were a flurry of action. He raised his gat, screaming, "There's not room enough in this genre for the both of us, Screwdriver!"

"There can be only one," I snarled, my trenchcoat flaring behind me.

Simultaneous gunshots echoed down the hallway.

We stood there, staring at each other for the obligatory minute, making the reader wonder which of us got shot.

From behind me a voice spoke, "Excuse me. Is this one of

your bullets?" Raymond Chandler stepped into the pool of light and pointed to his third eye.

"Yeah," said Hammett. "It's mine."

And then they both fell face first onto the cheap carpeting.

I pulled out my checklist. I'd already scratched off Poe, Conan-Doyle, Christie, Parker, Leonard, Fleming, Dixon, Keene, Don Ho, Mussolini, Gandhi, Jesus, Lennon, and got the assist on JFK (but then again, everyone got the assist on JFK). Now that I'd gotten Hammett and Chandler, the only one left was Spillame. And the way that this plot was twisting, I'd probably get my "shot" in a couple of chapters.

I had just enough time to switch papers with Hammett when the lights snapped on. Airport security hup-hupped into the corridor, screaming, "Bork dis ka ka glaje!"

I pointed to Hammett's still bleeding corpse. "There's your man, boys. Bag him, and tag him."

The security team hup-hupped over to the body while I slipped through Gate 37 and onto the plane.

I heard one of them yell, "Dis ka glaje, bork!" as he triumphantly held up Mrs. Namkuntabootikinte's passport. I smiled as the stewardess took my ticket. I stopped smiling when her friendly "Bork!" told me I was sitting in the non-smoking section. I laughed at her and took my seat. Sitting next to me was Mrs. R. J. Reynolds, a kindly old lady in an iron lung.

I offered her a Lucky, and she shook her head, declining. "I never smoke," she wheezed, "that crap. I only smoke quality tobacco products from Winston-Salem. "

Shrugging, I lit up. "Yeah. Winston tastes good…"

"Like a cigarette should," we finished together. Our eyes locked, and I felt the hot spark of passion like a Zippo struck against a trouser zipper.

The stewardess came and told me to put my butt out. I told her to butt out. She got huffy and stormed off, looking for the head stewardess. Her twelve-inch heels caught on the iron lung's extension cord, pulling the plug from the wall socket.

The old lady gasped, and reached her hand out to me. I guess she'd changed her mind, so I gave her my last Lucky and pulled out the Havana that Principal Sodom had given me back in high school. I lit my smoke and sat back.

Next stop: Rhode Island, U.S.A.

CHAPTER SIX

A voice came over the intercom: "Kirk to (*hic*) *Enterprise*. Kirk (*hic*) to *Enterprise*! God, I've always wanted to (*hic*) say that on the intercom. Anywaysh, this is Captain Kirk. Really. It-it's not a joke. For twenty-(*hic*)-five yearsh, I've been piloting the only Stockholm-to-Washington flight. And (*hic*) in those long, long twenty-five years, I've flown the only (*hic*) Stockholm-to-(*hic*)— Where was I? Oh, yesh. Everybody going to (*hic*) Rhode Island— though I don't know why you'd want to—please move to the front of the airplane. The stewardesh will give you each a parachute. In fact, everybody might want to grab their lug-luggage and (*hic*) move to the front of the plane and get a chute. Why? Why, you ask! Well I'll tell ya! Me and my bird are goin' out in a blaze of glory! No retirement for Captain Kirk, no, sir! No wrinkling skin sitting on the Murrell Inlet beach, no shuffleboard at the old-age home, and none of those huge black glasses for this Captain. Nope, uh-uh.

"So, drinksh are on the house. If you (*hic*) look out your left-side window, you will see the house that the drinks will soon be on. (*Ha-ha-snort*) We are currently flying at twenty thousand feet. (*Hic*) We are currently flying at nineteen thousand five hundred feet, nineteen even, eighteen thousand five hundred. Have a nice day. And thank you for flying with us today. Come fly the friendly skies with us again. We'll get you there, we care, we love to fly and it shows, something special in the air, less fare, more care, our spirit will lift you, absolutely, the proud bird with the golden tail, the wings of Kilimanjaro, exclusive service to exotic gems, we really move our tails for you, up, up, and away, you'll love our hypoallergenic nuts, positively guaranteed to get you there over night. Trust us."

Using Mrs. Reynolds as a battering ram, I made my way to the front of the plane. As I was about jump out the door, a stewardess with heaving silicone bosoms stopped me.

"What!" I snarled.

"Would you like a parachute, sir? We've found that they help."

"I knew that," I replied, releasing my grip from the iron lung.

Mrs. R.J. Reynolds asked, "Phil (*wheeze, wheeze*) throw me your lighter and a parachute."

Before I could respond, the plane hit an air pocket and lurched to the left. Mrs. Reynolds rolled out the door and into the chill night air over Newport, Rhode Island.

I grabbed a parachute from the stewardess with the heaving silicone bosoms and sprang out the door, chasing Mrs. Reynolds. The stewardess screamed, "Buh-bye," as I fell through the night.

Curling into a tight ball, I dropped after Mrs. Reynold's plummeting lung. While freefalling, I discovered an extra deck of Luckys in my trenchcoat and lit one up. The air whooshing by me as I plummeted caused the cigarette to burn fast. I only had time for a couple of drags, then I strapped the parachute to my back, just like I'd learned in The 'Nam. I never thought I'd be glad that they'd made me go to jump school, but I was now.

When I caught up to Mrs. Reynolds, she was gasping and wheezing terribly. Her sagging, wrinkled bosoms were heaving as she tried to draw air into her lungs. I held onto her iron container and popped my chute.

The silk billowed, but we continued to drop like an overweight elephant weighed down by an Italian mother-in-law. She looked at me through ancient, wrinkled eyes, and I wordlessly agreed. Instead of whining or crying about the busted flush life had dealt her, she held up a gnarled fist, and the cigarette I had given her on the plane was clenched between bony fingers.

She rasped, "Newport. Why did it have to be Newport? Why couldn't we have jumped over Salem?"

"Sure, kid," I replied, and gave her a light. And let her go.

Relieved of the weight, my descent slowed, and I knew I would live. I watched the glowing ember of her cigarette descend like a shooting star as she fell away from me and into the city of Newport.

***<u>AUTHORS' TRAGIC ASIDE</u>:** *Co-pilot Lieutenant Lance Cleftchin, the All-American, boy next door, smashed his way into the pilot's cabin and rendered Captain Kirk unconscious with a single mighty blow. Cleftchin brushed back his blond hair from his steel-blue eyes and rubbed his broad, masculine chin as the plane continued spiraling toward an abandoned farmhouse. Sweat poured from the Lieutenant's furrowed brow as he fought the plane's control stick, veins standing in bold relief on his massive arms. Betting his life against Captain Kirk's swansong, Cleftchin slowly but surely began leveling the big, steel bird out.*

Just when it looked like he wasn't going to be able to pull the plane out of it's spin in time, the controls responded, and the underside of the plane passed over the abandoned farmhouse, knocking the wind vane from the roof, saving all of the airplane's passengers from fiery death.

Then, before Lt. Cleftchin could blink his eye, the plane smashed into an elementary school across the state line from the abandoned farmhouse, and killed everyone in the building and plane.

Except for Cleftchin.

The former co-pilot and hero stepped out of the smoldering remains of the pilot's cabin and looked around. He found a Rolex watch attached to the bloodied stump of an arm lying nearby. He slipped the watch onto his own wrist, and then skulked off the scene, admiring his new watch and thankful for his good fortune. When Lt. Cleftchin reached a road, he found himself trying to whistle in harmony with the aimless tune emanating from the sky above him. Looking up, Lt. Cleftchin had just enough time to recognize Mrs. Reynold's plummeting iron lung before it, him, and his new Rolex all stopped ticking. In a shameless product placement plug necessary to make the movie version of this tale financially feasible, Mrs. Reynold's looked at her Timex, and noticed it had taken a licking and just kept ticking. And that she was outside Newport city limits.***

I landed beside an old pick-up truck and shrugged off my parachute. Rather than repack the silk, I thoughtfully left it for archaeologists to discover a thousand years from now.

A short, pale man, dressed in black and wearing a beret, got out of the truck's cab and walked toward me. He stopped a couple feet from me and finished his cigarette. The foul scent of clove assaulted my nostrils. He flicked the butt, pulled another smoke from his pack, and looked at me from behind his Ray-Ban number fives.

"Hey, man, can you spare some flame?" he asked in a toneless voice.

I gave him a jumpstart from my Lucky and asked, "Where's he live?"

"Who, man?"

"Don't give me that crap, mister . . ."

"Goyle, man. Garfield Goyle. Call me Gar."

"All right, Gar," I continued, "where's The Platypus?"

"Never heard of him, man. Wanna drink?"

I accepted. He had a wet bar in his pick-up. Gar selected a bottle of two-hundred-year-old brandy and poured two snifters.

He threw the stub of his clove cigarette into a pile of dried hay, raised his glass, and offered a toast, "To the manly arts, man: drinking, fighting, and smoking. Got a light, man?"

I sipped the brandy and jumped another clove cigarette for him. The brandy washed over my gums, and I savored the liquor until my gag reflexes forced me to spit the brandy across Rhode Island's southern state line.

I fixed a tight smile to my face and went back to my questions. "There are only ten citizens in the state of Rhode Island, pal, two of them Senators, one is a Congressman, and one is the Governor. And you're telling me that you don't know The Platypus."

"Eleven, man, eleven citizens."

"Not if you don't tell me where the Platypus is."

"That's like clever, man, but dig: The rivers of time have dried up on the white-man because the old dog learned a new trick. Also, I'm sheriff of this state and I'm, like, taking you in, man."

"Hah," I laughed, "what's the charge? I've got too many friends for a bum rap to stick."

"Dig, man: If a stitch in time only saves eight, will the sun refuse to rise? Anyway, you left your para-type-chute on my turf, man. Littering carries the death penalty in this state, grok?"

I tipped my hat back on my head and loosened my jacket. "Well, as long as you're going to kill me, Sheriff Goyle, how about spilling the beans on The Platypus?"

He finished his smoke and started a new one, not asking for a light this time; chaining the smokes and throwing the old one into an old gas can. "Alright, man, dig me and grok: How big you think this state is? You're like standing in everybody's backyard, including his. That's his house over there. The big pyramid with the floating eye thing. Like on the dollar bill. I think it was George Washington's summer pad. I know he slept there, anyways, man."

He stopped talking as Richard started. I emptied the magazine as lead filled the empty space below the pompon on his

Tonight's Episode: Slaughter of the Sacred Herd

beret.

He gurgled and said "Meditations on Death, by Gar Goyle: ... The Statue of Liberty shaves her armpits when no one's looking ... Toupees become fruitful, and multiply . . . Hitler lives in Sweden, disguised as an Italian endocrinologist . . . If I'm the state coroner and mortician, who buries me . . . At last I grok! You are the second coming! You Phillip . . . you're the son of God! I should have realized when I saw that you bear a striking resemblance to Steve Martin . . . Of course, God looks like Stacey Keach, so that means your mother must be . . . aaargh, I die at last! What did one frog say to the other frog?"

I grabbed him by his shirt, pressing my face 3.14 inches from his, and screamed, "Wait! Who is my mother, damn you?"

"Croak," was his only response, and then he died.

I took off my hat and scratched my head. Croak, I thought, that doesn't sound right. I was adopted by Frank "The Screwdriver" Linguini when I was seven and a half after leaving . . . The Croaks? No way; Gar had lied to me. Let's hope he hadn't lied about The Platypus.

I helped myself to another drink, trying to figure out my next move. Then, I helped myself to another. The next thing I knew, the wet bar was dry, and I had a plan: I was going to assault Fortress Platypus, and put an end to this novel before it dragged on any longer. I was starting to get a migraine. Of course, that could have been the smoke and fumes from the fire that had spontaneously ignited from the dry hay pile next to the old gas can.

I must have been a dramatic vision as my hatted and trenchcoated silhouette walked away from the flames licking at the night sky toward the glowing pyramid on the horizon.

Two minutes later, I was standing on the front porch of Fortress Platypus, located on the northern border of Rhode Island. Without giving myself a chance to change my mind, I stabbed a finger at the doorbell. Heavenly choral music sounded from inside the house.

Dammit, I hate heavenly choral music.

The door handle twisted slowly to the right. The door creaked open revealing a darkened room inside.

King Burger stepped out from behind the door and said, "Can I help you, little boy?"

"Sure, pal. Got a light?" I paused a moment and then asked, "Aren't you in jail on child molestation charges?"

Without missing a beat, he replied, "That bastard Donald McRonald framed me. Goddamn Roofies in the Happy Meals?!? Fucking genius. Besides, I've got a good lawyer. Eddie Shyster; know him?"

"The only Eddie Shyster I know shines shoes in DC and teaches law in New York."

He produced a lighter from the voluminous folds of his garish red and yellow costume, and asked, "Can I bum a cigarette from you? Ever since the boss gave it up, he won't allow us to have any in the house."

I gave him one, and we lit up. We smoked for a moment in silence.

King Burger threw his cigarette butt down and ground it out with his pointy shoes. "You'll have to leave your cigarettes and any fire-arms you may have with me. Boss' rules, you—"

Richard ventilated his Highness. Nobody takes my smokes.

I reloaded and combat rolled into the dimly lit foyer. Nothing happened so I continued combat rolling through the darkened house into a spotlit living room, and into the middle of a Pin-the-tail-on-the-Ken-doll game. Some young punk tried to make an ass out of me by using my butt as a pincushion.

I shot the tail out of his hand, and the bullet lodged in the birthday cake. I stood up and asked "Alright, who's the birthday boy?"

A defiant "What's it to you, pal," came from behind. I whipped around and discovered a familiar-looking eight-year-old pointing a familiar-looking gun at me. The room was dark, with only the light of the birthday candles illuminating his features.

"Lose the heater, pal," he demanded.

Something told me he was serious. I dropped Richard onto the floor.

"Now, kick it over here."

I did. I knew that kid; he stood there in his little trenchcoat and hat, unlit Lucky dangling from between his lips and gun in hand. *But from where*, I wondered. *From where?*

"What's your name, kid?"

"Jimmy Spillane, last-of-the-real-boys."

"Well, you're sure a real tough guy, Jimmy. What do you want to be when you grow up?"

His little chest swelled, and he said, "I want to be a real-man private investigator, or a lumberjack. Got a light, pal?"

As I reached in my jacket to get the lighter, the kid's finger tightened on the trigger.

"Easy, pal. Nice and easy."

Nodding, I brought out my Zippo.

Someone flipped on the lights, and from behind me, I heard a gravelly voice. "Reliving the good times, Glory?"

I turned around and saw The Platypus standing next to Benito Mussolini. Both had guns; The Platypus had drawn his, and Mussolini had his tucked into the waistband of his lederhosen.

"Hi, The Platypus. Can I call you The?"

His voice was as rough as his deeply grooved features. "You can call me Mickey for the few minutes you have left to live. Or," he smiled thinly, "Dad."

The air caught in my lungs like dolphins in a tuna net.

"You always treat guests this nicely, 'Dad'?"

"Generally."

"Well, you're a lousy host, but you've got the gun, so that makes it your move."

The Platypus looked at his Rolex, and said, "We wait. Our next guest should be arriving any minute now."

A trim figure in forest green tights landed on an open window ledge. A bow and quiver of arrows was slung over his shoulder, and a red feather stuck out of his hatband.

He placed his hands on his hips and exclaimed jauntily, "Welcome to Sherwood Forest!"

Flame lanced from Mussolini's luger. Red flowers blossomed in Robin Hood's forest green tunic. Standing there, he bled profusely onto the window ledge. His legs buckled, and he fell backwards, and off the ledge.

I looked at The Platypus. He looked at his watch and shrugged, "That wasn't who I was expecting." He tapped his watch to make sure it was still working. "Piece of crap. Shoulda bought a Timex. He should be here any second."

As if on cue, Batman landed on the same windowsill that Robin Hood had just fallen from. As he released his bat-rope, his feet slipped on the blood of the Prince of Thieves. Forward momentum caused his legs to shoot out from underneath him.

With a blood-curdling bat-scream, the caped crusader fell three stories onto his pointy-eared head. There was an audible pop as his neck snapped, and he died instantly, crumpled and lifeless at my feet.

I looked at The Platypus and asked, "Him?"

The Platypus shook his head. "Any second, though."

Batman's position on the ledge was replaced by a portly guy wearing green bikini briefs, a canary yellow cape, and fairy booties. On his red breast, a rhinestone "E.P." had been crossed out, and replaced by a black "R." He dropped his robin-rope and grabbed for the windowsill.

I glanced at The Platypus, "Him?"

He nodded.

Robin looked at the blood and yelled, "Don't shoot! I'll do anything! Confess to the Lindbergh kidnapping, take credit for Watergate, the outbreak of Psoriasis, eight hot dogs but six hot dog rolls per package, the last season of American Idol, anything! Don't

Tonight's Episode: Slaughter of the Sacred Herd

shoot, oh, god, please don't hurt me! Please," he sniveled.

"Get down here," The Platypus demanded.

The pudgy "boy" wonder lowered another rope that he pulled out of his utility sideburns. When he'd finished sliding down, Spillane motioned him over to join me. Robin nodded, and after picking Batman's pocket for his wallet, came over to me.

Spillane said, "Lose the mask, fairy."

Robin reared back, "Who you callin' a fairy, ya web-footed weirdo?"

I nudged him with my elbow. "You do look kind of gay in that outfit. Even I haven't worn pantyhose and bikini briefs since I was seven and a half, and a girl."

Heraldic trumpet music sounded from some distant corner of the room. A duck on a wire dropped with the note stating the word of the day was, "duh," and Groucho Marx waddled out and said "Well, it took you long enough." And then to someone offscreen, "He may look like an idiot and talk like an idiot but don't let that fool you. He really is an idiot."

Did I say "Since I was a girl?" Yes, I had, and I was. It was all coming back to me now.

Robin looked at me and said, "That's right, Phil, you were born a girl, and I," he paused before tearing off his bandit mask, "I'm your Momma!"

I exclaimed, "Norm?"

Mussolini squealed, "Elvis?"

The Platypus added, "Richard?"

Norm nodded, "You're all right. I was born Richard Steinman and gave birth to a little girl: you, Phillip are really Glory Steinman! After you were born, I gave you to Spillane to raise so I could pursue a career in Rock 'n' Roll as The King: Elvis Presley.

"I faked my death in 1977 because I was finally ready to be a mother, again. So I found you. But Stephanie Streeter, Spillane's first wife, knew my secret, and was blackmailing me. So I faked my death again, to put her off guard. Somehow she found out I was alive. I couldn't go living under threat of blackmail anymore, so I killed her."

My head was spinning like a 45 RPM record as all the pieces of the puzzle started to fit together. Groucho said, "Mind if I don't smoke?" and evaporated.

Elvis/Richard/Momma continued. "But don't think too harshly of me, Phil, I did it to be with you! I knew you'd never believe me if I came right out and told you that you were my daughter. I had to give you that box, and set you on the trail so that you could find out for yourself."

I stammered, not wanting to believe it, but hearing the ring of truth. "Then who's . . . who's my father?"

The Platypus cleared his throat. "Let me explain, Glory. Stephanie and I were unable to have a child, so I left her for your mother. When you were born, I was a struggling, young writer that wanted nothing more than to have a son. When Richard gave birth to a girl— that's you, I couldn't take the disappointment, so I left.

"Years later, when you were seven-and-a-half, and still Glory Steinman, Richard informed me, (blackmailed, really) that she was giving you to me and to give you a better home than she could. By then, my novels were quite popular in the Bible Belt. It would ruin me if it had come out that I had a bastard child. I had no choice; but I still wanted a boy.

"You and I hopped the first flight to Sweden, where Adolph, here," he jerked a thumb at Mussolini, "an old friend of mine, performed the controversial pre-pubescent sex change operation in secret."

I lit up a Lucky, my hands shaking like a leaf on a tree.

The Platypus/Dad/Mickey continued. "You stayed with me for about six months before running away to the protection of Frank 'The Screwdriver' Linguini. I couldn't touch you while you were under mob protection, but once you left for college, I saw my chance. There I tried to convince you several times to come back. You wouldn't listen, so, afraid that you'd remember everything, I put a contract out on you.

"I'm sorry, Glory, but I have to kill you. And Richard. I have to kill everyone that knows, or I'll always have it hanging over my head, and never get a moment's rest."

Mussolini's eyes went wide as Spillane turned his gun on him. "That means you, too, Hitler. Drop the piece. I hope you're wearing clean lederhosen, 'cause you're about to have an accident."

Shocked by the sudden turn of events, Hitler complied. "Ach, ja, mine charade ist uber. I am nicht Benito Mussolini, ich bin ein Berliner. Ich bin Adolph Hitler.

"Ich was a vealthy painter mit oodles of money. Eine tag, vhile on ein job in Munchen ven ich discovered that mein Jewish accountant had made off mit all of mein marks. Ich vas poor und destitute. Ich swore upon mein mutter's grave dat I vould get him if ich had to kill all of de Jews in Europe to do it."

Holy crap! Did everyone have to have a soliloquy in this chapter? I was on my third deck of Luckys. At this rate, I'd die of lung cancer before we got to the end of it.

Hitler/Mussolini continued. "Unfortunately, ich had gotten ein fraulein pregnant, and she gave birth to a girl. When I gave that little girl a sex-change operation, the fraulein took that little boy, changed his name to Spillane und fled to America!"

The gun wavered in The Platypus' webbed hand, "Wh-what?"

"Ja, Mickey, you are mein daughter! It seems 'Like mutter, like daughter,' ja?

"Then I wrote a book und became famous. 'Like father, like son,' ja?" Hitler smiled as The Platypus' seemed to shrink.

"After der war, I changed mein accent und appearance, fleeing to Sweden, to become a surgical endocrinologist. Ich habe missed mein family. Ach, mien charade is over!"

I lit another Lucky and cleared my throat with a shot of bourbon. "Well, I guess that makes it my turn to tell a long, drawn out soliloquy about my life. Here goes: I was born a girl, became a boy, smoked, drank, became a man. As a man, I smoked, drank, and killed a lot of people. I don't think anyone can blame me, as I was obviously a product of my environment. Now there's nothing left to do except kill all of you!"

The Platypus chuckled evilly and swung his pistol toward me. "That's going to be hard to do, son, with no blood in your body."

Hitler used the opportunity to make a play for Spillane's gun. I dove for my rod and heard a gunshot. As I rolled into a combat crouch, Spillane trained his gun on me.

Gramps Hitler was dead on the floor.

I inhaled on my Lucky and smiled. "It's a draw, Dad. Either we both die, or we both walk. What's it gonna be?"

Richard broke into the conversation, a worried tone in his heavy, southern drawl. "What about me, Glory?"

Without taking my eyes off Spillane, I said, "Mom, you're a weirdo, and a pervert. I'm going to kill you after I off Dad, who is also a weirdo and a pervert."

Richard smiled a knowing smile and said, "He may be a weirdo and a pervert, Glory, but he ain't your father. You can't kill me, because only I know who your real father is!"

Spillane blanched. "What?!"

I fired and Spillane dropped to the floor with a heavy thud. I turned my gun on Mom.

"Spill it, Mom, who's my father?"

"You're father is—"

A shot cut off Mom's reply and tore Richard from my hand. I looked up. Jay and the entire D.C. National Guard were on the window ledge, guns drawn. What they were doing in Rhode Island was beyond me.

"Drop the gun, Phil. I'm taking Elvis in for the murder of Stephanie Streeter."

Jay pointed his service revolver at Mom. "Hands up, fatboy!"

EPILOGUE ALPHA

I stood behind a heavy, drab curtain at "Orcah," trading shots of Canadian Club with the Cameraman. I was feeling the liquor, and the Cameraman, a small man, was matching me drink for drink; he must have been pretty far gone by now. He looked familiar so I asked "Have we ever met before?"

"Barbecue Sauce. I used to love it. Now the sight of it makes sick." This time he drank straight from the bottle. "She looks at me with those piggish eyes and a bottle of 'Famous Dave's in her cloven tentacle." He shuddered, "It's one her favorite things."

"Right. Mine, too. But have we met before?"

The Cameraman took a longer pull from the bottle. "At first I thought it was innocent. She wanted to hire me as her Refrigerator Doorman. I thought I was moving on up, to the east side, like Ralph Hart."

My eidetic memory coughed up a glowing fur-bulb of recognition. "Right. You're Carlton, my Doorman. I'm more of a Lucky Strike guy myself." I fired one up.

"Rhoda?" He looked at me with bleary eyes. "Is that you? You look good. Haven't aged a day. You've come back to save me?"

I paused and took a thoughtful drag on my Lucky. "I thought your name was Garfield."

"You wouldn't believe what I saw in her refrigerator. It was

Ralph Hart. Hell, I didn't even know he was missing. And you know that hand he always had out for a tip?" He shuddered again, suddenly cold. "It was covered in Famous Dave's."

"I haven't seen you around in a while," taking my turn with the bottle, "what have you been up to lately?"

"And you know what else was in there? Marge Simpson! Her blue hair was matted with coleslaw." Carlton shrugged. "But the job came with health insurance, so, I thought 'What the Hell'?"

"Job? You got another job? How the hell am I supposed to get in to my building? It's not like those doors just open themselves. What's next, firing all of the elevator operators? Savages. I don't want to live in a world where a man has to open his own doors, smoke outside in designated areas, and apologize for wearing trouser shaped Depends undergarments."

We were two sips from the bottom of the bottle when suddenly everything went red. Carlton staggered to his feet. "My camera! I've got to get back to my camera." He guzzled the rest of the bottle and then wobbled off to his station.

Red, the color of blood. I could taste the rage in my mouth like Famous Dave's barbecue sauce. I thought of Johnny.

Johnny had died on a talk show just like this taking a question that had been meant for me. It was the Maury Povich Show. A paternity test had gone bad. Before I could duck the question, Johnny stepped in front of it. There was nothing I could do. It was a loaded question. His life poured out of him in a red stream as dark as the fury that rose in me like the audience for Orcah just coming on stage for her mid-morning purge, binge, and monologue. She regurgitated her first guest, Harrison Ford, encased in a Carbonite block. He looked strangely at peace. "Hoo ha ee, Solo. Me cock choo. Ha ha ha."

A little rat-like creature named Gailascious Crumb cackled maniacally and she dragged the floating platform off-stage.

I was slated to go on after Orcah finished her next two guests. I couldn't believe that I was playing second fiddle to a couple of hack authors whose only claim to fame was an out-dated detective parody genre novel. They thought they were pretty damn clever. Unfortunately, so did a lot of people; it had been number one on the New York Times' best sellers' list since Orcah had featured it on her Book Club. They were big in the Amazon, too, but that didn't make any sense.

I pressed my ear to the curtain, but I couldn't make out anything over the audience's raucous laughter. I parted the curtains a little so I could see what was going on.

Orcah sprawled on an oversized, I-beam reinforced couch behind her desk, sipping from a steaming vat and pouring barbecue sauce on a bikini-clad Carrie Fisher. Next to her sat the authors, cheesy smiles stretched across their faces from ear to ear. They looked vaguely familiar: both wearing smart looking, black trenchcoats; one of them wore a black fedora, the other a pair of Ray Ban Metals.

Orcah opened the gash in her face and spoke through rows of shark-like teeth, "My first guests are the authors of that satirical detective novel: *Slaughter of the Sacred Cows*. Please welcome Deus X. Machina and his evil twin."

The audience exploded with applause. Carrie Fisher made eye contact with me and thoughtlessly mouthed "Save me." I took another shot of Canadian Club.

Sheesh, dames.

After the applause died down, Orcah said, "Well, I'd like to cut right to the chase, boys: Are either of you single? Tender? And how about dinner?"

They both looked uncomfortably at Carrie Fisher who inaccurately scrawled "save mee!" in barbecue sauce next to her on the floor. Clearly her father, legendary actor Eddie Fisher, had neglected her education as he shamelessly pursued his career, which is probably how she ended up chained to a talk show host, dressed like Lindsay Lohan at Studio 54, modeling her new line of home-monitoring ankle bracelets and accessories.

"Can we talk about our book first?" asked the shaded one. Without waiting for a response, he continued, "Our protagonist is a transsexual, sociopathic child of God and Elvis. He believes that he is the world's greatest detective, kind of an idiot savant thing without the savant. It's taken decades to write, and we're damn proud of it."

"Elvis? You don't say?" Orcah rumbled and regurgitated a sequined jumpsuit. The authors looked at her in horror.

"What?" she said. "He was a worthy adversary. I had spilled a vat of peanut butter and barbeque sauce on my chins and he came at me with a hungry look in his eyes. It was eat or be eaten! I had no choice!"

He turned to the camera manned by Carlton, which was wildly swinging to and fro, and said, "So don't pick it up at the library, don't wait for paperback release; down-load it now or kill a tree and buy the over-priced hardback edition. We need the money desperately! Our children are orphans, for God's sake! Help them! Help us! Get out there and buy! Buy! Buy!"

The oozing colossus repeated her question, "Are either one of you single?" Carrie Fisher nonchalantly signaled the words "save me" with semaphore flags. I silently mouthed back to her: "I'm your biggest fan." Then I gave her a wink and went back to watching for my cue.

The Hatman stretched his arms and subtly pointed at Shades from behind his back, "Phil smokes and drinks his way into the hearts of millions as a role-model for young, impressionable children."

Shades broke in, "I saw that!"

Carrie Fisher was using the distraction to casually lubricate her manacles with barbecue sauce and try and slide them off.

Hatman's face became naive and ingenuous. "Saw what?"

"The finger thing! You pointed at me!"

"Did not!"

The towering mass of flatulent protoplasm turned on Shades, "So you *are* single? How about dinner?"

Shades recoiled in horror and snapped, "I'd rather gnaw my arm off after picking my nose with a chain saw!"

Carrie Fisher began offhandedly gnawing her arm off.

Hatman said "I'd rather eat what you pick from your nose with a chainsaw."

"Now boys, she grunted demurely, don't fight over lil' ole' me. There's plenty to go 'round."

Orcah began what I could only assume was her mating dance in undulating rhythm with Carlton's drunkenly swaying camera. The authors dove behind Carrie Fisher. As the world watch in rapt attention, she regurgitated Carmen Miranda's tutti-frutti hat.

"Too much fiber," she explained. Then, too weak from food deprivation, she gave up and sat back down.

Hatman reached out and tried to pluck a banana from the hat, but Gailascious Crumb skittered up and began wrestling him for it. Just when it appeared the creature was going to be successful, Andre the Giant went to offer his assistance by handing Shades a folding chair. Shades shook his head, smiled knowingly, and then clubbed the weird rat-thing on the head with Carrie Fisher's arm, knocking the creature unconscious. Hatman held up the banana triumphantly and, examining it briefly, said, "Chiquita, of course."

Orcah popped the limp rat-like body of Gailascious Crumb into her maw, and then turned to Camera Three. "Our next guest is the famous Private Investigator who proved that Elvis was still alive. Please welcome, Phillip Screwdriver, *last of the real men private investigators!*"

The curtain parted as it flowed around my broad shoulders like Batman's cape. This was it: my big moment of fame. Something every girl dreams of since childhood. Stepping out onto that big old stage with the whole world watching. I stepped out into the spotlight to the applause of a single pair of hands. In the distance, a wolf howled and a baby cried. Crickets began chirping, and I heard a pin drop.

"Please, please," I said, holding up my hands. "I'm just a

humble private investigator, here on earth to save your souls from eternal damnation. Or something. I ask nothing in return except booze and cigarettes. And hats. I really like hats. So maybe add 'cuts in line at the haberdashery' to that list, with the booze and smokes. You know how crazy it gets there when a new fedora hits." I paused. "And a license to smoke in elevators or a government building or a kindergarten classroom—anywhere! Really, people, going outside to smoke in winter isn't good for your health. And besides, it was just one match. Sure it was in a glycerin factory, but you didn't have to go and change the warning label on a pack of smokes because of it! Oh, and I'd like to spend a little more time in Sweden." I stepped toward Orcah, and then stopped. "And for the love of my Dad, stop making changes to Star Wars! Really, Lucas? Stop the madness. No more adding in people that weren't even born when you first made it. That's just stupid."

Another step, and then a final thought occurred to me.

"And one more thing, as long as we're on the subject of how civilization can repay its enormous debt to me. I want the lifeless skulls of the two voices I keep hearing in my head. And I want them on a platter."

The blood drained from the faces of the two authors. I knew these men, but from where? From where?

Wait! The parking lot by my office, outside Mom's condo; it was the same two guys. I whipped out the manuscript that they had dropped several chapters ago. It was the story of my life! These were the two men who had been jerking my chain around all these years. These were the voices in my head. Well, two of them.

"Wait," pleaded Hatman, holding up his hands. In one, he held a suspiciously flaccid yellow gun.

"Yeah," chimed in Shades. "We can explain."

Orcah belched up Don LaFontaine, who said, "In a world gone mad…"

She smiled at Camera Two. "A world exclusive. The Son of God meets his creators. I guess now is as good a time as ever to bring this back to me! Please, everyone in the studio audience, reach under your chairs."

She couldn't fool me. I knew what they were going for. I tried to look casual as I drew Richard . . .

EPILOGUE OMEGA

It was a dark and lonely corner where no one but me could hear the sad, melancholy notes of a blues harmonica crying into the solitude of my prison. The haunting melody gave dreadful weight to the gloom of the shadows. I listened to the music for a while, and then opened my eyes, searching the darkness of my cell.

At the edge of a black stage, behind cold steel bars, the murky light from a solitary lamp shone upon a lone man—and a solitary rat. The man sat on his metal cot, playing the harmonica, and that harmonica sang a song that my soul would sing, if only my soul had a voice. The rat waited with weasel-like anticipation, his alto saxophone slung at the ready as portentous as a loaded gun tucked into the garter of a femme fatale in Act 1 of an off-off Broadway production of *Cats*.

The rat had traded his leather jacket emblazoned with Mother Teresa French-kissing the Pope for a striped prison jumpsuit and a pair of Wayfarers. I stumbled toward the somber musician and saw that he wore a black-and-white-striped London Fog trenchcoat, the same style I wore. He wore a matching striped fedora that was pulled low, obscuring his face.

The musician stood, turned half away from me, and lit a cigarette, cupping his hands against a non-existent wind. A cold fog fell between us, and I felt myself melting through the cell bars, almost stepping on the rat.

I read the numbers on the back of his trenchcoat.

As the harmonica player turned to face me, the rat placed the mouthpiece to his lips and turned away as he began to blow *Memories*. Before the man's face was exposed by the glimmering light, I knew who he was. And I knew that my soul did have a voice.

I was the musician playing that harmonica.

That was obvious. But where did the rat come in?

I must be dreaming, I thought. I couldn't be in two places at once, could I? I didn't play the harmonica, either. Or do I? One time, in band camp, I learned to play the gobble-pipe, but I'd never played the harmonica. No, I wasn't the man. I was the rat! Or had I just watched one too many episodes of *The Muppet Show*?

Weighing the evidence, I decided I was in a dream sequence written by my new authors. Yeah, that's right: new authors. I'd killed the original untalented jackasses controlling my life, right there live on "Orcah." I remembered the night that landed me in Hoosegow. When I'd come onstage, I'd recognized the creeps that had written my life into a twisted tragedy—and some dame that kept trying to get me to unshackle her from Orcah. I did what any other rational private detective, when faced with similar circumstances, would do: I ignored the dame and sent the two of them speeding to Hell on the forty-five caliber express train.

I didn't want to kill Orcah, but she made to eat the deceased, screaming something about not letting dinner get cold! I knew that I'd walk the final mile if anyone had seen me pull the trigger. Then I remembered the studio audience. *There could be no witnesses*, I thought as I turned toward the audience. *There could be no witnesses.*

The memory of that fateful night danced just inside the shaft of my prison light as I opened my eyes. I remember panting: I was breathing hard as my chest heaved, my lungs gulping greedily for air. There were no witnesses, I thought, until I remembered the camera.

As soon as I turned toward Camera 3, Carlton screamed

"Gimme three steps," and made for the door. Always the doorman, I expected he'd be waiting when it came time for me to leave. As I stared directly into the camera, and into the faces of millions of American couch potatoes, a snarl had come unbidden to my lips.

"There can be no witnesses," I'd rasped, my voice hoarse from screaming. "There can be no witnesses!"

I hadn't remembered how many times I'd said that phrase, but the prosecuting attorney at my trial did: one million six. Jesus Christ! Jay pulled a few strings, and offered me a deal on the murder-two raps; I just had to plead insanity. I of course said, "No," and looked at the rat who nodded in agreement.

The trial went well. It helped that Carlton had testified as a character witness for me. When he said, "I'm Carlton, I was his doorman," Rhoda, the jury foreman, wept. When Carrie Fisher said, "He's on a mission from God," John Landis, the Judge, nodded in understanding. When Orcah rose from the grave and said, "He tastes like chicken," all of the women in her sway smiled knowingly.

My wandering thoughts came back to the present. I wondered why I was doing my jailtime in a dream. Oh yeah. Otis and his unpaid elevator smoking tickets. There were just some things that the American Legal System is not willing to tolerate. I wondered why my whole life seemed to be a series of dreams knotted around a nightmare. I guess it's the Patch for me from here on out – at least in the elevator.

I loosened the knot of the black and white striped tie a little, thankful that it wasn't a noose. At least, not yet. I lay down on the hard metal cot, and went to sleep, hoping I'd wake-up.

I was gently snoozing when a firm hand shook me awake. I opened my eyes to Eddie's teeth, shining in the dark. "Boss? Oh boss, wake up!"

"What, Eddie? What in Dad's name could you want to talk about at this time in the morning? What time is it anyway?"

"It's time to tie up the loose ends, boss. I comes to apologize to ya's. I has to explain now, 'cuz I didn't gets a chance in Chapter

Six. First off, I'se real sorry 'bouts dat World War Two thing."

"What are you rambling about, Eddie?"

"Well, boss, you sees, I was a poor Irish immigrant wit' a talent fo' numbers, living in Germany. I tried to git work as an accountant, but seein' as how I weren't Jewish, no one hired me!"

"Yeah, and . . .?" I lit a Lucky. This spiel looked like it was going to be a two-packer.

"Well, boss," Eddie continued, "I tolds Massah Hitler that Eddie O'Countant was about as Jewish as they come, an's he hired me. When Mama needed that breast implant operation, I took me some petty cash and split town. Now, I heards that Massah Hitler was most irate 'bouts all dis. He was bound not to be's too understandin' bout Mama and all, so I changed my race and went to the States!"

"What are you talking about, Eddie? I've seen you in the showers--"

I was cut off when Hitler appeared enshrouded in flickering Höllenfeuer. "Ach, Eddie, I'm hurt. You thought that you could not come to me mit your problems? I would have understood, und given you the money. But," he said more slowly, "did you say that you are *not* Jewish?"

"Well, Massah Hitler, I'm sorry to say, but I'se Irish Atheist."

Hitler looked paler than usual. Distracted, he said to someone behind him, "Can't you see I'm on long-distance? Get that verdamnt pitchfork out of mine butt. Und turn off that Goddamn 'Yo MTV Raps!' Ach du lieber! I don't care what I did. No one should have to watch Kanye' West's Ground Hog Day special for all eternity! " Hitler turned back to us, "So, where were we? Oh, yes: I slaughtered six million innocent Jews for nothink?"

I blew smoke rings, and Eddie shrugged, "Guess so, boss."

Hitler's eyes widened and he sucked on his moustache for a minute. He appeared shocked, and then philosophic, like he was going to say something profound. "Mein bad!" he said at last. He shrugged his epaulet-laden shoulders and then disappeared in a puff of smoke. I flicked my butt into Hell just before the Verizon operator broke the connection.

"Anything else, Eddie?"

"Nope, boss. Be seein' ya!"

Eddie let himself out, and I went back to sleep, wondering if the authors were now grateful that I had killed them because they would never be able to avoid being labeled racists after the Amos 'n' Andy shoeshine bit and now claiming a black, formerly white Celtic atheist accountant, now pretending to be a black lawyer, was responsible for the Holocaust. Then again, maybe they had done the impossible. After this got out, both the Black Panthers and the Aryan Nation would want their heads. Maybe they would team up to get it accomplished, and, in doing so, realize that maybe they weren't so different after all. Because if they could come together over something like this, then they could come together and make the world a better place. Ebony and ivory, living in perfect harmony, singing "Kum Ba Yah" around the spitted heads of the authors while the Black Panthers danced "The Monkey" at the sly suggestion of some redneck from the Aryan Nation and the Aryan Nation skinheads stumbled about arrhythmically after being told they, too, could dance and that was all a myth used to separate brother from brother. Just like Dad had intended before He kicked them out of the Garden of Eden. Heavenly.

Nah.

Well, at least they hadn't denied the Holocaust. Of course, there was always the sequel to consider. Maybe Dad would raise the Authors from the dead like my Big Brother had done with Lazarus. Hell, nobody had updated the Book for years. Best selling book of all time and nobody had thought to write the sequel? Jesus, Mary, and Joseph! What a gold mine. You'd think with all the Jews in Hollywood somebody would have tapped that vein! Let's see, I'm thinking Madonna for the Virgin Mary. We might finally have a movie she's in that doesn't tank worse than "A Certain Sacrifice." I would have said "Dick Tracy" but hey, give some respect to a guy in a fedora and trench coat. Imagine the casting couch for the Virgin Mary. Hmmmm.

Hopefully, Eddie and Hitler were the last loose ends to be tied up in the next few pages.

I should be so lucky.

Morning came with the rattle of keys in a lock. Instantly awake, I shot bolt upright in bed. I was in a well-lit room, with a sky-blue and white ceiling. Paintings decorated my walls with green meadows and a urine-soaked crucifix by some impressionist everybody thought had talent.

The doorknob turned and an orderly walked in reeking of "Scent of Action" aftershave. Orderly, hah! That was the last word I'd use to describe the hairless ape that stared at me, open mouthed. Drool fell from the left side of his lips and onto the plate of food he carried. Hair drooped from his nostrils, and his stomach bulged over top of his too-tight, white slacks. He looked dirty, slightly differently gifted, and he dug deep into the back of his trousers to scratch himself. At least he wore Latex gloves. Sure they were fingerless but, hey, he'd at least made an effort.

A puzzled look was on his face when he said, "What's wrong? It's only breakfast as usual. Today, the kitchen's serving up your favorite: spit-pea thoup!"

I suddenly knew this guy; he was "Happy Joe" Kumquat, the son of Jay's police chief. His father had wanted him to be a top cop, and called in his last marker with the police commissioner and gotten "Happy Joe" a shot in the academy. He'd failed miserably. After seeing the movie "Police Academy" he was sure that the best way to graduate with honors was to position himself under the podium for the commissioner's commencement speech. It might not have been so bad, if only the "C.O.P.S." camera crew hadn't been there filming. After a botched guest appearance on "Steven Seagal: Lawman" where he'd driven a tank over a puppy to bust up an Arizona cockfight, he'd dropped out of sight. I'd never known until

I landed here what had saved "Happy Joe" from a lifetime career as a fluffer on "Ice Loves Coco" or a King Burger management trainee.

"Hi, Joe," I said casually, "Can I bum a smoke off you?"

"Nope, nope, that's against the rules! You'll have to wait 'til group for that!" he chuckled, patting the pack of Marlboro's in his shirt pocket. "Besides, these things are killers!"

"We get along well," I said, cutting in and sparing myself a lecture. "C'mon, Joe, how about just one?"

"Nope," he repeated. "I'm no doctor, but I'm going to help you with the only problem I can: your smoking. The rest is up to the doc's. But here," he said, looking around shiftily, and then palming me something. "It's Lucky Strike nicotine gum."

LSMFT. I chewed a few times before placing the wad under my shoe for later.

Problems? I thought as "Happy Joe" set the tray down before leaving, *Yeah, I got problems.* The doorlock clicked. *But I've always had problems.* My troubles stretched way back to childhood, around age seven or so.

You know how these "problems" get started. In the beginning, somebody wants you to try it, just one or two; they think it's cute. You start experimenting with different brands, and different kinds, until you find one that feels right. It was encouraged in church, at weddings, and social gatherings. There was no harm meant by any of it, but after that first taste, I became hooked.

I did it more often. I duplicated the key to my parents' cabinet, taking small amounts they wouldn't miss. Just a couple of shots, you know what I mean. As I grew older, and my habit got worse, I'd do it at parties. I forget what people called it back then . . . oh, yeah, "casual gunplay."

The neighbors began to wonder about me when the cats and dogs disappeared. By then, it was too late. Now, when I was out on dates, it became expected of me. I was now a "social gunplayer." None of my friends thought anything was wrong; they thought it was normal, and through peer pressure, encouraged my habit.

I was a goner. I'd made excuses for myself, told myself I was in control, a human safety, and that I could stop anytime. But I was wrong. Dead wrong.

Now, when I'm not in an asylum, I do it for a living. My name's Screwdriver, Phillip Head Screwdriver. I'm the *last of the real men private investigators.* And the second Child of God.

"Happy Joe" broke me out of my reverie. He'd opened my door without me hearing.

"Group time, Phil, let's go," he said.

"I'm busy," I replied. "Go away."

"Okay, but I guess I'll just have to finish these smokes by myself!"

You dirty bastard, I thought. "You don't fight fair, Kumquat. I'll go."

Group session was usually all right, but there were some real losers here. I wondered what I was doing in with this bunch.

I smoked a "Happy Joe" special and looked around the room. I saw my parents and they saw me.

Mom and Dad were an interesting pair. God was tall, broad-shouldered, and majestic; robust at an ancient age, with the Heavenly Host flitting about his crown like gnats. He wore a flowing white robe that was belted in golden starshine His smile outshone His belt and made the room glow bright like the morning sun. Everyone smiled with Him. He was what you'd call a "people person." A bass guitar was strapped to His back.

Elvis (or Norm), my mother, was not as tall, but was much darker. He looked like he might have once been handsome, but increasing weight and the ravages of drug abuse and death had scarred his face. His smile was lopsided and his side burns were large and bushy. He gyrated his hips as he walked, trying to look casual as he tossed a blue, Viagra wrapper in the waist can. Until that point, I thought my mother was carrying a microphone.

259

"Hi, Mom, Dad," I said, shaking my head at God. "What'd I tell you about that 'Holier-than-thou' look? C'mon, ditch it."

A frown lined Dad's smooth face. An angel wept. "But, my son, I am holier than thou."

"Uh-uh. It's bad for our image. Make with the heavy metal duds."

Dad said, "Shazam," and a bolt of lightning stripped away His robes and sandals, replacing them with a cardigan sweater, turtle-neck, corduroys, and loafers. He looked amazingly like Jerry Seinfeld. I could see how the witnesses had made their mistake.

I smiled. "Well, that's better than your 'Godfather' look. By the way, couldn't you have come up with a better alias than Frank Linguini?"

God shrugged. A seraphim spun the cylinders on a revolver, put the muzzle to his head and pulled the trigger. Click. "What can I say? I was on the lam. Eddie's not as good a lawyer as I thought."

A thick German accent sounded from beneath us. "Not a very good accountant, either!"

I smiled. "Ready to rock?"

God walked past me and onto the stage. He plugged His bass into the amp and nodded. "Yes, my son; I am ready to rock." A Cherub ejaculated.

Elvis, with surprising agility for a man of his girth, leaped onto the stage. He placed his microphone into its stand.

Twisting his hips and sneering while he spoke, Elvis said, "An' I am a-ready to roll! I even forgive you for testifying against me. I just want to be your mama!"

I grabbed my saxophone and dark sunglasses while our drummer, Ray "Scarecrow" Bolger, a former Mafia kingpin, and some new guy came onstage.

"Hold it," I said. "You, New Guy, what're you doing?"

"Good afternoon, Glory-of-God," the man said. His voice had a lilting and lofty tone, smooth and soft, yet strong and powerful. "My name," he continued, holding aloft a trombone, "is

Gabriel, and I play The Horn."

I asked God, "He any good?" and jerked my thumb at Gabriel.

God chuckled before nodding His head. "Yes, yes indeed, Glory. You might say he's a showstopper!" An Ophanim tittered.

I nodded my okay and noted that we were all wearing our dark RayBan Number Fives. Every band needs an image. We'd stolen ours from the Blues Brothers.

The amps came to life and a powerful hum filled the room. The walls vibrated with raw sound-energy and bulged almost to the breaking point.

God hit the first chords and then said, "Wait, something isn't quite right." He snapped His fingers and a Dominion told a Virtue to produce a dark and stormy night. The lights dimmed. Lightning flashed and the drummer echoed the thunder. We were jammin' (to the tune of *Jailhouse Rock*):

"Jehovah threw a party in the Looney Bin
Prison band was there makin' records spin.
Joint was goin' crazy and began to swing!
Should've heard them screw-loose fruitcakes sing!

Chorus:
Let's Rock!
Everybody Let's Rock!
Every inmate in that crazy place,
was a freakin' certified basket case!

Screwdriver played the tenor saxophone,
Gabriel was blowin' on the slide trombone
Drummer boy from solitary went crash, bang, boom,
The whole rhythm section's from the rubber room!

(Chorus)

Schizophrenia said "Co-Dependency,
you've the cutest symptoms I ever did see,
I sure would be delighted with your company
Come on and do the St. E. rock with me!"

(Chorus)

Oedipus was sittin' with a guy named Tom
Just telling a lot of stories a-bout his Mom,
Tom said "Hey fella, I think you're really sick
If you can't have you're mama try a different chick!"

(Chorus)

Good ol' Happy Joe said "For Heaven's Sake,
No one's lookin'; now's a chance for a smoke break!"
Phil turned to Happy and he said: "Nic' fit;
I wanna stick around while I get mine lit!"

On the last verse, Gabriel smiled, lifted the golden trombone to his lips and blew. An earth-shattering note erupted from the metal tubing, leaving everyone stunned. It was the perfect chance for a jailbreak: crumbling walls fell, crushing my limited edition Piss Christ and framing the morning sun rising over the storm-washed valley. Freedom was right there, but that was just another word for nothing left to lose. Plus, no one could move.

"Not bad," I said.

The only person to recover was an obese woman who wore a Viking-maiden outfit. Long, braided, blonde pigtails fell from beneath her horned helmet as she waddled from the ruin, crushing concrete debris beneath her sandaled feet. We all watched in rapt attention. She drew in a deep breath, bosoms heaving.

And The Fat Lady sang: **"Bork!"**

Tonight's Episode: Slaughter of the Sacred Herd

ACKNOWLEDGMENTS

We'd like to acknowledge all those people, particularly our spouses, who have tolerated and even supported us this last quarter-century as we wrote this ~~Great American Novel~~ book. Also, we'd like to acknowledge the Vikings and their gods, Elvis Presley, Mickey Spillane, Gene Roddenberry, Elisha Otis, Oprah Winfrey, Adam West, London Fog, the Scarecrow (we always liked him best), and everyone else we were inspired by. It's all in good fun and we appreciate your sense of humor and understanding.

And we'd also to like to acknowledge that smoking is bad for you. Don't do it.

Phillip H. Screwdriver, *Last of the real men private investigators*, will return in:

Thunder Bowl

Authors' Note: This is a working title. We reserve the right to change it at our whim. Please keep checking www.lastoftherealmen.com for samples and teases.